Leap of
perception

The Transforming Power of Your Attention

Penney Peirce

Foreword by Martha Beck

ATRIA BOOKS
New York London Toronto Sydney New Delhi

BEYOND WORDS
Hillsboro, Oregon

ATRIA BOOKS
A Division of Simon & Schuster, Inc.
1230 Avenue of the Americas
New York, NY 10020

BEYOND WORDS
20827 N.W. Cornell Road, Suite 500
Hillsboro, Oregon 97124-9808
503-531-8700 / 503-531-8773 fax
www.beyondword.com

Managing editor: Lindsay S. Brown
Editors: Sheila Ashdown, Anna Noak
Copyeditor: Jennifer Weaver-Neist
Proofreader: Claire Rudy Foster
Design: Devon Smith
Composition: William H. Brunson Typography Services

First Atria Books/Beyond Words hardcover edition May 2013

ATRIA BOOKS and colophon are trademarks of Simon & Schuster, Inc.

Beyond Words Publishing is an imprint of Simon & Schuster, Inc., and the Beyond Words logo is a registered trademark of Beyond Words Publishing, Inc.

For more information about special discounts for bulk purchases, please contact Simon & Schuster Special Sales at 1-866-506-1949 or business@simonandschuster.com.

The Simon & Schuster Speakers Bureau can bring authors to your live event. For more information or to book an event, contact the Simon & Schuster Speakers Bureau at 1-866-248-3049 or visit our website at www.simonspeakers.com.

Manufactured in the United States of America

10 9 8 7 6 5 4 3 2 1

Library of Congress Cataloging-in-Publication Data:

Peirce, Penney.
      Leap of perception : the transforming power of your attention / Penney Peirce. — First Atria Books/Beyond Words hardcover edition.
        pages   cm
      Includes bibliographical references.
      1. Attention.   2. Perception.   I. Title.
      BF321.P446   2013
      153.7—dc23

2012051366

ISBN: 978-1-58270-390-9
ISBN: 978-1-4516-9513-7 (ebook)

The corporate mission of Beyond Words Publishing, Inc.: *Inspire to Integrity*

This book is dedicated to the misfits, rebels, and rabble-rousers,
to those who feel they were born at the wrong time, or in the wrong family,
who use their differentness to do good;
to the poets, artists, dreamers, mediums, and mystics,
to the inventors, innovators, and change-agents,
to the leaders of integrity in all fields,
to the teachers of every ilk;
especially to the spiritual teachers who have come again and again
to patiently reframe the wisdom lessons for each new time.
I thank you for courageously carving the path for us today.

Contents

Foreword by Martha Beck   vii

To the Reader   xi

About This Book   xxi

PART 1: Rediscovering Perception

1 Acceleration and Transformation   3

2 The Path to Expanded Perception   19

3 How Do You Know?   35

PART 2: Skillful Perception for Transformation

4 Unlearn Habits of Old Perception   59

5 Recognize the New Perception   77

6 Navigate the Transformation Narrows   95

Contents

PART 3: New Attention Skills for the Intuition Age

7 Practice Direct Knowing 115
8 Practice the Spherical-Holographic Reality 135
9 Practice Undivided Attention 155
10 Practice Flow Attention 179
11 Practice Unified Field Attention 197
12 Practice Collective-Self Attention 219
13 Practice Shaping the Imaginal Realm 239
14 Practice "New Human" Abilities 259
15 Practice "Pretend Dying" 279

Final Thoughts 301
Acknowledgments 307
Notes 309
Glossary 313

Foreword

When it comes to books about spiritual and personal development, I am a very hard person to please. I grew up in a religious community bursting with good intentions, pearls of wisdom, and a great deal of what I later came to see as utter nonsense. Then I got three social science degrees from Harvard, where I learned to question absolutely every claim made by every author I read. Harvard also exposed me to a sort of dogmatic materialism, a cultural denigration of anything that could not be measured in purely physical terms, which struck me as woefully shortsighted in a post-Newtonian scientific era. Physicists had proven that matter and energy are in fact different manifestations of the same phenomenon, and I doubted even the doubters.

I left academia to become a self-help author, unintentionally motivating many other writers in that genre to send me their work. Nowadays, I receive several new manuscripts, galleys, and hardcover volumes each week that I stack in a pile I call "Books for Which I Did Not Ask." Some of them are terrific, but many more are just well-meaning regurgitations of a sort of verbal pabulum. My process for them has three steps: (1) read a few chapters; (2) roll eyes; (3) donate book to a home for the bewildered. I know I should respect people who worry about cleansing their auras as much as I do about tooth decay, who consult psychic gynecologists when their chakras feel muddy, or who spend whole chapters attributing their writer's block to the fact that Mercury is retrograde (Mercury, as far as I can tell, is virtually *always* in retrograde). But I don't.

My point is that between battle-hardened skepticism and jaded overexposure, I am an extremely tough critic of books written by people like Penney Peirce. I am skeptical to the point of outright hostility.

However.

The thing about Penney's advice is that it works. Instead of making vague positive statements, she gives specific counsel with pragmatic steps that readers can use to create specific outcomes. True, both the instructions and the outcomes have to do with the reader's subjective experience, and most aren't physically measurable. Do I have more calm and peace when I follow her advice? Yes. Do I experience the world as if all humans, including me, are going through a transformation that requires a leap of perception? Yes. Do Penney's instructions make me more intuitive? By using them, can I more accurately "see" situations that are far away, either geographically or in the future? Do these perceptions test well when I check the details in the physical world? Yes, yes, and yes.

I might not believe a word Penney writes—except that pretty much everything she describes is happening to me, too. We've never met, but our experiences seem to be marching in perfect synchrony. The day before she asked me to write this foreword, I told my literary agent that the only book I'd want to write would be something called *The Leap*, and I was pretty sure I wasn't the one who had to write it. Well, you're holding that book in your hands right now, and that probably means you're marching to the same exciting, joyful, delighted tune that so enthralls Penney and me.

Most writers who take on this issue describe it in terms that reveal a rather shallow and cursory experience of energetic transformation. Reading their books is like trying to use a guidebook to a city—say, Manhattan—that the author has seen in movies but never visited. They're describing something real and fascinating, but their information is skewed by preconceptions that have never bumped up against real-time experience. *Leap of Perception* is like a guidebook written by a native New Yorker. Penney has walked and driven and taken the metaphorical subway through this territory. She knows how to hail a cab, where to find great restaurants, which landmarks are worth seeing. When you follow her guidance, you actually get to the places she describes. And the place she describes—the world on the other side of the "leap of perception"—is a magical, wonderful place. You're probably going there already, on purpose or accidentally, by choice or by happenstance. This book will make the trip much easier, much more joyful. I recommend that you consult it often, as I intend to.

I'll finish by quoting Penney's own words: "Whatever or whoever has real presence is authentic, trustworthy, convincing, vital, magnetic, universal in some way, and naturally attention-getting and attention-giving." I doubt she knew as she wrote this that it was a verbal self-portrait, but it perfectly describes this book and its author. I'm so grateful that Penney has offered this to the world—so that I can feel someone holding my hand as I make my own leap of perception. Her other hand is also extended to you. Grab it, hang on, and leap.

Martha Beck, PhD
November 16, 2012

To the Reader

There is almost a sensual longing for communion with
others who have a large vision. The immense fulfillment of the
friendship between those engaged in furthering the evolution
of consciousness has a quality impossible to describe.

Pierre Teilhard de Chardin

Eventually time proves to be our friend. You think you know what
you're doing until a revelation unfolds and you see what you're
really doing. Then another urge and revelation come, and you see one
more facet of the picture. Another comes, and soon you see the connections. If you pay attention, you notice that a cohesive, intelligent pattern
to your life is materializing rather deliberately. You realize there's a
higher wisdom guiding your story, and you learn to trust it.

In my unfolding story of coming into greater consciousness, I think
back to a time when I'd been teaching intuition development for several
years and noticed I was feeling bored. Though I was still in love with
intuition, and the experience with people always came alive in new ways
that entertained me, I felt a nagging urge to change. "What's my next
courageous act?" I asked myself. "It's time to write a good, classic book,"
my inner voice responded.

At that time, my colleagues and I were on a pioneering, leading edge trying to mainstream intuition, that magical sense of knowing something directly without reference to logic or proof. Even saying the word "intuition" to an unprimed professional or businessperson could cause ridicule and rejection. We were constantly seeking credibility, and vocabulary was everything. I walked on eggshells to prevent people from labeling me as a "psychic" or an airy-fairy New Age channeler, and discounting me as someone who lived in a dream world. I remember latching on to the word "demystify" to help describe my motivation. I was going to demystify supposedly supernatural abilities and the superstitious beliefs that kept us locked in limited ways of thinking and knowing! I was going to help make intuition *normal!*

So I followed my guidance and wrote *The Intuitive Way: The Definitive Guide to Increasing Your Awareness.* I had Post-it notes all over my workspace: "Each sentence is a jewel; each paragraph must come alive." "The words must carry the experience of the truth." The act of writing that book wove many idea-threads into a lovely tapestry inside me, and my own intuition deepened. It registered in a more physical way, teaching me what it really meant to "be in my body." I became much more sensitive and empathic, and lo and behold, I demystified intuition for *myself* in a way I hadn't known I needed! How our souls trick us sometimes!

Welcome to the Present Moment

My next book was *The Present Moment: A Daybook of Clarity and Intuition,* and in it, I had to come up with 365 stories and ways to apply intuitive knowing. "I have plenty of stories!" I told myself. I listed them; I had thirty-three. Shocked, I moaned, "How will I ever think up 332 more of these?" So I did what I could do and wrote the thirty-three I had. I was staring for what seemed like forever at the new blank page and the blinking cursor, when out of the blue the phone rang. It was a woman from Texas who wanted to tell me a story about some intuitive children she was teaching, and it was the perfect piece number thirty-four for the book.

It kept on that way, the stories coming just as I needed them, as long as I kept my attention in the present moment. If I jumped ahead to look at, say, November, and groaned about how-will-I-ever-get-that-far, the momentum stopped. Back to the blank page and blinking cursor. When I re-entered the present moment and felt cheerful and expectant, the supply resumed effortlessly. Once again, writing was initiating me into a higher understanding. Someone summed it up quite well: "Worrying is praying for what you don't want." I was experiencing firsthand, in a precise way, how the mind and the moment can stop or start the natural flow of ideas, creativity, and energy.

I continued to write—two books on dreams—and meanwhile, I cultivated the habit of paying attention, in the present moment, to the subtle intuitive signs and inner messages my dreams and life experiences were bringing. I was teaching myself about the mechanics of consciousness, and much of my education came from doing clairvoyant-empathic life and business readings for clients. I could see patterns of consciousness—how problems had formed, how they were being maintained, and how they could be solved or cleared—in other people that I couldn't see in myself. It became evident that many problems could be solved, or transformed into nonproblems containing useful energy and information—not necessarily with physical action or by applying cleverness, effort, and control—but by using perception in a skillful way. More and more, it seemed that our lives were a function of our imagination, attitude, choices, and open-mindedness.

Glimmers of Transformation

My insights accumulated and fit together like pieces of a big puzzle. I began using my intuitive, empathic ability to *feel into* life—to sense the currents of what was happening energetically under the surface of reality—and interpret how those flows might materialize as events in the world. As I practiced this year after year, I could feel life accelerating relentlessly. Waves of buzzy energy and higher consciousness rolled through my body, causing me to experience an initially uncomfortable process of intensified psychological and spiritual growth. My colleagues, friends, and clients were experiencing this, too. I paid attention and tracked the nuances of this process.

A larger understanding dawned: I was not just helping people open intuition and improve their lives—we were *all* undergoing a profound *transformation of consciousness*. At first I wasn't sure what this meant. What was really happening to us? I knew viscerally that transformation was more than mere change—in fact, it was dramatically, radically different. My intuition told me we were shifting into a whole new kind of reality, becoming a new kind of human being. Life would function according to new rules. The whole thing was so much bigger than I had suspected! From this point on, I focused entirely on discovering what these new forms of expression would be like and how transformation would come about.

I became so excited about every new perspective I gained concerning the transformation process that I wanted to write a book about it immediately. And I did write many book proposals over a period of years, but each one was premature. A new series of insights would soon eclipse my previous view and add more important detail.

I knew I was being psychically anxious, pushing the river, wanting to get to "the real thing"; I also knew I needed to be patient and continue observing and experiencing. The fruit wasn't ripe yet.

Finally, it felt like a good time to write an advanced version of *The Intuitive Way*. Intuition had become much more mainstream, and I thought it was time to address the topic of empathy. The acceleration of energy in the world was, after all, causing us to become ultrasensitive and often overwhelmed by information, negativity, and the sheer stimulation of life. As I contemplated the topic of empathy, I saw that it related to the transformational shift we were all making. Our increased sensitivity to energy was allowing us to pick up *energy information*—insights contained in the very vibrations we received from people, situations, and even events at a distance—with our budding empathic ability. What we needed now were the heightened intuitive skills to decode this preverbal, nonrational data.

To the Reader

Frequency and Personal Vibration

All these ideas wove together, and it turned out that empathy was just one aspect of what the next book wanted to be about. In *Frequency: The Power of Personal Vibration*, I detailed the stages of the transformation process and the symptoms of each phase, then sketched a rudimentary picture of what it will be like when we live in a transformed reality. It addressed the new "energy reality," how everything and everyone has a particular frequency of energy, how we can change our vibration to produce varying experiences, and how we can work with our vibration to improve life and smooth our transformation. It was the right time for *Frequency*—the vibration of the world had risen to a level where the concepts could make sense and seem like the next useful thing.

Even so, the process of writing *Frequency* stirred me up. It often seemed to write itself and it shocked me, challenging many of my old reality constructs. I felt as though I were being rewired and repatterned at a deep level as the words appeared on the page. When I finished, I couldn't remember what the book was about! It wasn't until I went on the book tour and had to talk about it repeatedly that the material slowly integrated into my daily life. As I became saturated by the experience of keeping my vibration at the level of my *home frequency*, or the soul-in-the-body state, my life effortlessly changed for the better, just as the book had described.

Looking back on my process of writing, it's fascinating to see how the "deep me" knew things before my conscious mind knew. The understanding of a complex body of material was doled out in bite-sized insights, in a sane sequence and a timely way, as if my soul were helping my personality match the vibration of the times and the new knowledge, right as it was emerging, so I could experience the vibration and make it real. This is what I mean when I say that time is our friend—how eventually we see how compassionate the growth process really is. The vibration of the times, of our own selves, and of the information, is resonating harmoniously like a beautiful chord. And of course, this growth process doesn't stop! After *Frequency*, new insights continued to emerge.

To the Reader

A concealed or slumbering identity, not yet recovering itself,
still remembers or conveys by the intuition its own contents
and the intimacy of its self-feeling and self-vision of things,
its light of truth, its overwhelming and automatic certitude.

Sri Aurobindo

On to the Next Thing: Attention and Perception!

Sometimes, I see and hear certain words; they stand out in books and conversations as though highlighted in bright yellow. For the past few years I've been noticing the words "attention" and "perception" everywhere. My inner self seemed to be laying a breadcrumb trail of concepts, directing me to examine attention, perception, and consciousness next. I wanted to drill down below the explanation put forth in *Frequency* to understand the inner dynamics of how consciousness could transform. What was the role of perception and attention in smoothing our transformation process? I could see that where there is consciousness, there too is perception, revealing the territory.

Skillful perception was a term I'd heard described years ago by some of my Buddhist friends that resonated in my core and remained in the forefront of my mind. As I understand it, skillful perception is a concept connected to the three pillars of Buddhism—virtue, mindfulness, and wisdom—that advocates using the mind properly to heal your own wounds while not adding more pain and suffering to the world. This made sense to me because I had seen how so many of my clients' problems were caused by an unconscious use, or even misuse, of attitude, decision-making, fixed beliefs and opinions, and a lack of intuition and trust. And certainly, much of the pain we experience is due to this same unskilled use of consciousness by others. I sensed that skillful perception could reveal a more sophisticated, expanded consciousness—the kind that would characterize our transformed reality and new sense of self. Learning to use consciousness—perception and attention—skillfully became my new fascination and primary focus.

A Live Connection with the World

I began to see that *attention* is intimately interwoven with the overall act of perception itself. It is the adjustable lens of perception—the tool we use to make consciousness into knowledge, to understand the many dimensions of ourselves, and even to materialize our life. I could feel how the skillful use of attention and perception could do so many amazing things, and how this was the key to personal transformation. I also saw how our attention skills were atrophying due to today's technology-dependent culture. Everywhere I looked I saw people in the throes of fragmented, shallow attention and "attention deficit disorder." Yet I sensed that somewhere inside us, perhaps deeply buried, we do recognize a need for true reality and the unity that attention can bring.

I remember something poet David Whyte said in a talk years ago, that "attention is a live connection to the world." It is this live connection that keeps intuition open, and reveals unity and the Flow—all important factors in the transformation of consciousness. In my various visionquest experiences, in the quiet desert or on a mountaintop, I have often experienced this live connection. If I stared at a plant for a sustained period, for example, and "felt into" it, I could feel it seeing and experiencing me. As I merged with it, it merged with me. I knew the world from its point of view and it knew the world from my point of view as if we *were* each other, which we were! Those visionquests were experiences of using attention consciously and perceiving skillfully to remind myself of universal truths.

As time passed, more revelations poured into me about the skillful use of attention and perception to aid transformation. I began to feel in my body how energy and consciousness were aspects of the same thing, and how they immediately affected each other; I began to call it *consciousness-and-energy*, for lack of a better term. Interestingly, the science of neuroplasticity became popular about this time, introducing the idea that consciousness and focused attention can affect the brain, a refinement of the older idea that the brain determines consciousness. There was increased public interest in the brain's structure, and the roles and capabilities of the brain's left and right hemispheres. Science and psychology were coming closer to each other—and to spirituality, too.

A New Book Takes Shape

The end result of this buildup of insights was a solid conviction: the transformation of our personal self and life is absolutely doable, it is not that difficult, and we can do it in our lifetime—by using our perception in more "modern," updated ways. Now I was ready to write a new book! *Leap of Perception* finally crystallized, and as you will see, it weaves together many almost futuristic ideas about how consciousness-and-energy functions, all relating to furthering your personal growth toward transformation and living in a transformed world. As usual, I've been going through the process I'm writing about as I write it. I'm in it with you—clearing and polishing the perceptual lens, seeing through the illusion of solidity into the consciousness-and-energy world, and practicing the faster, more holistic ways of perceiving and knowing.

> In times of change, learners inherit the earth, while the learned find themselves beautifully equipped to deal with a world that no longer exists.
>
> Eric Hoffer

If we can learn to use perception wisely, there are two big benefits. First, we can more easily and quickly navigate the difficult phases of the transformation process. We're breaking longstanding, deeply ingrained habits of perception to instigate new ones, and this is incredibly challenging.

Second, once we get there, skillful perception can help us adapt to life in the transformed reality and function successfully according to the new rules. The more "early adopters" who embody and model this new way of life, the greater the influence of the new, and the more quickly and effortlessly the next wave of people can slip into the enlightened reality. And so evolution will progress, with geometrically increasing ease, until we're all living in a new, high-vibrational, consciousness-and-energy world. This is the dream I feed with my attention.

It is these two big benefits—easing your transformation process and living successfully in the new transformed reality—that I focus on in *Leap of Perception*. The sooner you learn the principles of new perception and practice the new attention skills, the faster your life will streamline and take you to magical heights.

Making the Leap of Perception—Together

The transformation process is unveiling expanded consciousness for each of us in our own way, with our own sequence of events and timing. Yet it is increasingly obvious to me that our stories are echoing each other more, and our paths are joining. We have answers for each other, we precipitate lessons and solutions for each other, and we are truly interwoven in this evolution of consciousness. Together we are bringing forth the new reality, and we are beginning to experience the communion inherent in the huge vision that is drawing us all in.

As Teilhard de Chardin said in the opening quote, we have a sensual longing for spiritual friendship—and spiritual family—and this experience is indeed showing up now as our collective consciousness expands. The deep familiarity this new state of interconnection brings is just one byproduct of the astonishing reality that's coming, as we make the perceptual leap into what I call the "Intuition Age."

About This Book

You cannot stand apart from a reality and do any more than present diagrams of it. You will not understand its living heart or its nature.

Seth (as channeled by Jane Roberts)

It seems I've actually been writing a trilogy on the transformation of consciousness without realizing it. The trilogy began with *The Intuitive Way* and expanded with *Frequency*; now I'm furthering the explanation with *Leap of Perception*. *The Intuitive Way* is a comprehensive course on intuition development, and intuition is a foundational skill that all spiritual growth rests upon. *Frequency* describes the transformation process in detail, and how you can work with energy and your growing ultrasensitivity to shift your reality to a better state. *Leap of Perception* takes you into the deep waters of the changes in perception itself, demonstrating how the new, transformed reality differs from the reality you're so familiar with.

In this book, you'll learn to identify and change the geometry of your perception from the older, linear way of thinking to the new, spherical-holographic model. You'll discover how too much left-brain perception can make you feel stuck and how to shift out of that stuckness; and you'll understand how transformed consciousness feels and behaves, and what you can do to develop the new attention skills that will give you the edge for greater success—and joy—in your life. Our focus is: *What is the perception of the future? And how do we get there now?*

My Intentions

I enjoy translating abstract-conceptual ideas into common sense, practical application. This is why I like writing guidebooks, because they offer simple practices that help you physically and emotionally experience the ideas I'm describing. If the material doesn't seep all the way into your body, my experience is that you don't really absorb it for the long term. *Leap of Perception* is one of these guidebooks. I want you to be able to integrate the book's content deeply into the fabric of your being. Perhaps it would be more accurate to say that I want to usher you into the memory of what you already know intimately, in every dimension of yourself, because it is who you are and always have been.

In *Leap of Perception*, I realize I'm addressing ideas that can at times seem futuristic and even unreal when you perceive them from today's "old" perception. As you make the shift in perception I'm describing, it will all seem absolutely understandable. So I want this book to stimulate your imagination and open you to thinking in new ways. It's OK if the material just stirs you up and makes you a little uncomfortable; resolving unease often leads to change. Basically, I hope you'll be able to feel into what transformed perception might be like.

Tips for Understanding This Book

This is a book you can read from start to finish and a process will unfold in you. You can also open it anywhere to read a sentence or a paragraph for a little boost or a problem-solving insight. It is intended to serve a variety of purposes and personal goals.

In addition, to avoid reinventing the wheel, I've occasionally woven together bits of explanation from the two previous books in this trilogy with new material to make a more complete and fluid understanding. And yet, this book stands alone; you don't have to have read the previous two (though ultimately, it would be helpful).

The content of *Leap of Perception* may seem dense if you try to read it too fast or if you skim it. The material is often profound, yet it's also simple. If you read slowly, stay in the moment, and feel into it as you read, you'll find many things clicking.

As I wrote this, I found an interesting thing happening. The book's organization began in typical outline form but soon showed me it didn't want to be as linear, logical, and left-brained as the usual nonfiction book, where a nice, neat process of discrete points A, B, and C progresses in an orderly fashion to a final conclusion. A more right-brained, spiraling rhythm surfaced instead, wherein each point became an aspect of the other points; they were fairly inextricable. To speak of one point meant I often needed to mention the others, too. I found myself touching a bit on one idea, then coming back to deepen it, then coming round again to take it further and connect it with its related ideas. Threads of ideas wanted to weave continually throughout the fabric of the whole book; they didn't seem content to be mentioned just once. Please keep this in mind as you read.

Also, I wanted to mention something about the "voice of authority" in *Leap of Perception*. I am not a scientist; I am not an academician. My early background is as an artist and designer. My expertise comes mainly from direct experience over many years with the spiritual realms—with insights gleaned via intuition and synthesized in my own odd sort of detailed mind, which holds large amounts of data and finds pleasure in seeing interrelationships and commonalities among many kinds of diverse information. I think the advances in the sciences are very interesting, and I like to ground insights from my firsthand experience in scientific findings. I often find that the things I "discover" on my own (without reading about them first) have been described by masters, mystics, and sages in ancient times and from varied religions, in slightly different terms. If an insight occurs across many cultures and time periods, I pay attention.

My bias is always toward subjective experience. You yourself are the expert on what works for you, and I feel strongly that you will recognize truth when you hear and feel it, no matter what science says. I have the deepest respect for original thinkers and balanced, integrated spiritual teachers. I know it often takes hearing something three times to have it sink in and that it takes different points of view—different kinds of teaching—to round out the wisdom. And I know that, for me, profound openings in my own understanding often come from a single phrase that shifts my perspective even half a degree.

In *Leap of Perception* I am primarily concerned with helping you relax your left brain so you don't identify with it, but instead are free to move into right-brain perception and beyond. Once you can do that, you can return to your left brain to make sense of things without getting stuck there. This is the only way you'll be able to understand the new transformed reality and the attention skills that accompany it. You need to be able to use heightened sensitivity to know what's coming.

Documenting Your Progress

By keeping a journal and writing about your experiences, "noticings," and insights, you can track your process of growth. This is a guidebook with exercises, and a journal is a perfect place to record the results you achieve when you do the exercises. What insights did you have? What difficulties or surprises did you encounter? What questions arose as a result of the exercise? Between exercises, you might write about the things you notice during the week or the themes filling your dreams. You might ask yourself a question and use *direct writing* to answer yourself. To do this, just write directly from your core, with a totally open, innocent mind, letting a stream of words emerge as a spontaneous flow without censorship. Don't think ahead or second-guess what's being said, and don't read what you've written until it's finished; keep the stream going. You'll be surprised what you find yourself writing, because it will be fresh and heartfelt.

Be creative; draw diagrams and sketches in your journal. You might also have a section that serves as an idea journal, where you note things that have captured your attention—a song lyric, a synchronicity, a snippet of someone's conversation, an article, the silly behavior of a bird outside the window. Transcribe the gist of the inner dialogues you have with yourself. Write out the negative declarative statements your left brain makes so you can see these limiting thoughts on paper. Find elements of your life dream, your destiny. List your loves and favorites, your distastes. You can go back later and peruse; what has your soul been trying to say? What are you working on, *really*, in your inner world?

Noticing What You Notice, Trusting What You Receive

This book is about paying attention and noticing. There is always a good reason you notice what you notice, and I'd like you to seek that underlying reason as often as possible. I'd also like you to begin to notice *how* you're becoming aware of something. Is it through intuition? Your subtle inner senses? Is it through your belly, heart, spine, or feet? What is the vibration of the experience you're having? Does it match who you really are? What can you discern from the vibration alone? When you pause between periods of reading, intuitive insights may pop to mind. When you're out in the world, experiences may occur that relate to the chapter you're reading. Intuitive "ahas" can make the information particularly real to you.

The Structure of This Book

Leap of Perception progresses in three logical steps. **Part 1: Rediscovering Perception** lays a foundation for understanding the basic nature and principles of consciousness and perception. Before you work with specifics, it's best to know the lay of the land and get the terms straight. We'll summarize the process of transformation so you understand what's happening to you and the world energetically. We'll examine both the right-brain views of mystics and the left-brain views of scientists. How do the soul, mind, and brain interrelate? What is spiritual evolution? Just how does consciousness-and-energy function? How might perception expand beyond what you know as normal?

In **Part 2: Skillful Perception for Transformation**, we'll dive into the transformation process so you can polish your attention skills for a successful journey through the sometimes chaotic and upsetting transitional phases of the transformation process. Personally, societally, and globally, we're now in the midst of the most confusing part of what many people are calling "the Shift." We'll focus on recognizing and breaking old-perception habits, then we'll discern what "new perception" is and learn the series of consciousness shifts that reveals it.

Part 3: New Attention Skills for the Intuition Age delves into the expanded use of consciousness-and-energy. The transformed Intuition Age worldview is vastly different from what we know now; in fact, from our current level of understanding it seems futuristic. What is it like? To make the leap of perception that allows you to live in it successfully, you need to develop some new consciousness practices. There are new perceptual models and geometries, new ways to do things that are lightning-fast and multidimensional. New human abilities are likely to develop. When life is based on consciousness-and-energy, attention skills become the key to moving energy, creating, and experiencing more love, wisdom, and soul.

Key Terms I Use in This Book

I like to be clear about terminology, since today we experience many made-up words and widely varying terms used to refer to the same idea. Where I first use a term, it will be italic, and will include a definition or description nearby. Often, I'll pair a term with a parallel term that is commonly used to mean the same thing. For example, I might say: "The energy body, or etheric body, underlies the physical body." Or I might refer to a "realm," "dimension," "world," or "reality," paralleling those terms in various ways, since they all basically denote the same experience.

Most often, the terms I choose are based on common sense and are composed of well-known, ordinary words. They mean pretty much what you think they mean. For example, I use the hyphenated phrase "consciousness-and-energy" to remind you that the two ideas are intimately interrelated and affect each other simultaneously. I use the term "the Flow," capitalized, to represent the movement of consciousness-and-energy in and out of physical form, and from one state to the next in a cycle. The "unified field" is one big sea of consciousness-and-energy, containing everything and every possibility. An "inner blueprint" is the underlying pattern of thought, feeling, and energy that gives rise to a particular, matching physical form or reality. These things are fairly self-explanatory.

There are some concepts with subtle distinctions that I wanted to clarify. For example, I have discriminated between "consciousness" and "Awareness" (which I explain in chapter 2). I also differentiate "perception" as the general act of becoming conscious of anything, from "attention," which is the act of focusing on a specific thing to make it conscious.

If you become curious or confused by any term, or can't remember where you first read it in the text, rest assured you'll be able to find it defined in the detailed glossary at the back of the book.

Next, in chapter 1, I summarize the acceleration and transformation process, to give you a basis for understanding the rest of the book. You'll see how the changes you're experiencing are caused by a true leap of perception.

> Every book . . . has a soul. The soul of the person who wrote it
> and of those who read it and lived and dreamed with it.
> Every time a book changes hands, every time someone runs
> his eyes down its pages, its spirit grows and strengthens.
> Carlos Ruiz Zafón

Part 1

Rediscovering Perception

1

Acceleration and Transformation

The global recovery of archaic memories is causing a mind-bending
spiritual crisis that is reaching its apotheosis due to time
acceleration. It is so important to realize that time
acceleration is causing old *ways* to end, not our planet.
Of course, many people cling to the old ways.

Barbara Hand Clow

A new time is upon us! Whoo-hoo!! If you've been paying attention,
you've certainly noticed the volatility, dramatic ups and downs,
sudden breakthroughs and life changes, and the widening gap between
fear-based people and compassion-based people. Large segments of
society are progressing steadily into chaos as old systems and ways
of thinking fail to produce results. At the same time, other segments are
progressing toward spiritual and mental clarity, innovative solutions to
societal problems, and greater peace and abundance. It's an amazing
drama to watch and participate in.

These symptoms are the early signs of a sweeping change that is
transforming us into a new kind of human being, living in a new world,
with new rules. We are just now realizing that the changes afoot are different than documented historical changes; we are participating in a
profound process that has never been experienced en masse on earth.

We are experiencing the acceleration, or increased vibration, of individual and planetary consciousness—and this is giving rise to a new reality that will eclipse the pain, suffering, and density we have always accepted as normal. This is *transformation*.

I want us to be able to navigate this transformation process smoothly so we can come out the other side all wide-eyed and bushy-tailed, with a big grin on our faces! Then we can cocreate something truly amazing together on this lovely planet. This chapter summarizes the process of acceleration and transformation so you can recognize it in yourself, others, and society and not be disoriented or stalled by it. By understanding the overall transformation process, you can move through it and be a "thought leader" and role model for others. Then you can develop the new attention skills that will bring success in the new reality.

We'll start by examining the beginnings of the transformation process, then look at what we're transforming into. After that, we'll explore what happens in the process itself and how to navigate the various changes involved with the least amount of confusion and negativity. The points I mention in this overview will be fleshed out in depth in subsequent chapters.

Life Is Accelerating and So Are You

Transformation begins with an acceleration process; the vibration of the earth, and of our bodies, has been steadily increasing for many years. We're not sure why this is occurring—perhaps it's a cosmic source of high-vibrational energy that's flowing through our solar system—but it is measurable; the vibration of the earth itself, called the *Schumann Resonance*, has been increasing. When the frequency of matter increases, so does our ability to access a matching vibration of consciousness. Our minds expand. Life itself speeds up.

Barbara Hand Clow, in her enlightening book *Awakening the Planetary Mind*, describes a phenomenon predicted in the Mayan calendar concerning "time acceleration"—a function of the earth's increasing frequency. The Mayan calendar delineates cycles of time covering more than 16.4 billion years, divided into nine periods called "underworlds." The length of each underworld, or period of development, is twenty times shorter than the previous one, with the completion date for all nine occurring at the end of 2011. That means time on earth has accelerated twenty times faster in nine different increments, and the last was just one year in length. Obviously, we're now living in an extremely accelerated period.

> The future has a way of arriving unannounced.
> George Will

The Mayans understood the increasing frequency of the planet. What's interesting is that the dates of these underworlds relate closely to the earth's biological and evolutionary cycles, which science has just recently documented. Now that the vibration of the planet is moving so fast, everything seems to be happening in the present moment. With that speed comes emotional intensity. Things we haven't wanted to deal with—our fears—can no longer be denied, postponed, or kept in the past; they're immediate and in our face. Hand Clow says, "The Ninth Underworld during 2011 rips open the full vibrational response to nature, so our unresolved inner traumas are arising like great monsters in our hearts and minds."[1]

For years, you and I (and other energetically sensitive people) have intuitively experienced this acceleration as it increased the subtle frequency of our bodies. While on the surface it may have worried you, deep down you probably suspected you were preparing for something exciting and good—a shift in consciousness toward enlightenment, a new reality that might resemble heaven on earth. You probably sensed it wouldn't come without consistent work on clearing yourself of the unresolved inner traumas Hand Clow mentions, and certainly not without some upheaval in the world. It may seem odd, but I'd bet most of us have been secretly looking forward to it.

It's a Vibrational World Now

As you and the world vibrate at a higher frequency, your perception naturally expands; your worldview shifts as your vibration shifts. At a higher frequency, you become conscious of the nonphysical world and can now perceive yourself, everyone, and everything as energy rather than as slow, solid bodies or objects separated by empty space. In effect, you can "see through" or feel into the solidity of matter to experience the energy patterns inside. Everything is vibrating at its own particular frequency, and the world is full of a symphony of tones.

You notice energy inside and between everything; there's no space devoid of it. Then you discover that energy is connected to consciousness. You notice that when you change your energy level, your consciousness changes; when you shift your consciousness, your energy shifts too. You can feel how the resonance of different forms can be harmonious or dissonant when combined, and how there is a natural tendency to seek vibratory coherence.

As the world increases in vibration, processes become more instantaneous. Cause-and-effect ceases to be the primary rule for materializing results. What you want to create happens effortlessly, miraculously, with no logical explanation, in a twinkling. Everything is faster and easier. You experience the fact that much more is contained in the present moment than ever before—it is mushrooming to include increasing amounts of the past and future. If everything is in the moment with you, you don't have to wait for answers, assistance, or results. You just need to ask and receive.

Evolving from the Information Age to the Intuition Age

It may help to understand transformation by seeing it as the natural continuation of an evolution process that's been steadily progressing on earth for ages—literally 16.4 billion years, if we are to believe the Mayan calendar-makers. We know that adaptation and growth are inexorable. Species evolve, life evolves, and with evolution comes expansion of knowledge, greater functionality, more connectivity, and speed. Just look-ing into the recent past, we can trace our evolution from the Dark Ages to the Renaissance to the Industrial Revolution. The acceleration has now brought us from the relatively slow Industrial Age, with its emphasis on physical, mechanical, linear (cause-and-effect) processes, into the Information Age, which emphasizes knowledge, access to increasing amounts of information, the speed of mental processing and data delivery, and multidirectional, simultaneous interconnectivity.

Television and computers—high-frequency machines—marked the end of the Industrial Age and shot us into the Information Age. Now the internet and global communications media have accelerated life even more. The Information Age is so fast, and we have access to so much data, that we can barely keep up. Our minds, dominated by left-brain compartmentalization, are still trying to integrate the vast amounts of information in a linear way by multitasking insanely or by skimming along the surface, sacrificing depth for speed. This creates myriad stresses, from hyperactivity to bloated workdays (with insomnia at night) to "nature deficit disorder" as people remain glued to electronic screens.

As the Information Age speeds toward its leap into hyperspace and to the next breakthrough experience, we see that the old physical and mental realities are no longer expansive enough. They're too slow and antiquated; their methodologies are malfunctioning and failing to produce results. What used to work is now being superseded by a new age—a new reality with new methodologies. As this happens, the old constructs slowly integrate into a larger, more comprehensive context. My term for the emerging, transformed reality is *the Intuition Age* because unlimited, holistic, direct knowing is its hallmark.

The Intuition Age focuses on spirit, and you may already be experi-encing its nascent stages. You've known yourself as a body in the Industrial Age and a mind in the Information Age, and as the Intuition Age begins, you're remembering that, above all, you're a soul. One of my colleagues calls this flow toward transformation "the Soul Movement." A new, more rarified perception is emerging—one based on intuition and sensing frequencies of energy. This expanded perception takes you straight into the nonphysical world so you're able to see people as more than just physical beings—you now realize there is a powerful, inner spiritual component. And you know this is true for objects and space as well—everything is made of higher-vibrational consciousness-and-energy.

> There is no death; only a change of worlds.
>
> Chief Seattle

What Are We Transforming Into?

So, you're accelerating and transforming. What does that mean, really? It means your increasing vibration is giving you the ability to perceive much more of the way life *really* works, with more access to exciting possibilities and a hugely expanded sense of who you are. Your fundamental identity is evolving; you're becoming a new kind of human. After transformation, any remnants of that old self-protective, dominating, isolated, ego-self—that small identity we've always assumed was part of being human—disappears and a much greater self rises from the ashes like the golden phoenix from its funeral pyre. What was fear-based becomes love-based.

Transformation is the beginning of knowing yourself fully and loving what you are; you have a very real felt sense of your soul in your body, as your personality, all the time. Your consciousness-and-energy increase dramatically. You can access information from dimensions or frequencies of consciousness you didn't realize even existed previously. Your options increase, your human abilities increase. You are not the same person, yet you are more of who you really are. Then you leapfrog over that to become even *more* of who you are, and as this continues, you are pleasantly surprised each time.

The transformed you lives in a transformed reality where you understand how the inner, consciousness-and-energy world and the outer, physical world work as a seamless continuum. What used to be separate convenes—left-right brain, head-heart, body-mind, inside-outside world. These integrations expand you into new territory where the whole is greater than the sum of the parts. Compassion becomes the main evolutionary force, a crucial part of the new consciousness that ensures success and planetary survival.

When transformation begins, there's a tendency to first feel it as a purely *energetic* process. Your body is disturbed, there are stresses and time pressures—a "time famine"—and upsetting emotions affect you. The intensity may even affect your health. You experience how your energy affects your reality. As the process continues, you experience how the rising frequency is changing your *consciousness* too. You perceive more, learn more, and understand how your thoughts affect your reality.

The new consciousness is not a bodiless state; it is the transformation of our present body consciousness, which is limited by time and space, into a state of transformed body consciousness which is that of resurrection.

Bede Griffiths

As you successfully navigate the stages of opening, and your body adapts to the higher energy, you feel better. You get used to the new speed of life. Your emotions stabilize, and you feel happier, more harmonious, enthusiastic, and positive. The positive feelings beget a higher quality of thought; you stop complaining and criticizing, are receptive to new ideas, and are more curious. Positive imagination reemerges, serving a renewed desire to create things that resonate with your destiny. You realize you were previously using your imagination unconsciously to create negative situations. "What a waste of energy!" you say.

You see how your high-frequency thoughts and feelings are creating a better life, a more effortless reality. Living is more fun. Now you are a high-frequency personality, embodying more of your soul and spiritual truth in everything you do—and that facilitates your destiny, without willfulness.

How Transformation Works

"But," you ask, "how does transformation occur? Will it hurt?"

To achieve transformation, you first have to make a profound shift in the way you know things. How you make your world real to yourself must undergo deep revision. You can't just keep processing data the way we're doing it now—with an almost desperate need for speed. You need a new methodology that lets you naturally and effortlessly jump into expanded perception. This transformational shift, or leap of perception, requires new pathways through your brain, new habits of sensing and knowing, and seeing that your "brain" actually includes your heart, body, cells, and even the field of energy around you. You have a much greater sensing apparatus than you may have imagined. If you can't figure out how to "rewire" your brain and access the many new pathways in your nonlocalized brain centers, not to worry! The acceleration process is taking you there, revealing the insights one by one.

Transformation is a process composed of a series of shifts. If you understand and embrace the doable tasks required for each shift, you'll sail through the process. If you resist, the process will happen anyway, and you'll be dragged along, kicking and screaming. So, no, transformation doesn't hurt—unless you block the Flow.

I previously mentioned how the increasing frequency in the world increases your ability to perceive more, to see through the surface of physical reality into the nonphysical consciousness-and-energy reality. *Entering the nonphysical world is one of the first big steps in the transformation process.* Just think about your normal daily reality: you are absorbed in brushing your teeth, making breakfast for your kids, listening carefully to your coworkers, remembering to buy everything you need at the grocery store, exercising after dinner, and reading your page-turner novel before bed. It's easy to get lost in these mundane details and think that's all there is. But there is always an inner reality close at hand. When you remember to meditate, or pray and bless others, or revere nature as you stand in your yard staring up at the full moon and stars, you deepen yourself, dropping through the physical world; you activate a mystical connection to the ineffable.

You must enter the inner world to be able to transform yourself. And this is where intuition becomes so important, because intuition is the means by which you know and navigate in the nonphysical world. In the consciousness-and-energy reality you don't think logically; you sense, feel, and know directly. You're merged with what you experience. With intuition, you discover principles of oneness and learn to function in the *unified field*, or infinite sea of consciousness-and energy. All ideas, resources, and realities are available and possible in the unified field, so your consciousness increases exponentially. In the nonphysical world, everything is interconnected, mutually inclusive, and supportive. Experiencing the truth of unity reveals the dynamics of the Intuition Age.

Eventually, you become comfortable living in both the physical and nonphysical worlds, perhaps rocking back and forth between them for a while, then feeling how they are simultaneous, affecting each other instantly. *Experiencing this merger of the inner and outer is the next important step in the transformation process.* For example, you might instantly feel how a sarcastic comment you make about a friend to her face shuts her down emotionally. Your physical action creates a nonphysical effect that has ripples: both you and your friend feel worse than you did before, and that contracted inner state inhibits full self-expression in the outer world. The inner inhibition continues until one of you says something in the physical world, then instantly, the inner state changes, energy flows again, and expanded self-expression resumes in both of you.

Being permanently rooted in the center of the present moment is yet another important part of the transformation process. When you live permanently in the present moment, there is no more projection—no more casting your attention along lines to other points in time and space that seem separate from you. There is no more separation. The past and future are inside the present moment, too, along with all ideas and everything else in your reality. This causes you to experience a natural change in the geometry of your perception. You see that the old, *linear perception*—perception limited to timelines, cause-and-effect processes, and lines of thought—doesn't function well anymore, and you begin to experience life as a ball, or a sphere, surrounding you equally in all directions. We'll go into the mechanics of this crucial shift in much more detail later.

It's important to remember that when the physical and nonphysical realities are merged, and when everything is in the present moment, any change always occurs simultaneously in both worlds. *Every nonphysical perceptual shift corresponds with a matching shift in your physical brain, body, and daily life—and it happens instantaneously.*

Transformation Can Feel Scary at First

The transformation process is not an all-at-once thing that blows you out of the water. There are many small shifts, and each one takes some getting used to; you're basically unlearning a long-standing habit and relearning a new one. The process often begins unconsciously and becomes more deliberate as you go along. It resembles the mythological hero's journey through the underworld, and it takes time to understand what's happening to you. Let's examine how it may affect you in the early stages.

Accelerating energy rolls through you in progressively intensifying waves. Initially the higher vibration feels foreign and can upset you—it's actually changing the way your body, emotions, and mind operate, and it can cause you to unconsciously clamp down in resistance. Wherever you clench or contract yourself in fear, the energy backs up and causes a problem—or magnifies a problem you already have. If you adapt to each wave by matching its vibration, however, it passes through without disturbing you, and you evolve with each intensification, becoming more and more clear. It's like a swollen stream building in velocity and strength as it gathers downhill momentum—it flows easily through the open channels, but as it encounters logjams, it breaks them apart and carries the debris downstream to be dispersed in the ocean.

Chapter 1: Acceleration and Transformation

The stream is the accelerating consciousness-and-energy; the logjams are fears, fixed beliefs, lies, chronic physical congestion, blocks, or pain; and the ocean is the unified field.

Most of us are used to living with suppressed fear, in denial, as a sort of make-do comfort level. We use strong fixed beliefs, opinions, and habits as cover-ups so we never have to feel our core rage, panic, and pain; we just live in our head, on autopilot. But this is not possible anymore. The transformation process evolves your consciousness from fear to love. That means you have to dissolve the fears and heal the emotional wounds that are in the way—by understanding them. And *that* means you have to face them, feel them, and decode them, which most of us dread. Each time an intensified wave of acceleration rolls through you, it dislodges low-frequency consciousness-and-energy, or suppressed fear, from your subconscious mind. Needless to say, you may experience varying forms of discomfort!

> One does not become enlightened by imagining figures
> of light but by making the darkness conscious.
>
> Carl Jung

As deep fears and pains rise from the subconscious, related memories flood into the conscious mind in present time. That means you re-experience them as brand new fearful or painful real-life situations that closely parallel the original ones—which were never completely experienced, integrated, and released. Drama and trauma abound! If you haven't embraced the clearing process, there's a tendency to resuppress and redeny what's uncomfortable. You may try to push it all back down into the substrata with various fight-or-flight behaviors.

When the heightened energy scares you and you clench and resist it, it builds up force like water behind a dam, pushing harder. If you continue to choose and validate resistance rather than the Flow, life becomes intense and difficult, fills with negative experiences, then explodes, creating dramatic breakthroughs and breakups of old patterns.

Awareness requires a rupture with the world we take for granted;
then old categories of experience are called into question and revised.

Shoshana Zuboff

The Turning Point: Surrendering to the Pause that Refreshes

The effort of avoiding and resuppressing subconscious blocks eventually wears you out, and the exhaustion can make you feel disillusioned, unmotivated, and hopeless. But actually, this is good! You're at the turning point. The last gasp of the negative path to transformation is when you're finally so tired of resisting and controlling, and so overwhelmed by complexity, that you stop; there is nothing more you can do. It's the end of progress, and willpower alone won't work. Wallowing in negative judgments and interpretations just drains you.

You're forced by the process to simply be with what's happening—to be with yourself and with the fears and pain. You must experience the state you're in directly, without voting on it or having to act. By simply "being with" life and "letting things be" as they are, you return to an experience of your own "being"—your soul—which was always present under the distractions. This is when you engage with silence and enter the nonphysical reality. And this is when your intuition opens. Now your soul can shine through, shedding light on everything. Revelations emerge. Understanding and compassion dissolve the fears. There is release, relief, and a return to joy. You feel *so much* better!

This is the turning point in the transformation process—when the fixed mind surrenders and precipitates a huge expansion into the consciousness of the heart, body, unified field, and the wise, evolutionary Flow. Your new shining identity emerges, along with a new world. After this, you're more deliberate about practicing the consciousness-and-energy skills that help you stabilize your new Intuition Age perception and reality.

Transformation Can Feel Exhilarating and Enlivening!

You have a choice at every point along the way to evolve smoothly and rapidly, in harmony with the planet and the Flow, or to evolve jaggedly, with self-created pain and suffering. When you embrace the heightened energy and the clearing process, the Flow moves through you, lifting you to a higher vibration and increasing your love, understanding, and health. It's easier then to engage with what emerges, without judgment or recoil—it's all useful data. A surfacing fear simply points to an area that needs sweetness, compassion, and patience. And as you "be with" the fear, it unclenches, tells you its story, and you gain a calm perspective. The energy becomes contented, like a small child comforted by its mother. Smiles return.

One of my colleagues went on a pilgrimage to Tibet, and while she was there something mysteriously shifted in her. "It's hard to describe," she said, "but it's like I just became myself. It felt like I stepped over the forty-nine yard line into my own territory." I've found her comment echoed by many others. Something they all say is, "There's no description of what this is like, of what happens to you. I thought I was going crazy at first! I was different but more real, more relaxed, and more excited—all at the same time."

> Keep your feet on the ground and keep reaching for the stars.
>
> Casey Kasem

I know only too well that even when you've begun to see the light, you can still be affected by other people's fears and still wrestle intermittently with societal beliefs in sacrifice and suffering. You gain insight then backslide a bit, like Sisyphus pushing the rock up the hill every day only to have it roll back down at night. This is natural. Making the new transformed reality normal requires a repeated choice to maintain your personal vibration at the level of soul, or what I've called your home frequency. We're breaking an old habit—unlearning and relearning the principles of how we live, create, and grow—and it requires practice.

Entering the World Again as a "New Human"

After the turning point, you feel who you are as a soul. You know how you want your life to feel, you have a new set of criteria for making choices, and you trust your intuition to guide you. Problems you thought were so terrible before change effortlessly, turning into opportunities. The Flow becomes your best friend, and you don't want to lock down any ideas—you want to leave space for everything to evolve and improve naturally.

As you review your successful navigation of the difficult stages in your transformation, you see that your success was due to the way you used your attention. You made choices, consistently, to *not* activate old habits that were holding you back and causing you to suffer. You notice that this practice changed your life for the better. Good opportunities, people on your wavelength, and interesting new creations emerged from your home frequency. It becomes second nature to be vigilant concerning what you notice and how you use attention. Now you want to refine your attention skills even more to be able to know and do what's possible in the Intuition Age.

At this point, you should now have a loose sense of where we're headed, what the Intuition Age can bring out in you, and how skillful perception can play an important role in helping you move through the transformation process. We'll go into all this in greater depth throughout the book, until transformation becomes real for you and you can begin to settle into your life as a "new human." In the next couple chapters, we'll dive into the territory of the nonphysical world so you can understand the subtle processes of how consciousness-and-energy functions.

> There is no way to bring about the outer perfection we seek other than by the transformation of ourselves. As soon as we succeed in transforming ourselves, the world will melt magically before our eyes and reshape itself in harmony with that which our transformation affirms.
>
> Neville Goddard

Just to Recap . . .

Time is accelerating and this causes the energy of the physical world and your body to accelerate, too, which causes a process of transformation of consciousness to occur. At first it feels disorienting as higher frequency energy pushes suppressed fears to the surface and your subconscious mind empties like Pandora's box. You may experience various uncomfortable, even painful symptoms, but the goal is to embrace and understand the fears—so you can clear them. Then you can replace them with love and clarity, which speeds and eases your growth.

Your consciousness is increasing, and you're perceiving more of who you are and how reality functions. You're seeing into the nonphysical world, understanding how everything physical is really made of consciousness-and-energy, how everything vibrates at varying frequencies, and how the physical and nonphysical worlds are really one unified field. You are evolving into a new kind of human being who will live in a new reality according to new rules. I call this transformed reality the Intuition Age. By understanding what occurs at each stage of the transformation process, you can move through the process with less distortion.

2

The Path to Expanded Perception

We are perceivers. We are an awareness; we are not objects; we have
no solidity. We are boundless. The world of objects and solidity is . . .
only a description that was created to help us. We, or rather our *reason*,
forget that the description is only a description and thus we trap the totality
of ourselves in a vicious circle from which we rarely emerge in our lifetime.

Carlos Castaneda

We all have one thing in common: we grow, we expand. And even
if our progress stalls temporarily, the evolution process jump-
starts us again. In this chapter we'll explore our evolving nature, which
is really the story of how perception expands to reveal more of our true
self and the higher functioning of life. We live in a time of transformation, and that means perception is quickly leaping from the low road to
the high road, ushering us into an amazing new understanding of
everything! Let's map out the route.

What Is Perception?

Perception is a mechanism that reveals the territory you can explore in
both physical and nonphysical life. What's interesting is that your frequency—your level of consciousness-and-energy—affects your perception

and determines what you can know. Remember that consciousness and energy are flip sides of the same coin, aspects of one another that immediately affect each other. When one increases, the other does too. So the higher your energetic frequency, the broader and deeper your consciousness of life. That's why the acceleration and transformation process, with its intensifying energy, is increasing your capacity to perceive and know more.

You might think of perception as a combination telescope-microscope with a lens that can change focus to view anything from the most distant stars to the tiniest microbes. The frequency of your consciousness-and-energy, just like the power of the lens, brings various worlds into view through the scope. The highest frequencies enable you to see beyond the physical world into the nonphysical world. As your perception becomes more refined, you can clearly see how nonphysical reality affects physical reality.

The Expanding View of Self and Reality

Some basic questions arise as you contemplate the territory of what's possible to perceive. "Who am I? What is reality? How does life work?" As your frequency increases, you're able to perceive more aspects of self, more dimensions of reality, and more nuances of the dynamics of life. For example, at a slower frequency, you might perceive "self" as a body made by inherited genes, run by a brain. You might see "reality" as a physical world of time, space, and matter filled with objects separated by empty space. You might see life functioning along timelines divided into segments of past, present, and future, with processes occurring relatively slowly because of cause-and-effect thinking.

At a higher frequency, you might perceive an inner, nonphysical world of sensation and emotion, thought and wisdom, or imagination and energy that adds dimension to the physical self and the reality you knew before. At this level you experience self as a being made of consciousness-and-energy, more fluid and interconnected with reality, which is also made of consciousness-and-energy. Life functions in the present moment, and much faster.

Chapter 2: The Path to Expanded Perception

As your frequency continues to increase, your perception follows. Now you see how the inner, nonphysical reality blends seamlessly with the outer, physical reality. The worlds are concurrent and intermingled, and their integration changes your experience of self and reality yet again. The physical and nonphysical worlds are in the same moment and cannot be separated; cause and effect occur so rapidly they become one thing. This merger is akin to moving into a new dimension of life, and this is the shift we call transformation.

> When two things are held in mind at the same time,
> they start to connect with each other.
>
> Rick Hanson

After this, you experience yourself as a soul, and the DNA, body, and brain as functions crystallized out of the soul's wisdom and memory. Reality might be the larger effluvia of your own consciousness-and-energy patterns, combined with those of all other sentient beings. Form, once so solid, now becomes a porous collection of vibrating, shape-shifting particles, and there are no boundaries anywhere, just different frequencies occupying one unified field. Time becomes one vast present moment and creativity is instantaneous. You now understand that self and reality are so intertwined that they create each other and actually are each other.

So, to summarize, you begin with a rather simple experience of self and reality based on the external physical world, and as your frequency increases, you perceive the internal nonphysical world. First, you oscillate back and forth between them, but as your frequency continues to increase, your perception shows how the worlds blend and interpenetrate, transforming you and your reality. Now there are more possibilities and you discover principles of how things work that were invisible and incredible before. It's natural for perception to evolve in its sophistication. At one time, low-vibrational perception had us believing the world was flat, the sun revolved around the earth, and women weren't real people! Now we can see that all people are souls, equal in the fact that we exist. We can understand the cosmos as something experiential in addition to seeing it as galaxies reached by traveling through space at the speed of light.

Mystical Breakthroughs

I have always had an active inner world, but a few years ago, the interpenetration of my physical and nonphysical self and reality was brought home to me in a fairly shocking waking vision. At the time, I was visiting my mother and her husband, both close to ninety and both quite vital, curious, and witty. I enjoy spending time with them because I can slow down and merge with their relaxed lifestyle. On this visit I learned that a few of their friends had died, and loss was in the air. I was also experiencing a wave of intense energy that was giving me insomnia.

One night after tossing for hours, I turned on the light and sat up in bed, cross-legged, staring into space. I was just *being* but without protest or irritation of any kind. That's when it happened. I inhaled and the room disappeared! I was still present in the center of my reality, but I was now a ball of light floating in space, nothing below me. Space itself supported me spherically from all directions. Though my body had dissolved along with the room, I could feel myself with the same familiarity I always have concerning my own presence. I was basically at peace, still just being.

Then I exhaled and the room came back. My eyes were wide open, and when I glanced down, there was my body. I inhaled, and presto! The room dissolved again, and I was back to being a radiant ball of light with no particular personality. This rocking in and out of form continued until I became bored with the game. I thought, "Maybe this is what it is to die. You just blink out of the form reality and 'come to' in the light-and-energy reality. You see yourself differently but still recognize your core vibration."

I had a split-second realization that maybe I was breathing my physical reality into being, inhaling and retracting it back into my greater self, then exhaling it back into form again, like blowing up a balloon. Perhaps I could also change it while it was in the inhaled state, exhaling it slightly differently, in whatever way I chose. This experience had a profound impact on me. It dissolved any residual fear of death I had, and helped me feel the intimate connection of the physical and nonphysical worlds—the inner and outer self and reality. The waking vision showed me that I spanned both realities and was "alive" in both.

· · · · · · · · · · · ·

Try This!
Open and Close Your Eyes, and Breathe

1. Find a comfortable sitting position, and make sure your head is level.
2. Notice the many details of the space you're occupying. Notice your body.
3. Notice that you've been in your busy daily consciousness and it has a particular feel. It might feel buzzy, dull, ambitious, upset, or even loving and peaceful.
4. Pay attention to your breath. Let it move all the way in, turn, flow all the way out, then turn and flow back in. There's nothing important that you have to do or know right now.
5. Close your eyes slowly as you inhale. Imagine you're inhaling the reality of the room, your body, and your daily personality. It all dissolves into the unified field and you rest comfortably in a quiet, comforting, dark (or bright), spacious reality. Let your breath pause as long as is comfortable. This is your inner world, the beginning of your own state of higher consciousness.
6. Now exhale slowly, opening your eyes gradually as you do. Imagine you are exhaling a new reality similar to the previous one, but perhaps with a slightly higher vibration. Imbue what you experience with love and appreciation, even with a feeling of innocent wonder.
7. Inhale slowly again while closing your eyes and withdraw all your attention from the outer reality. Let it dissolve. Feel a timelessness in the nonphysical world and let yourself be simple and pure. Gather that purity into yourself and attune to it completely.
8. Exhale again while opening your eyes, imagining you are blowing up the balloon of the three-dimensional world that your body and personality are

(Continued on next page)

(Open and Close your Eyes, and Breathe, continued)

living in. Send the vibration of the inner, higher dimension of consciousness into your "movie" to animate it. With each breath, let it improve.

9. Continue this way for as long as you want, and notice any revelations that surface. Make note of them in your journal.

• • • • • • • • • • • •

Evolution Is Unrelenting

Because of mass agreement about reality being only physical, it's difficult to challenge the view and break free of its grip. I'm fairly certain, though, that you've had experiences similar to mine, where you felt or saw yourself (or others) as energy, light, and higher consciousness. Perhaps you were flying in a dream and it felt *so real*, or your grandmother came to stand at the foot of your bed to let you know she just died. Maybe you were healed by intergalactic beings, or saw the radiant aura of a tree flash on and off.

I've spoken to countless people who tell stories about the bleed-through of a higher frequency reality into their lower frequency one. The interjection comes when evolution determines that you need a jumpstart to expanded perception—and it changes you. When she was eight, my mother was staying at a farm for the summer. A traveling healer stopped by and in minutes dissolved a large bump on her forehead, just by placing his fingers on it. It stunned her and opened her to life's mysteries, and I'm sure it has been a factor in her healing herself later in life of four different kinds of cancer.

These openings to expanded perception sometimes require an accident or shock to silence the chattering, daily "monkey mind" and sideline it temporarily, yet sometimes the experience happens in the midst of an ordinary moment. It demonstrates that there is another level of reality beyond the one we think is "it." In ancient cultures and esoteric societies, this is called *initiation*, a rite of passage that propels you into a higher frequency of consciousness and a new level of power and responsibility. Almost universally, when people experience this sort

24

of breakthrough, they say they prefer the high-frequency, mystical experience because it feels magical, natural, and deeply comfortable. The magnetic draw of our consciousness-and-energy upward in frequency is powerful and unrelenting; evolution will take any opportunity to break through stuckness.

> And the day came when the risk to remain tight in the bud
> was more painful than the risk it took to blossom.
>
> Anaïs Nin

It's also possible to raise your frequency and move beyond the perception of physical reality by meditating. Meditators who have learned to experience the nonphysical realms often advocate letting go of the experience of I, me, and mine. It helps expand your perception to encompass a larger sense of self. Zen Buddhism has this focusing phrase: *Nothing left out.* By taking your attention off your small individual self and world, you can see things, people, and possibilities you previously excluded, which you were unable to experience and know. When you re-include them in your world, your perception increases. There is another expression from Buddhism: *Nothing special.* This implies that no experience should be revered above another, that if nothing is special then everything is special; everything is equally valuable as an experience. By not attaching to specific realities and resisting others, your perception is open to know anything and everything.

> To study the Way is to study the self. To study the self is to forget the self.
> To forget the self is to be enlightened by all things.
>
> Dogen

From Awareness to Consciousness to Awareness

One of my favorite wise people, Sri Nisargadatta (1897–1981), taught about our evolving perceptual journey through the realms of consciousness-and-energy. He said that *consciousness* includes all that we can possibly imagine or know; that it is a fundamental sense of presence, a feeling of being, of existing—it is the experience of "I Am." He also taught that there was something beyond consciousness, which he called "*Awareness*," or "*the Absolute*." It is the enlightened state known by various names: nirvana, moksha, kensho, satori.

While consciousness comes and goes, oscillating with duality, Awareness is pure, unmoving, and unified—without duality of any kind. Nisargadatta describes it as a "shining," an uncaused mystery. It is consciousness unaware of itself. We toss the word "awareness" around, using it interchangeably with "consciousness," yet it is really so much more. Awareness is both the original state out of which we emerge and descend toward physical life, and the final state toward which we evolve and ascend. Note that I use the term "consciousness" throughout this book, and "Awareness" (capitalized) to refer to our place of origin and completion.

Nisargadatta first had students move through various levels of "extinction," where concepts of self were jettisoned. They needed to realize they were not what they usually think they are: memories, habits, or possessions. To be only a personality is a very small, false identity made of ideas. Students needed to "extinguish" or release the idea that they were their body, that they were their mind with its constant kaleidoscopic flow of beliefs and fantasies. This "attainment through extinction" or "progress through pruning" is a common practice in Zen as well. After letting go of all the "stuff," what's left is simply the experience of being, of consciousness itself, of the "I Am." We'll talk about how to do this in chapter 15.

An eternal instant is the cause of the years.

Sri Aurobindo

Nisargadatta then had students focus on the idea of "I Am" until they realized they were the entire unified field of consciousness itself out of which all ideas and forms come and into which they return. They moved from a sense of *only* being the limited body and personality to being the soul, then to being a collective consciousness or soul group, then to being the soul of the world, then the entire unified field, and finally, the consciousness of the universe.

You'd think being one with the unified field would be enough, but the next interesting step came as Nisargadatta made students aware that consciousness always includes some sort of duality. If you are conscious, it is always *of something*; there is an object—even with the highest, crystal-clear consciousness. And if you identify yourself as the "I Am," you can then also realize *I am not the "I Am."* Then you can understand that there is something beyond consciousness, beyond the sense of existing as a soul! This is Awareness, the ultimate reality that ever was and ever will be. Awareness is there before the "I Am" consciousness appears; it is what enables consciousness to come into being, and it is the end goal—the experience of coming home.

> You thought yourself a part, small;
> whereas in you there is a universe, the greatest.
>
> Hazrat Ali

So, our consciousness (and its counterpart, energy) emerges mysteriously from Awareness, or the Absolute, then descends in frequency in a process called involution, literally "turning inward" or spiraling down toward physical reality. Once here, we experience what I call *immersion*, a phase in which we seek conscious recognition of our spiritual nature while fully embodying in the physical world—the soul-in-the-body state. During this phase it's possible to feel trapped and stuck. Eventually, when our frequency increases enough, we begin the cycle of upward, outward turning—the expanding phase of *evolution*, where we consciously integrate higher and higher dimensions of consciousness—until we return to Awareness and total unity.

In the following three sections, we'll look at what happens during these phases on the path to expanded perception. We'll examine involution (consciousness descends, or decreases, in frequency from Awareness to matter), immersion (higher consciousness saturates matter), and evolution (consciousness ascends, or increases, in frequency from matter back to Awareness).

Involution: The Journey from Heaven to Earth

Involution is the journey of consciousness-and-energy downward in frequency from Awareness into matter. Awareness surpasses even the universal mind and unified field. Without identity, without duality, it is unable to be conscious of itself. It "shines" and mysteriously gives rise to consciousness, which has duality, or subject and object, and can thus perceive and have a point of view. As consciousness emerges, so do the concepts of self and reality. We often call this the emergence of "the Word," the vibration of the original Creation: consciousness and energy combined. Consciousness and energy are integral to each other and together they form the original substance of the universe, which is a unified field.

In the involution process, consciousness perceives in gradually slowing cycles, or successive levels, that can be likened to rungs on a ladder or layers of an onion. These different frequencies are often called *dimensions*, and the slower the frequency, the denser and more individualistic the consciousness-and-energy. When consciousness slows enough, it crystallizes or fragments into physical reality, which results in the experience of solid form in time and space.

> The Tao gives birth to the One.
> The One gives birth to two. Two gives birth to three.
> And three gives birth to the ten thousand things.
>
> Lao Tzu

Involution occurs every time a baby is born. You experience mini cycles of involution every time an idea or an imagination pops into your mind from out of the blue and you take it from conception to completion as a physical result. Every time you wake in the morning after having been asleep and lost in dreams all night, and each time you finish a sentence or make a decision, you perceive the involution phase on our path of perception.

Immersion: On "Pause" in Physical Reality

The second part of the journey is immersion, when we have descended in vibration and successfully created a physical self and reality. The journey into matter is an adventure; the challenge is to bring higher consciousness fully into physical reality—to saturate matter with spirit and the personality with soul. This can be a joyful, creative, sacred, loving experience full of beauty and awe, or it can be an experience of resistance and suffering.

> All wants to float. But we trudge around like weights.
> Ecstatic with gravity, we lay ourselves on everything.
> Oh what tiresome teachers we are for things,
> while they prosper in their ever childlike state.
>
> Rainer Maria Rilke

This phase is when most of us become stuck, immersed in the density and low-frequency vibration we have created. We identify with the world of seemingly solid form and forget our true nature as beings made of fluid consciousness-and-energy. We forget that we're descending/involving and ascending/evolving. We think physical reality is all there is and we can feel psychically trapped.

Here's how it happens—see if you can feel into the process: Physical reality gives rise to the idea of separation, separation gives rise to the experience of fear, and fear gives rise to the fixation or contraction of consciousness-and-energy due to resistance. Contraction slows and stops the flow of consciousness-and-energy, which produces pain. Over time, fear and contraction give rise to erroneous, negative thought and emotional habits that create a fog of ignorance and confusion around the personality. The soul has difficulty penetrating the fog to bring truth and inspiration, and the conscious mind—the point of view or perceptual lens of the soul—can only see the clutter, which contains no high-frequency consciousness. At this point, you can forget you even have a soul.

You may temporarily forget the experience of the higher frequency reality, or spirit, but deep down you know it's there. Because you perceive the world of form as separate from you, it's easy to define the nonphysical world as separate too—as "up there" in heaven. Actually, the higher frequency reality is right inside matter. Higher consciousness breaks through the thick fog of illusion at opportune moments to bring glimpses of this truth. Each mystical breakthrough or initiation opens you to the nonphysical world and triggers a yearning for memory and experience of the higher reality; you *want to* expand. These are the openings that remind you it's time to evolve. As souls, we are already "enlightened." We are always who we have been in all the higher dimensions, and at our core we always exist as pure Awareness. At the end of the immersion phase, this truth creeps back in.

> Inspiration may be a form of superconsciousness, or
> perhaps of subconsciousness—I wouldn't know. But
> I am sure it is the antithesis of self-consciousness.
>
> Aaron Copland

You experience the negative aspect of the immersion phase when you feel helpless, isolated, uninspired, or resistant. If you're anxious, too revved up or too sluggish, or in need of proof and control, you're caught in the negative side of immersion. On the other hand, if you're enjoying the spontaneous flow of creativity and discovery, feeling joyful and lucky to be alive, honoring the beauty of the physical world, or experiencing love for others, you're feeling the positive side of immersion and are making the turn toward evolution. It's suffering and resistance that keep you in the immersion phase.

Evolution: From Earth to Heaven Again

When you no longer resist physical reality but love it instead, a process of psychological and spiritual growth, or the evolution of consciousness, begins. You attune to sequentially higher and higher levels of vibration, increasing your wisdom and love as you go. As your sense of self evolves, high-frequency perception shows how interconnected we all are and your identity becomes more inclusive. You recognize that you belong to a soul group of like-vibrational beings; then soul groups merge into larger groups and you become more of a global collective consciousness. Eventually your perception expands to reveal that you are really one great consciousness containing all individual lifetimes throughout all time and space. As evolution approaches Awareness, the unified field becomes the entire self and reality.

Creativity and art are instrumental in turning the Flow from immersion to evolution. As your consciousness increases in frequency, you focus more on beauty, and creativity shifts from a focus on survival to become inspired art and design. You reach for ideas that benefit people and the planet in the evolution process; being creative this way is a spiritual experience itself, aiding your expansion. Joyful service, not sacrificial service, is another force that aids evolution.

> The Law of Wonder rules my life at last,
> I burn each second of my life to love,
> Each second of my life burns out in love,
> In each leaping second, love lives afresh.
>
> Rumi

Attention, too, helps turn the Flow from immersion to evolution. You learn to train your perception on unifying ideas, connecting yourself to the world and finding the soul and higher consciousness within matter. Intuition is also important—it accesses higher consciousness and facilitates the experience of it. By focusing on similarity, interconnectedness, and large patterns of ideas, intuition reveals greater possibilities and brings the mystical breakthroughs that crack open trapped consciousness and free it to flow again. It is intuition that ushers you into the highest perception and allows you to complete the journey into unity.

You experience evolution every day in small ways. Every time you open to new ideas and the unknown, or dream and work with your imagination, or open your heart to express generosity and faith—you experience tiny evolutionary acts. Learning and love, in all their forms, are signs that you're evolving.

The Rocking of Consciousness Is Constant

The process of involution, immersion, and evolution is always happening. There are long cycles of it and short ones too. Consciousness is blinking in and out of form every millisecond. The *many-worlds theory* in quantum mechanics says that all possible alternative realities exist at once in the unified field of consciousness-and-energy, and each idea represents an actual world. When attention focuses on a single idea, the many worlds fall together to become that particular reality. The wave condenses into the particle. In effect, this is involution reaching the immersion phase. When you take attention off a physical reality, it "collapses," or dissolves, into the nonphysical world, and all possibilities come into existence again. The particle dissolves into the wave. This equates with the evolution phase of our journey in consciousness.

You are "born" into matter and "die" into essence. You imagine a vision, then make it real. You become bored with a reality, pull your attention out, and it disappears. You are fully involved in the moment, concentrating, then you space out and "come to" again with new thoughts. Consciousness is continually moving in and out, or up and down in frequency, according to a greater wisdom and plan.

What's unique about the time we live in now? We're approaching the end of the immersion period, reaching full saturation of spirit in matter—the merger of the physical and nonphysical realities. Our perception is increasing to a point where we can experience ourselves and our reality as form and consciousness-and-energy simultaneously. This is huge! We are entering a period of conscious evolution as a new sort of hybrid human. The key thing is you don't have to wait for evolution to happen, because it's taking you along with it right now. You can just relax and leap!

In the next chapter, we'll drop further into the territory of perception and examine the processes involved in how we know what we know. We'll look at some of the discoveries made by brain science, and we'll draw distinctions between two geometries of perception: old, linear perception and new, spherical-holographic perception.

Chapter 2: The Path to Expanded Perception

Here all is one, united in a simple vision of being. All the long evolution
of life and matter and man, all my own history from the first moment
I became a living cell, all the stages of my consciousness and that of
all human beings, is here recapitulated, brought to a point, and I know myself
as the Self of all, the one Word eternally spoken in time.

Bede Griffiths

Just to Recap . . .

Perception reveals what's possible to know in physical and nonphysical life. It's like a combination telescope-microscope you focus with attention; how much you see depends on the frequency of your consciousness. Higher frequency consciousness-and-energy fine-tunes perception, allowing you to see into the nonphysical realms, and ultimately, how the nonphysical and physical worlds intimately blend with each other. If you are stuck, your soul (higher consciousness) may spontaneously break through to bring inspiration and revelation when you need it.

We are on a journey of consciousness. We emerge from the unified state called Awareness, and descend in vibration in a process called involution until our consciousness "crystallizes" in time and space in the physical world. At this point, the adventure is to saturate your physical self and reality with higher consciousness until the physical and nonphysical worlds become one—a phase I call immersion. Then transformation occurs and we realize we are free. At this point, evolution begins.

Often we get stuck in the physical world due to resistance and fear, but we are living in a time when the immersion phase is just about finished and we are beginning to evolve consciously. As we evolve, we experience successively higher levels of consciousness-and-energy until we finally return to Awareness, the experience of "home."

3

How Do You Know?

People with high levels of personal mastery do not set out to integrate
reason and intuition. Rather, they achieve it naturally—as a byproduct
of their commitment to use all the resources at their disposal. They
cannot afford to choose between reason and intuition or head and heart,
any more than they would choose to walk on one leg or see with one eye.

Peter Senge

In this chapter, we'll explore some of the exciting ideas to come from
neuroplasticity, the science that deals with how your brain can grow
and change. We'll also look at two inner blueprints or models for ways
to perceive—each a "geometry of perception." One is linear, one is
spherical and holographic, and they both figure prominently in understanding how your perception is shifting in the transformation process.

How we know is a hot topic of late; there is much debate among scientists, and even information technology geeks, about the mind and
brain. To me, this is symptomatic of the accelerating end times of the
Information Age, where humanity's worldview is still largely immersed
in the physical and mental realms yet poised to make the leap into
unknown territory. I heard some young men on the radio postulating
about three-dimensionally photocopying the brain and reducing it to
binary code so we could live, Matrix-like, in a virtual reality. I'm

thinking, "Why don't we just penetrate fully into the reality we have and see what we discover? Why don't we add some dimensionality?"

How Scientists and Mystics Perceive Consciousness

Many neuroscientists are convinced that the brain makes the mind, that it's even responsible for spiritual experiences. Neurobiologists are examining how the brain makes neural patterns and turns them into mental patterns that become "movies in the mind." And they're looking for an explanation of how the brain creates a sense of self, which is central to the act of knowing. This is fascinating stuff!

It's true that there are varying balances of brain chemistry—levels of neurotransmitters, neuromodulators, and neuropeptides—that affect the feeling tones of our experience, from states of pleasure and well-being to states of pain and suffering. It is also true that brain scientists can connect neural activity with near-death experiences, dreaming, and meditative states. But is neural activity the cause of consciousness?

On the other hand, mystics, through direct experience, maintain that the body and brain materialize out of the high-frequency fields of the soul as it slows itself down through successive levels—what in metaphysics we commonly refer to as the causal, mental, emotional/astral, etheric, and physical realms. In this view, there is a "body" that corresponds in vibration to the frequency of each level, and your conscious mind, personality, and physical body are replicas of your higher fields of memory and knowledge, with their unique proportion of love and fear.

Many spiritual teachers say your unique pattern of personal emotion and knowledge survives death and returns upon reincarnation. Once you're born, the unseen pattern plays out. Many of the talents, events, and major lessons in your life are determined by *karma*, the residual misunderstandings and imbalances you carry over with you from previous lives. So, in the mystics' perception, an underlying consciousness-and-energy blueprint shapes your brain; your brain then helps shape your outer reality; and that reality, in turn, influences the inner blueprint, which is cocreated with all other people.

I'm sure the mystics didn't describe the brain with terms like amygdala, anterior cingulate cortex, reticular formation, parietal lobe, hippocampus, and hypothalamus. Instead they gathered knowledge by *becoming* the workings of consciousness-and-energy, and they represented brain functions as a blooming lotus, an eye opening in the center of the head, or a cobra rising through the neck and head, spreading its wide hood. Though their imagery was poetic, they tracked the processes closely, and they understood the transformation of consciousness. Psychologist Carl Jung summed it up when he said, "The collective unconscious contains the whole spiritual heritage of mankind's evolution, born anew in the brain structure of every individual."[1]

> We are not human beings having a spiritual experience.
> We are spiritual beings having a human experience.
> Pierre Teilhard de Chardin

The Involution and Immersion Views

As we enter the Intuition Age, we are exploring the connections between two views: (1) spiritual reality creates the mental, and the mental creates the physical; and (2) physical reality creates the mental, and the mental creates the spiritual. Both are correct, yet each is a byproduct of a particular perceptual view. The first is the view seen through the filter of involution, of consciousness descending in frequency to become physical. The second is the view from within our state of immersion, as consciousness saturates the physical world and everything looks mainly physical. Though the cycle is turning now and starting to evolve into the Intuition Age, we're not quite there yet. When we truly enter the evolution phase, we'll have a new, much more integrated view of the brain, mind, *and* soul.

While you're in the physical world, you identify yourself as body, brain, mind, and personality, so it's natural to think that the physical self generates everything—that the brain must be the cause of consciousness. These days, though, a growing number of physicians, neuroscientists,

37

and neuropsychologists—people like Rick Hanson, Dan Siegel, David Eagleman, Candace Pert, and Jill Bolte Taylor, to name a few—also have an active inner, spiritual life. They are doing important work in bridging the physical and nonphysical worlds—and science and spirituality—as we ready ourselves for transformation and evolution. They are helping us see that the brain has an effect on consciousness *and* consciousness has an effect on the brain.

James H. Austin, a neurologist, neurology professor, and Zen practitioner, is among these professionals. He describes how the brain develops to give us a sense of self: In the fetus, the brain initially wrinkles in the back, in the visual cortex. After birth, the nerve fibers leading into the infant's visual cortex are the first to be covered with protective layers of myelin. By eight months, the white matter has moved farther into the center and front of the brain, and at one year the protective myelin sheaths are mature in the temporal lobes. The neural paths are hooking up, but the child still lacks the experience of the personal.

At eighteen months, an important threshold is reached. The long subcortical association pathways link all the brain's lobes together, and distinctions can be made between self and other. The child becomes self-conscious and recognizes her image in the mirror. With the onset of the "terrible twos," corresponding language surfaces: No! Mine! Me. You. Are our brains working alone, or are they following an inner consciousness-and-energy blueprint in these stages of development—stages that correspond with the soul gradually materializing itself as a finite personality in time and space?

Over time, we add countless layers of identity, from beliefs to career to possessions, and become attached to them. We get stuck in the immersion phase of the consciousness journey. Austin, a practiced meditator, says, "If, in a flash, an enlightened state of consciousness is to dissolve all such ties, it must extensively revise the way impulses usually flow in many circuits in the brain."[2] From what we're learning about the fluidity of the brain and the acceleration of the physical body and world, this massive change may be more possible than ever before. In other words, the physical structure of your brain may well be able to change to accommodate the inner blueprint of what happens in transformation and evolution.

> The great news is not only that the brain makes new connections throughout the life span, but there's some evidence to show that you can grow new integrative pathways.
>
> Dan Siegel

Signs of Evolution: Neuroplasticity and Human Adaptability

Not long ago it was a common assumption that the brain had only so many cells and they died progressively as we aged, unable to be replaced. We were doomed to lose our faculties and be forgetful, doddering fools in our dotage. But there have been some amazing discoveries that have shown the brain to have a resilient and nearly magical design. Biologist Fernando Nottebohm demonstrated that the brain of a male songbird grows fresh nerve cells (*neurogenesis*) in the fall to replace those that die off in summer. Building on his work, researchers have since found that humans (and other adult animals) share this ability to produce new brain cells.

In the 1920s, neurosurgeon Wilder Penfield's research concluded that all our experiences are recorded in our brain, from the most impactful events to the tiniest detail of a mundane observation. After that, Karl Lashley discovered that surgically removing various segments of rats' brains had no effect on their memory, concluding that memory is not just supported in certain areas but stored everywhere, evenly distributed throughout the entire brain. Following this, in the 1960s, Karl Pribram, a neurosurgeon and psychiatrist, read an article about holograms, put two and two together, and realized that the brain was functioning holographically concerning memory—with the "whole in every part." Later he discovered that the visual cortex functions the same way: even a very small piece of the visual cortex can reconstruct the whole of what the eyes are seeing These are mind-blowing—or *reality*-blowing—ideas that contribute to the opening of our consciousness to evolutionary perception.

Thanks to neuroplasticity, we now know that the brain changes in response to physical and emotional experiences, that the very stimulation of experience causes neural firing and the production of proteins that help create new neurons and connections among neurons. We know that when there is a growth of new neurons, there is also a growth of myelin, the protective fatty sheath that speeds nerve transmission. With increased speed, consciousness can increase. With new neural pathways, there is growth and evolution.

Negative life experiences, however, can shock the brain into fearful contraction. A repetition of similar fear-based experiences can cause sets of neurons to fire together, and then, as the saying goes, they "wire together," forming unhealthy perceptual habits. People can develop chronic limited brain chemistry and the negative thought and behavior patterns that parallel it—helplessness-thinking, depression, drug addiction, aggression, and neuroses. The reverse is also true. Positive experience can stimulate the brain to expand its functioning and renew itself. In fact, attention alone can stimulate these changes.

. . . .

Try This!
Light Up Your Brain to Help It Change

1. Close your eyes and quiet yourself. Breathe in and out easily, with a slow, regular rhythm.
2. Picture your brain and imagine there are various places throughout that are wired together. Some seem dark and shadowy, or perhaps empty, as though there's an absence of energy. There are other places that are radiantly giving off light.
3. Focus on the light places and as you pay attention, allow the light to intensify and increase. See it radiating into and through the clumped, dark, and empty places.

4. Let the light gradually change the unhealthy patterns by equalizing the amount of light until it is evenly distributed throughout your brain. You might see your brain as composed of millions of particles of glowing fairy dust.
5. Just sit with this image and experience it. Let the light work on you—it knows just what to do to heal the imbalances. Be at peace.

• • • • • • • • • • • •

Neuropsychologist Rick Hanson says, "When your mind changes, your brain changes too."[3] When you can see the workings of your mind more clearly, you can focus on mental behaviors that break unhealthy thought habits and help grow new connections and healthier, more evolutionary perception—because *how you focus your attention shapes the structure of your brain.* This is encouraging news! You are no longer condemned to a dead-end life of suffering due to negative mental and behavioral patterns. What's detrimental is now reversible. And yet, mystics have always understood the positive effect of perception and attention, focused at the frequencies of higher consciousness, on our experience of self and reality.

> The events which you observe are determined by the concept you have of yourself. If you change your concept of yourself, the events ahead of you in time are altered. . . . You are a being with powers of intervention, which enable you, by a change of consciousness, to alter the course of events—in fact, to change your future.
>
> ### Neville Goddard

I look at the developments in neuroplasticity as symptomatic of the end of the immersion phase of consciousness. We've been learning to bring full awareness into the physical realm, to see how matter behaves when its frequency increases. Now we're discovering that the brain's processing is not only linear but holographic. It isn't just a lump of gray matter but a vibrating mass, with every part equally capable and equally responsive to consciousness-and-energy. As we combine the physical and nonphysical worlds, and fully enter the evolution phase of consciousness, the brain and mind transform and become multidimensional.

Perhaps we'll experience the brain as a magic crystal from outer space, capable of shifting itself from form to *diamond light*—the vibration of the soul—and back, accessing patterns of consciousness through resonance and projecting those patterns as holographic movies, like the message from Princess Leia in *Star Wars*. Perhaps we'll discover that our neural pathways are lines of light composed of an infinite number of tiny sparkling holograms, capable of instantaneous transmission of vast amounts of knowledge from the unified field.

In the next sections, I want to introduce you to the mechanics of two different geometries of perception. You may not notice that you hold a geometric model, or inner blueprint, of the way you see consciousness-and-energy flowing and behaving. But the model you hold determines the way you know yourself and the way you allow reality to function. The first model, *linear perception*, is based on the geometry of the line and it relates to physical reality. The second model, *spherical-holographic perception*, is based on the geometry of the sphere and the hologram and it is the kind of perception that emerges when we live equally in the nonphysical world. It is the perception that will predominate in the transformed reality of the Intuition Age. Before we detail the two models, let's do a quick review of the territory of your brain.

The Basic Territory of Your Brain

Your brain has evolved over time in three stages, with each successive level bringing a more sophisticated kind of perception. So you actually have three different brains wrapped up in one amazing package. Each segment of the brain vibrates at its own frequency and reveals its own unique experience of consciousness-and-energy.

The first and earliest brain at the top of the spine is the *reptile brain*, which contains the brainstem and limbic system. Perception focused at this frequency pertains to instinctive survival, basic attraction-repulsion responses and fight-or-flight emotions, as well as pleasure-pain experi-

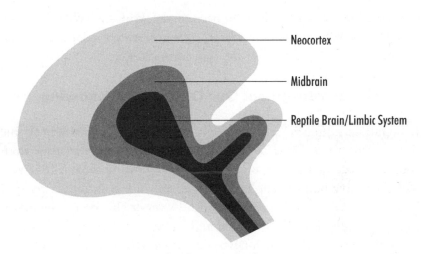

Fig. 3-1: The Three Levels of Your Brain

ences. This part of the brain influences the endocrine system and hormones, as well as the autonomic nervous system.

The next level, the *midbrain*, or mammalian brain, focuses on sensory perception (especially vision and hearing), motor control, and alertness. It also helps you feel connected to the world through similarity and affection.

The top level, the upper *neocortex*, with its left and right hemispheres, handles language and the perception of abstract-conceptual ideas. The *right hemisphere*, which develops first after birth, focuses on the essence of things—on nonverbal, holistic pattern recognition (seeing the big picture before the details), visual-spatial processing, subjective skills, and creative abilities. Intuition, or direct knowing, is its primary mode of perception. The *left hemisphere* focuses on rational, sequential, logical thinking; analysis of differences; and linguistic processing. It makes sense of experience and makes learning conscious.

The two hemispheres of the neocortex ideally work together when they're balanced—with the right brain accessing insight and higher consciousness, the left brain processing and quantifying this information, then the left brain releasing control back to the right, and so on.

Consciousness has a tendency to become stuck in the left brain, however. We'll talk more about this later, since achieving a balanced left and right brain is so important for the transformation process.

Linear Perception: Our Old Way of Knowing

In a rather simplistic sense, perception seems to progress in a line through the three levels of the brain. Energy information rises from your body along the line of the spine, progressing from animalistic instinct to our human capacity for logic and higher intuitive, mystical insight and wisdom. Consciousness-and-energy also progresses down from the higher brain to the body, and we perceive visions and how to make them real. Since the inner reality affects the outer and the outer affects the inner, I can't help but wonder whether, in chicken-or-egg fashion, this linear progression of perception through the body and brain causes us to see life itself as functioning in a linear way. Or is it vice versa? For now, let's become familiar with linear perception as it progresses up and down through your body and brain.

The Ascending Flow of Linear Perception

Body information, or sensation in the form of nerve impulses, rises up the spine. This ascending flow from the body is a process that pertains to becoming conscious of the workings of self and reality, navigating through life, and learning. In the inner world of consciousness-and-energy, the *kundalini*, considered by yogis to be the subtle energy of the universal self, also rises up the spine when activated with meditation and attention. Both the physical and subtle energies sequentially activate the seven major consciousness-and-energy centers, or *chakras*—from your tailbone to the top of your head—bringing a progression of feeling states and insights related to self and reality.

As the rising energy, which carries consciousness as energy information, enters your brain, the reptile brain at the top of the spine is the first point where the information becomes recognizable, albeit in a rudimentary way. You may have immediate instinctive responses of expansion (attraction) or contraction (repulsion or fight-flight); these arc your *truth and anxiety signals*. You might experience excitement and motivation, desire and curiosity—or perhaps boredom or wariness. There is no language center in the reptile brain, so you experience these states as physical-emotional, kneejerk responses. You are aware of yourself as a body, and are concerned with safety and sexual attraction. You notice your senses of smell and taste.

As the consciousness-and-energy progresses to the midbrain, you perceive via your senses of touch, hearing, and vision. You notice connections between yourself and others, between ideas, or even between the inner and outer senses—for example, external hearing and internal *clairaudience*, external touch and internal *clairsentience*, and external vision and internal *clairvoyance*. You experience sympathy, affection, and empathy, and are able to feel into situations or objects to know about them. Intuitive perception begins. At this stage, information is still experiential and preverbal.

> I picture the artist as someone deep-sea diving, holding her breath
> and bursting out of the water into the air six minutes later, one hundred feet
> from where she began, with sun catching the water spray. . . .
> The good thing is that the artist can move through experience,
> learn from it, and not be caught by it.
>
> Natalie Goldberg

Next, moving from the midbrain to the neocortex, as the rising energy information reaches the right hemisphere, it becomes part of a big picture or pattern that may relate to other patterns. It's experiential and nonverbal here, and you feel expansive; a symbol or symbolic event might unpack its inner meaning. The right brain is also the seat of the imagination; your intuition may access and connect a series of thoughts and impressions all at once, taking you into a higher level of consciousness. Right brain perception gives you a sense of yourself as a being, or soul, beyond the personality.

As energy information reaches the left hemisphere, perhaps simultaneously, it takes on meaning and language. You may experience an "Aha!" as you focus on definition, connect the insight to previous facts, fit it into a system of knowledge, and describe it. Left brain perception gives you a sense of being an individual personality, and it can produce the experience of ego.

• • • • • • • • • • •

Try This!
How Does Your Reptile Brain Tell You What's True or False?

1. Write about the subtle sensations and sensory impressions you have in your body when you hear something that's true or when you know something is right for you. Where do you feel it? Does the sensation move from one part of your body to another? These signals register in your reptile brain. Common truth signals include tingling or chills, bubbling warmth, leaning toward something, feelings of expansion and energy rising in the body. Perhaps you feel something click into place or "ring" true.

2. Write about the subtle sensations and sensory impressions you have in your body when you hear something that's false, or when you know something is not right for you, or dangerous. Where do you feel it? Does the sensation move from one part of your body to another? These signals also register in your reptile brain. Some common anxiety signals: contraction in the solar plexus/pit of the stomach, tight chest or throat, cold hands and feet, feelings of solidity or heaviness, leaning away from something, something "smells fishy" or "leaves a bad taste."

• • • • • • • • • • •

Try This!
Do You Use All Your Senses Equally?

1. Write about your predominant sense. How do you usually first notice things? Are you visual—do you receive a flash, a whole vision, or a "movie"? Are you auditory—do you hear a little voice inside, notice energy

in people's voices, hear important messages in song lyrics? Are you kinesthetic—do you feel "vibes"? Do you sense things as hot, warm, cool, cold? Do you feel into things to know them? Perhaps you have a strong sense of taste and smell. Rank your senses in order of predominant use.

2. For the least used, list three to five ways for each that will help you pay more attention to life, and actively practice developing them for the next few weeks. Using all your senses equally can speed the processing of energy information through your brain.

• • • • • • • • • • • •

The Descending Flow of Linear Perception

Consciousness-and-energy from the higher, nonphysical dimensions descends in frequency to materialize as form. This descending flow is about creating and receiving guidance and direction from your soul, with the energy information first impressing itself in your right brain as a pattern or inner blueprint via imagination and inspiration. It is experiential, though intuitive insights do bounce briefly to the left brain to register as concepts. The descending flow then moves into the midbrain, activating the visual sense first. The light bulb goes off, giving you that flash of insight, and you receive a vision. The idea takes on a bit of reality, then the Flow moves through the other senses, fleshing out the vision so it becomes tactile and feels real. Perhaps you can even taste or smell it.

The consciousness-and-energy continues to descend into the reptile brain, and your body becomes excited and motivated. There is desire and attraction. The creative process is set in motion, sometimes impulsively, and soon the idea materializes. During the whole creative process of the descending flow, your body continually sends ascending signals—progress reports—back to the left brain, where the process registers as real, is categorized, regulated according to past experience, and communicated about. The left brain plays an important role by focusing and concentrating attention, making choices along the way, and using its logic and analytical ability to measure success.

The relationship between the hemispheres does not appear to be
symmetrical, in that the left hemisphere is ultimately dependent on,
one might almost say parasitic on, the right, though it seems to have no
awareness of this fact. Indeed it is filled with an alarming self-confidence.
The ensuing struggle is as uneven as the asymmetrical brain
from which it takes its origin.

Iain McGilchrist

The linear geometry model of perceiving makes sense, doesn't it? It feels familiar. It's sequential and logical, and fits with the way we're used to understanding life. Linear perception is a stage along the way to a new kind of perception that is already emerging—spherical-holographic perception. When we achieve this new perception, we won't lose our linear way of thinking—it will simply be absorbed into the newer model and will adapt accordingly.

• • • • • • • • • • •

Try This!
Where Does a New Idea Register?

1. Think back over the past few weeks and use your journal to list some times when you received an idea or urge.
2. Notice whether the idea or urge came from the reptile brain as an attraction or a repulsion and whether your body moved directly into action without thinking. Or did the idea come from your midbrain via one of your senses, or from a resonance with another person? Did the idea come from the neocortex, via your right hemisphere, giving you an impression of a pattern or concept that then registered as a vision? Or did it come from your left hemisphere as a "should"?
3. Pay attention for the next few weeks to which area of your brain is accessing consciousness and where you habitually notice incoming information, noting the patterns in your journal.

• • • • • • • • • • •

Spherical-Holographic Perception: A New Way of Knowing

Because the world is increasing in frequency, you may be experiencing reality in a new, faster, more multidirectional way that supersedes the sequential, one-thing-at-a-time, linear processing we've come to know so well. Today—right now— we're shifting to a new inner geometry of perception—one based on the sphere and the hologram. *This new model develops in two stages*—first comes spherical perception, then holographic perception is revealed and the two modes merge inextricably.

With spherical perception, every point of view can expand and contract spherically to include more or less of the unified field of consciousness-and-energy, with everything contained in the present moment. With holographic perception, any part of the brain, any part of life, and any point of view can contain the entirety of the whole self and whole reality. As I mentioned before, science is gradually discovering that both your brain and the universe are like a hologram.

Before we move on into how the change in geometries of perception occurs, let's take a minute to really understand what holograms are and how they function. Basically, a hologram is a three-dimensional photographic image made with lasers, much the way our two eyes produce one three-dimensional image in the brain. If a holographic image is cut in half and illuminated with a laser, each half still contains the whole image. Continue to divide the images and each bit will always contain the whole. So every part of a hologram contains all the information of the totality. And it is this "whole in every part" idea that helps us understand an entirely new way of organizing life.

Physicist David Bohm suggested that subatomic particles remain in contact with each other in spite of separation in space because their separateness is an illusion; they may actually be holographic bits of a greater hologram. If we take this to its logical conclusion, it means that everything in the universe is interconnected via deep internal commonality, sharing and echoing one great order. Even time and space can't be broken down into separate fundamental principles. In a holographic universe, all times exist at once and our core consciousness is in all things, everywhere. This means that three-dimensional reality—our physical world—is really just a projection of this greater consciousness, or order, or "superhologram."

Reaching spherical-holographic perception is a process, with stages of development, or incremental shifts of consciousness, where each stage grows from the previous one. The first stage grows out of linear perception. In the next sections I want to relate these experiential shifts of consciousness to the way you experience energy moving through your brain and body. If you can imagine the changes in your brain and body, you'll be applying the principles of neuroplasticity, and it will help usher you into the new perception more effortlessly. See if you can feel into the stages and their resulting shifts of consciousness as I describe them.

Stage 1: Vertical and Horizontal Integration of Your Brain

Something interesting happens when you use all the parts of your brain consciously and equally. When you pay attention to both the ascending and descending linear flows of consciousness, and when you notice them registering at each stage of their progress until there are no gaps, no blind spots, no parts you skip over, the flows become even, fluid, and continuous. You learn quickly (ascending flow) and materialize imaginations effortlessly (descending flow), and the two functions feel simultaneous. This is the *vertical integration* of your brain.

You can also balance and equalize your left and right hemispheres. This is the *horizontal (bilateral) integration* of the brain. The interpenetration of activity in the left and right hemispheres, through the connecting fibers of the *corpus callosum*, helps you be just as good with imagination and creativity as you are with intellectual rigor and detail, just as satisfied with ambiguity as you are with definition and proof. You can access the nonphysical realms with intuition and deal with the logistical mechanics of the physical realm equally well. When the two sides of your neocortex integrate, it helps you experience being the soul in the body.

When both the vertical and horizontal linear flows of consciousness integrate, a sudden shift precipitates. The image that comes to mind is the Celtic cross with equidistant arms. *Your whole consciousness converges at the crossing point, or centerpoint, of those flows, and you experience centeredness.* With centeredness comes collectedness, presence, knowledge, and power. Your whole worldview changes. It's the beginning of spherical perception. This is a life-altering experience of deep integration that brings feelings of communion, the divine presence in all things, and belonging intimately in the unified field while still maintaining the sacredness of your individuality

Stage 2: After Integration, The Centerpoint

At this stage, you no longer think in linear terms, with your soul "above" your body, your body "below" your mind, or people outside you, "over there." Your position is not so relational. You are stable, always in the center of a field of consciousness-and-energy, which you now experience as existing spherically around you in all directions. What you're aware of in any given moment is inside the sphere with you, and there is nothing beyond the sphere.

In many metaphysical and spiritual traditions, there is a special spot in the center of the brain, often identified as the pineal gland or the root of the *third eye*, that is considered to be the centerpoint of consciousness and higher vision in the body. It is a connecting link between the physical and nonphysical worlds, and has played an integral role through the ages in developing intuitive abilities. The pineal gland manufactures melatonin, controls the various biorhythms of the body, and is activated by *light!* It may indeed be the intersection point of your vertical and horizontal brain-flows, and with the right kind and amount of attention it may help you leap to a new level of consciousness.

When you achieve integration of your brain, you may suddenly feel energy and light radiating from this spot, as though it's a tiny white hole through which the diamond light of your soul enters the physical world. You can also intentionally focus your attention on this powerful centerpoint and activate it with the principles of neuroplasticity. By doing this regularly, perhaps as part of a meditation practice, you can increase the frequency of your consciousness and accelerate the integration of your brain functioning.

focus: a central point of energy, from "hearth, fireplace,"
used in postclassical times for "fire" itself

Stage 3: After the Centerpoint, Multiple Centerpoints

The centerpoint in your head lets you perceive yourself as a soul with higher consciousness. Looking out from here, you can sense thoughts and wisdom radiating from you in all directions. After that, another shift spontaneously occurs: your point of view moves via resonance to another important center—your heart. Your viewpoint has descended a bit further into the physical world, and you now know yourself as a soul with enlightened sensitivity and feeling. You can look out from this vantage point and feel consciousness-and-energy radiating in all directions, producing the experience of love, compassion, and empathic communion.

It's not uncommon then to shift even further down in the body via resonance and feel the centerpoint at the base of the tailbone—where mystics say the serpent of the kundalini energy is coiled. This centerpoint gives you the experience of being physical, of understanding all animals and forms of life on earth. If you look out from this vantage point and feel consciousness-and-energy radiating in all directions, you're likely to understand the vastness of the vital force itself.

Now an amazing thing happens. *You suddenly feel yourself in the center—as the center—of everything and anything.* This is the beginning of holographic perception. You gain a different sense of self: you are the centerpoint of the entire unified field of consciousness-and-energy, no matter what position you take, no matter where you go, and you can always know the whole. In other words, *the center of anything is the center of everything.* You might then experiment with being in the center of anything so you can know the world from other perspectives. You aren't limited to just one center but have access to multiple centerpoints and endless ways to understand reality.

Having multiple centerpoints allows you to experience yourself as the soul focused in the center of higher vision in the brain, in the center of love in the heart, in the center of vital force at the tailbone, and in the center of each organ, each chakra, and each cell—they are all points of view and frequencies of perception for your soul. And each reveals its own kind of understanding. You can be the whole body as a unified brain center, and you can be the centerpoint in the middle of the earth, knowing yourself as a global mind.

The visible body just happens to be where the wave function of the organism is most dense. Invisible quantum waves are spreading out from each of us and permeating into all other organisms. At the same time each of us has the waves of every other organism entangled within our own makeup.

Mae-Wan Ho

But the evolution of your perception doesn't stop there. You begin to understand how the microcosm (the tiniest bit of the hologram) is the macrocosm (the superhologram) and how they are connected via resonance. You see that any centerpoint is both a collapsed sphere and a potential sun—that the point and the sphere are versions of each other, rocking back and forth between nonphysical and physical reality. Each centerpoint contains the encoded information to become a radiant field of consciousness-and-energy. The grain of sand is the earth, the child's sparkler is the star. And you can begin to feel how each center and its corresponding spherical field contain all other centers and their fields. Drop a million pebbles in a pond and their ripples overlap, merge, and contain each other until they all become the size of the pond.

· · · · · · · · · · ·

Try This!
Find Your Center, Feel Your Field

1. Close your eyes and quiet yourself. Breathe in and out easily, with a regular rhythm.

(Continued on next page)

(Find Your Center, Feel Your Field, continued)

2. Focus your attention on the geometric center of your head. Imagine a small opening of diamond light there, in the exact center, about as big as a pea. It is radiating light in all directions. Keep your attention focused on the light as it expands spherically through your brain and into the space around you.

3. Focus your attention on the center of your chest in your heart chakra, or in the feeling of your heart. Imagine a small opening of diamond light there, in the exact center, about as big as a pea. It is radiating light in all directions. Keep your attention focused on the light as it expands spherically through your whole body and into the space around you.

4. Focus your attention at the tip of your tailbone, in your first or root chakra. Imagine a small opening of diamond light there, in the exact center, about as big as a pea. It is radiating light in all directions. Keep your attention focused on the light as it expands spherically through your whole body and into the space around you.

5. Let the three spheres of light and energy merge into one. Feel your body as the center of this aura, or personal field of consciousness-and-energy. Let the spherical field expand through space as far as feels comfortable. Let yourself experience how everything you are aware of is inside your field.

• • • • • • • • • • •

Stage 4: After Multiple Centerpoints, The Field

Yet another shift occurs when you realize you can be in any centerpoint and a spherical field of consciousness-and-energy will occur around you, giving you access to the entire unified field. *Now you experience yourself as a spherical field of consciousness-and-energy projected from the centerpoint.* Your centerpoint becomes a big, living reality that you may first experience as your own *personal field* of consciousness-and-energy—your aura.

Picture a balloon blowing up around you, then shrinking back down to a point in your core, then blowing up again. You remain in the centerpoint as the nucleus but also feel yourself as the entire field of what's being encompassed; you know everything that's included inside the spherical field, and you can make it as big or as small as you want. Exhale and your world appears, inhale and your world dissolves. Another interesting aspect of this stage is that this field of consciousness-and-energy, your new self, contains *all* possible centerpoints, *all* possible ways of knowing, *all* possible experiences of self. You can move into any of them and still know everything.

> Human beings and all living things are a coalescence of energy
> in a field of energy connected to every other thing in the world.
> This pulsating energy field is the central engine of our being
> and our consciousness, the alpha and the omega of our existence.
> "The field," as Einstein once succinctly put it, "is the only reality."
>
> Lynne McTaggart

Now instead of thinking life is separate from you, you experience it as occurring inside you. The further you allow your consciousness to radiate, the higher your frequency becomes, the larger your sphere becomes, and the more time, space, and knowledge your personal field, or your reality, includes. You see that you are part of the unified field, and if you want to, you can expand to become the entire unified field. *You understand how the field is your original master organ of perception.* You experience yourself as all the centerpoints and the field simultaneously.

Wow! This is the stuff mystical experience has always been made of, but now it is to become the stuff of normal life. Though it may seem dizzying, you can have all these leaps of perception today and still be your physical self. You're living the experiment of creating an enlightened life on an enlightened earth. In part 2 we'll discuss ways you can speed and ease your transformation. Out of the old, and into the new!

> The body of heaven is extremely high. Open, round, immeasurable,
> it is boundlessly vast. Covering everything, containing everything,
> it produces myriad beings without presuming on its virtue, it bestows
> blessings on myriad beings without expectation or reward.
>
> Liu I Ming

Just to Recap . . .

Does the brain create consciousness or vice versa? The science of neuro-plasticity is helping bring the views of mystics and scientists closer together. It's introducing the idea that we can change our brain functioning via applied attention, but we need to understand the functions of the various parts of our brain first—to understand how we have understood perception as a linear function.

There are two "geometries of perception": linear perception and spherical-holographic perception. The first is indicative of an old way of knowing who we are and how life works, and the second is indicative of transformation. Linear perception is evolving into spherical-holographic perception via four distinct phases of growth, or shifts in understanding: integration, centeredness, multiple centeredness, and field consciousness. As the shifts occur, your sense of self and reality becomes more spherical and holographic, and less linear; processes of life become more cyclical and interrelated, and less linear. You can be in any centerpoint and understand life in new ways, and you can simultaneously know the totality of the whole unified field from any centerpoint.

Part 2

Skillful Perception for Transformation

4

Unlearn Habits of Old Perception

Analysis has at least three major limitations. First...you don't need it to find the big truths. Second, analytical tools have their limitations in a turbulent world. . . . Third, good analysis rarely motivates people in a big way. It changes thought, but how often does it send people running out the door to act in significantly new ways?

John P. Kotter and Dan S. Cohen

Linear perception is old perception. It makes us experience ourselves as solid bodies separated by empty space, and creates cause-and-effect thinking, which leads us to believe that creating anything in our reality must be a gradual, logical, relatively slow process. Linear perception gives us the illusion of "gaps" between things—between you and your goals, you and other people, and you and your soul. With linear perception everything is fragmented, and seeing separation leads to feelings of isolation. It is this experience of disconnection that keeps us stuck in fear and the immersion phase of our consciousness journey.

It's important that you be able to recognize the signs of old linear perception so you can disengage from it and feed your transformation instead. In this chapter, we'll explore some of the causes of old perception and the unconscious habits we've fallen into—habits that, with a little focused attention, we can change.

Tolerating Fear-Based Behavior

Because old perception is tied so closely to fear, it is often marked by unconscious reactionary habits we've developed to protect ourselves. When focusing on survival, it's difficult to feel our heart; empathy for oneself and others often seems to go underground. We feel the effects of old perception's reactionary habits every day, and though the experiences can be upsetting, we assume they're ordinary and grudgingly tolerate them.

Here are two examples: In the first situation, Samantha offered to give her friend Peter her copy of some tax preparation software after she used it. He took it. The following year, he hinted, "Did you buy the software yet?" She had and was finished using it. He said he was going to have to buy it. Samantha once again offered hers to him, which he said he would take. Then Samantha realized she was feeling slightly uncomfortable. Peter was her friend but in neither year had he offered to split the cost with her. He wasn't poor, and the product wasn't cheap. She might have given it to him even if he had offered to help pay for it, but when he expected to get it for free, she balked a bit.

Samantha wrote a kindly worded note to him, saying she felt uncomfortable about the situation and wanted to rectify things so it wouldn't damage their friendship; perhaps they could split the cost this year. He responded tersely with: "I'll buy my own copy." After that, he avoided her and their friendship ended. An old, *reptile-brain perceptual habit* had raised its ugly head. Both people felt offended, but Peter reacted with an attack (fight response), then abandoned Samantha (flight response). What could have been win-win became lose-lose.

In the second situation, the director of a women's organization asked Jane, an experienced teacher and speaker, to give a talk on empowering women to make change. She asked that it be done gratis, and in exchange Jane would receive publicity for her new coaching business. Jane gave a great lecture, but afterward, the director couldn't be bothered to thank her and brushed her off. Jane later discovered the same organization was paying a flashy trainer a hefty fee to do an intensive workshop on the same subject.

"Why didn't she hire me?" Jane wondered. "Didn't she see how good I am and how much I know?" Jane did not lack self-esteem but was humble, while the director had a get-something-for-nothing-and-therefore-don't-value-it-very-much attitude. The director was caught in an old, *left-brain perceptual habit* that measured success by ego expression—the more brash the confidence, the better. It blinded her to Jane's high quality. In both these examples, behavior rooted in unconscious, old perception was allowed to wound others, as though it were nothing out of the ordinary.

Expecting a World Steeped in Suffering

Even before the Industrial and Information Ages, brain science tells us our brains and perception were shaped by centuries of scarcity, trauma, suffering, and danger. A fairly new field called *fetal origins* studies the effects of the conditions we encounter in the womb and how our nine months of gestation may wire our brains for survival. More specifically, you may be influenced from the very beginning by emotional and chemical expansions and contractions coming from your mother about whether the world is safe, abundant, loving, and creative—or if it's a place of danger and pain.

Catherine Monk, at Columbia University, has been conducting research exploring how a pregnant woman's mental state and moods may shape her child's personality. She stress-tests pregnant women who are depressed or anxious and pregnant women with normal moods, then notes the effects on their fetuses. All the women show physiological signs of stress in response to the tests, but only the fetuses of depressed or anxious women display their own disturbances. Monk says the reason may be a genetic predisposition or that the fetuses' nervous systems are actually being shaped by their mothers' emotions.

It makes sense that the empathic connection between a mother and her unborn child would convey energy information through vibration that indicates either expanded states based on love, safety, and soul or contracted states based on fear, scarcity, and danger. Think back to our caveman ancestors, to early tribal cultures based on survival of the fittest and most warlike, to the days of agriculture when a bad year of drought or flood meant death. How many mothers back then were able to convey to their fetus a consistent experience of safety and expansiveness? It's not unreasonable to assume there could be a cumulative effect of the repeated stimuli of lack, greed, and cruelty on our DNA, where predispositions to negative emotion, deformity, or disease might become genetic. Notice how we validate the idea that if a parent is an alcoholic, or violent, or suicidal, the child is naturally expected to be that way too. On a large scale, globally, it's not surprising that many people equate being alive with suffering; it may be passed to us in our genes.

> So long as we are embedded in a learning, or block of learnings . . .
> we can't grasp the possibility of any higher mode of operation. . . .
> Fields are kept active by participation—the positive or negative
> aspect of that participation is irrelevant.
>
> ### Joseph Chilton Pearce

We are spiritual beings, emerging through birth from a realm of unity and love, where safety isn't even a concept, into a dense physical reality where we must accustom ourselves to everything that isn't what we know as truth. We must accept and convince ourselves of the strange idea of "survival" and of the resignations, negative expectations, and "co-miseration" that plague physical life. To a spiritual being, knowing nothing but freedom and eternal life, these are odd concepts indeed. No wonder life in this world is so confounding; to be here, in the body, we've had to give up everything we intuitively know to be true—everything safe, loving, and joyful—in favor of collective negative beliefs that seem so real. "Everybody else thinks life is hard, so I guess I should believe it too, if I want to fit in."

In the deeper parts of your brain, no matter that you're actively educating yourself about your true nature as a spiritual being, you still probably buy into some of this collective negative programming and unconsciously act from it. How can you inherit DNA shaped by generations of people who have suffered and trudged, and not be affected by the encoding? It's something that we as human beings have in common.

> If you've ever lived through an earthquake . . . you may have
> felt static energy reverberating in your body for days. Strong waves
> of emotional stress can affect the whole world in a similar way. . . .
> At the level of consciousness, we're all in this together.
>
> Doc Childre and Howard Martin

Antiquated Tactics and Worldviews

The fear-based reality to which we've resigned ourselves, to some degree was formed by our reptile brain's survival instinct and the tendency of our left brain to control reality by suppressing painful memories or knowledge that might contain disruptive emotion. Fight, flee, deny, and control. A wide variety of methods for dealing with fear have developed over time from these basic tactics, then cultural worldviews grew from the tactics.

Consider the ubiquity of war and its saber-rattling intimidation strategies, now used commonly in politics, business, and relationships. Consider the great credibility and power of scientific-mechanistic-academic thought, that co-opts or disparages intuition, art, dreams, oral wisdom, and personal growth. Or the hierarchical patriarchy that tries to control what it considers uncontrollable and thus dangerous: women, nature, mystical spirituality, outer space, truth, and anyone who seems too different. All these began as solutions to fear, but have with time actually perpetuated fear. In the Industrial Age we handled fear by strengthening materialism and patriarchy; in the Information Age we distract ourselves with a glut of media, data, and electronic devices that splits our attention into seemingly irreparable fragments, like Humpty Dumpty after his fall.

As we enter the Intuition Age, these tactics and their resulting worldviews feel antiquated, and the realities they precipitate are malfunctioning and failing. What worked to cope with fear in earlier, lower frequency times now limits our potential. Let's examine how the reptile brain and the left brain have shaped our perceptual habits, so you can recognize what might hold you back.

The following habits are the result of a small part of your brain dominating the totality of who you are, and they are usually very unconscious and automatic. If any of the following habits seem familiar, it's not that you're "bad" or flawed—you're just noticing an old tactic you share with many others, that you may want to clear. All of us have probably experienced all these behaviors at various times, and we certainly know others who do these things! We are all very nuanced in our combination of love and fear characteristics.

Very little knowledge comes by "instinct." By definition, instinct is that which is innate, invariable, unlearned, and fixed. . . . So far as anyone can test, measure, or prove, instinct doesn't account for much in humans. Biologists unanimously define as "instinctive" only a very few basic reflexive responses to stimuli.

Cathy N. Davidson

Old Reptile-Brain Perceptual Habits

Your reptile brain processes information at the earliest stage, when instinct is legitimately required for survival, and many of the tactics we developed to deal with fear have their roots in the reptile brain's pre-verbal, kneejerk reactions. The reptile brain has two modes: expansion/safety and contraction/danger. This leads to two reactions when fear and danger are involved: fight or flight.

These days you don't have to be in actual physical danger for these reactions to occur; you can be slightly reminded, in a very unconscious way, of a long-past danger by something fairly innocuous, like Peter feeling criticized for not being generous to his friend. Reptile-brain reactions may feel normal to the personality, but they aren't natural to the soul. Fortunately, you can learn to move beyond the various reptile-brain behaviors by seeing them for what they are—just habits.

The Adrenaline Habit

When the reptile brain decides a situation warrants fighting or fleeing, the amygdala triggers the sympathetic nervous system and the release of epinephrine, or adrenaline, so we can shift into emergency mode and take immediate action. Adrenaline is a powerful hormone and neurotransmitter that increases the heart rate and dilates air passages—and it can become addictive. "Adrenaline junkies" have a constant need for urgency. If we've been exposed to frightening situations repeatedly and have begun to think it's normal, we may actually crave danger and stressful experiences for the adrenaline rush they provide. With the intensity of our multi-tasking lives today, adrenaline addiction is common. In fact, we're often praised and rewarded for speedy, hyperactive, risk-taking behavior.

The adrenaline habit can manifest as the seduction of fear—we can be attracted by the very thing we're trying to protect ourselves from. Whether we jump out of airplanes, weave in and out of traffic at high speed, or unconsciously create situations that threaten to do us in emotionally or financially, we're under the spell of adrenaline. This habit lives for drama and anxiety. For example, we may repeatedly find partners who act out aggression or abandonment patterns that mirror the way our parents behaved when we were young.

> Projection and attack are inevitably related, because projection is always a means of justifying attack. Anger without projection is impossible. . . . The process begins by excluding something that exists in you but which you do not want, and leads directly to excluding you from your brothers.
>
> Helen Schucman (channeling *A Course in Miracles*)

The adrenaline habit also causes anger and rage responses to fear. Becoming aggressive and projecting unwanted feelings onto others in the form of bullying, blame, criticism, belittling, guilt, or punishment is a great way to deflect internal terror. We see it so often: the controlling husband, who grew up feeling abandoned, flies into a violent rage when his wife doesn't feel like making love or when she expresses an opinion different from his. Then there are those catty girls on reality television who have sarcastic, hair-trigger attack reactions to anyone who threatens their aura of superiority.

The Security Habit

A more subtle response is the urge to fortify and create impenetrability and security. In the "Three Little Pigs" fairy tale, the big bad wolf huffed and puffed and blew down the houses made of straw and sticks—but *not* the third little pig's house of bricks. We all would like that proverbial house of bricks, and the most common way to find it is by accumulating power through financial and materialistic means. The same is true for accumulating information and being an expert, or achieving cultural standards of beauty so others will be in awe. Our fixation on celebrities today is part of this reptile-brain drive for security through attractiveness. We might also find security by controlling others or by becoming indispensable. Being a people-pleaser, rescuer, or problem-solver fits into this pattern. So does acting superior, powerful, and aloof.

The Helplessness Habit

When life presents us with a string of wounding and demeaning experiences, it's natural to freeze under the onslaught like a rabbit in the hawk's shadow. Freezing can result in feelings of helplessness, paralysis, lack of motivation, or blankness. It's normal to feel hollow, or develop depression or an apathetic attitude. When we stop the flow of energy, our frequency drops. And when that happens we can become physically sluggish, drained, or sick.

There is a tricky version of this helplessness habit where we sneak in a little bit of controlling behavior. This is *passive aggression*, and it's sometimes difficult to notice. In this habit, we unconsciously decide to be right by being wrong, or to be in control by being out of control. We can be depressed or paralyzed, but it's someone else's fault. We can blame others by "guilt-tripping" them, yet if they try to help, we can say they're doing it wrong. We can praise people with sarcasm and insult them in the process. We can act out in aggressive ways and still pretend we're helpless or don't care.

The Avoidance Habit

One of the most direct solutions is to simply avoid situations that threaten us. After all, "ignorance is bliss," right? We can walk out of an uncomfortable situation, retreat into the past to reminisce, or "leave our body" and dissociate from the present moment altogether, spacing out into a mindless state. We can be forgetful, escape into fantasy worlds, or feign ignorance. We can abdicate responsibility and give authority to other people.

Addictive behaviors are another way to avoid uncomfortable situations. Alcohol, drugs, work, exercise, money, sex, food, sports, shopping, socializing, television, mystery novels, collections, cats, Star Trek conventions, and just about anything else can serve as our substance of choice for an addiction—and avoidance.

The Submission Habit

Finally, the reptile brain comes up with another coping mechanism. When confronted with an overpowering, threatening, or narcissistic person, we can stand our ground but be submissive and subservient. Show our vulnerable soft parts and smile innocently. Assume a cowering posture and nonthreatening tone of voice. Avoid eye contact. Basically, we keep our vibration a bit lower than theirs, making them feel good about themselves. With this habit we can become a master at charming, serving, helping, and finding ways to be needed and accepted. And what's wrong with these behaviors, we ask? Nothing—if they come from joy, love, and the natural flow of the soul. But when we confuse acceptance with love, and pleasing with survival, we end up sacrificing ourselves.

. . . .

Try This!
Find Your Reptile-Brain, Old-Perception Habits

1. In your journal, list the ways you are stimulated or motivated by adrenaline. Do you crave a certain kind of "high"? Do you react dramatically in opposition to

(Continued on next page)

(Find Your Reptile-Brain, Old-Perception Habits, continued)

certain things? Do you need a particular intensity to feel alive or attracted to someone or something? What situations make you project anger, blame, or punishment onto someone else?

2. List the ways you try to find security. What draws you to specific celebrities and powerful people? Do you use subtle forms of intimidation? How do you dominate and control people and situations? Are there things in your life you feel compulsive about? When do you stonewall others?

3. List the ways you shift into feeling helpless. What kind of people or situations can make you give your power away or feel severely frustrated? When do you feel paralyzed, unmotivated, blank, or stagnant? In what areas of your life do you feel negative, burned out, or apathetic? How do you tend to be passive aggressive when dealing with other people?

4. Now list the ways you run away from painful or uncomfortable situations, including those that involve particular people. List a few times you've allowed the past to dictate your present experience. When do you space out, leave your body, or feign ignorance in response to threats? How do you distract yourself from things you don't want to face? What do you consider your addictive patterns?

5. When do you seek to minimize threats by being agreeable and pleasing? What specific mechanisms do you use to make yourself seem invisible and nonthreatening? What "shoulds" have you internalized that govern your behavior, and to whom do they really belong?

. . . .

Old Left-Brain Perceptual Habits

We've shed some light on how your reptile brain has contributed to old perception, but what about your left brain? Remember that your left brain governs rational, sequential, logical thinking; analysis of differences; and linguistic processing. By itself it has no inspiration—its perception is based on compartmentalization and isolation, regulation, definition, proof, and description. If you're being smart, setting boundaries, managing reality, feeling like an individual, arguing a point and trying to be right, organizing and categorizing, or making declarative statements, you're in your left brain.

When you experience fear, the signals from your reptile brain ascend to your left brain, where the information is processed, forming rules and beliefs about what you must do to prevent similar situations. One of the left brain's primary rules is "never be overwhelmed by negative emotion," so it preemptively suppresses any potentially upsetting memories and knowledge. Let's look at the ways the left hemisphere of your brain contributes to old perception.

Many of us make judgments with our left hemisphere and then are not willing to *step to the right* (hemisphere) for a file update. For many of us, once we have made a decision, we are attached to that decision forever. I have found that the last thing a really dominating left hemisphere wants is to share its limited cranial space with an open-minded right counterpart!

Jill Bolte Taylor

The Logic Habit

Logic has its place and is a highly useful tool. But when we primarily identify with it, we lose touch with our totality. You've certainly encountered people who rely on knowledge and intellectual prowess. For them, proof and academic rigor are paramount, and information is power. In this left-brain mode, there should be no leaps of perception, no intuitive flashes—just objective, deductive, or inductive reasoning. If you make a point, it should be similar to points made by previous scholars. And though there's validity to common sense, it's too casual—too open to interpretation.

This perception habit fights fear by denying ambiguity. And, with an overemphasis on logic, we don't need to acknowledge "uncontrollable," wishy-washy emotions. Mistakes are not tolerated. We want to be right, which can eventually lead to being "dead right." In addition, living in a world of thought can prevent us from having a direct experience of life, or from effectively materializing visions. Even light, fluid ideas, if confined to the left brain, eventually become heavy, turning into beliefs and rules. Every decision and declaration the left brain makes cuts off half the available possibilities, and the world narrows to something dry, brittle, and uninspired. What's known and proven leaves little space for change, innovation, and growth.

The logic habit keeps us rooted in linear perception—in the belief in sequential, gradual progress. We are limited to thinking about what worked in the past, and this can make us tend toward conservatism and tradition, repeating what used to work, what used to be true. With this perception habit, we project past experience onto the present and future, and there is no concept of transformation.

The Isolation Habit

The left brain reduces direct experience to a described meaning and therefore tends to cut us off from life. That means our experience of self is reduced, too. With too much left-brain dominance, we experience ourselves as separate from an "outside world." The perception of separation—of us being small, and the world being huge and overwhelming—can cause our experience of individuality to turn to one of isolation.

It follows that when we feel isolated, the world becomes a source of danger. The left brain takes on the role of guard and protector, constantly monitoring the perimeter for problems. When we identify with the left brain, we can embody this sense of distrust, suspecting everything of potential harm. The more isolated we become, the more fragile we feel. With the focus on danger, we can become negative too, finding reasons why ideas can't happen or why we can't do something. After all, things will probably go wrong or fail, right? The left brain spins out an endless series of "yes, buts" and negative declarative statements. It likes to have roles clearly defined, with life functioning in comfortable hierarchies that diagram the flow of energy, influence, and power.

The Ego-Narcissism Habit

Born from isolation, the next left-brain, old-perception habit is the development of *ego*. We may have a mild case of ego—a simple overemphasis on the importance of our own individuality—or it can become more deeply ingrained and serious. We can identify totally with the functioning of the left brain—which by nature is separate from the world—and think we *are* the left brain. This is a sort of imprisonment, and our consciousness can merge with its captor (perhaps it's the energetic version of Stockholm Syndrome), and we can behave, speak, and think like our captor. We literally *become* the ego in its desperate, isolated, and glorified individualism.

> Half the harm that is done in this world is due to people who want to feel important. They don't mean to do harm but the harm does not interest them. Or they do not see it, or they justify it because they are absorbed in the endless struggle to think well of themselves.
>
> T. S. Eliot

As the ego, we tend to "believe" rather than think freely. We don't like to try new things for fear of failing, being criticized, and rejected. We rationalize why we don't take chances that would allow growth and draw on past information to cleverly outsmart our "rivals." We focus on our own needs first, to the exclusion of others, and have difficulty feeling or even understanding what "heart" is. I often hear my clients saying these disparaging things about themselves as though this is who they are, but really, it's just the ego speaking.

As the ego becomes more entrenched and fragile in its isolation, *narcissism* emerges, and we only feel comfortable when we can seduce or manipulate others to act in ways that agree with our worldview. If they don't agree, or if they act discordantly, we attack or abandon them until they come back and behave themselves. This is the left brain thinking it's the ultimate master of the universe. It's important to be able to recognize this pattern of perception and behavior, especially in others, so you aren't manipulated by it and don't identify with it. When you see the pattern operating, remember that it's not the person who is that way—it's the left brain that has become totally dominant.

The narcissistic habit of perception and behavior goes like this: glorify oneself (physically, sexually, and mentally) to impress others; seduce them with charm by making them think they're special and privileged to be with us; have them support us in our beliefs and habits; reward and reinforce that behavior, but if they stray, punish and intimidate them back into compliance or threaten to abandon them. When the above doesn't work, leave without a second thought, or get rid of them, then start all over with new, impressionable people. If these tactics ever stop working—if there is ever the realization that we are equal to others—the ego will start to "die." If we've identified with the ego, we may feel that *we* are dying.

> There is no witchcraft, no evil, no devil. There is only perception.
> Carlos Casteneda

The Willpower Habit

To maintain order and control, the left brain focuses our willpower. If we see the world as inimical and overwhelming, it can seem that the only way to hold our own against great odds, or to make headway, is to develop an iron will and use it like a machete to cut through the jungle. If we feel isolated, with no one to assist or care for us, we'll rally all our resources to survive. If we're fighting fear, our choices require force to prevent and counteract incoming threats.

Willpower is choice with added directional force. It appears when we forget that the unseen realms are supporting us, and that we can materialize whatever we can imagine, without forcefulness, simply by choosing a reality and focusing on it gently. Willpower often involves cleverness and subterfuge, especially when we believe we must somehow cheat, overpower, or impress others to win. Achievement through willpower eventually fails because it has no joyful motivation at its core; it's about achieving one reality to *prevent* another. If we're using willpower, our underlying belief is that the negative reality is the real one and it will eventually win out. In addition, willpower draws forth resistance from others, which makes our path even more difficult.

The Distraction Habit

Finally, to avoid fear and negative emotion, the left brain may distract us by multitasking and jumping rapidly from one focus of attention to another, and another, and so on. As life becomes speedier and more complicated, there is more to pay attention to, and we must cover ten times the ground we covered a few years ago. This chronic overload can offer shelter from personal and societal negativity. Speeding, hyperactivity, and a short attention span keep consciousness on the surface; there is no chance for deep diving into emotion. Neuro-marketers, who measure test subjects' EEG responses to certain words to target advertising more accurately, report that the word "fast" ranks very high in the function category and "speed" sets off extremely positive feelings.

• • • • • • • • • • •

Try This!
Find Your Left-Brain, Old-Perception Habits

1. In your journal, list examples of the ways you resort to logic, analysis, proof, or cause-and-effect thinking to avoid feeling something. What topics and positions do you argue about? How is your perception limited by too much focus on gradual progress or linear time?

2. Now list ways you feel separate from others and the world, or isolated. What or who don't you trust? How do you feel you might be harmed? What are some of your fixed beliefs? What can trigger you to act, in even mild ways, like a narcissist? How do you do that? In what areas do you feel you have too much ego?

3. Where in your life do you exert willpower to make something happen? What do you think might happen if you let up?

4. How do you split your attention? What do you routinely use as a distraction? How do you feel when you live on the surface of things?

• • • • • • • • • • •

Recognizing Unhealthy Contraction and Expansion States

The old-perception habits I've listed used to be comfortable because they helped us survive. Denial used to work. Now these habits limit and slow us down, especially when used as the *only* methods for achieving a successful life. The problem with these reptile-brain and left-brain perceptual habits is that they've become unconscious, ingrained, automatic defensive behaviors. They feed fear through their constant attention to it; they expect fear and exist to deal with it, so fear never really has a chance to be transformed. *What we resist persists.* By constantly paying attention to fear, and by trying to deny and suppress negativity, our vibration remains at a low level. Meanwhile, the vibration of the planet is rising dramatically, creating obvious dissonance and stress!

When you're in the Flow, there is an oscillation that contains the kind of contraction and expansion that promotes evolution. Healthy contraction is about focus and choice, while healthy expansion is about creativity, growth, and release. But with old perception, there's a tendency to contract in ways that lead to paralysis, or expand in ways that lead to hyperactivity. Both end in exhaustion. Old perception can prevent life from renewing itself easily or flowing into new cycles of creativity and growth. It slows and often stops the Flow, denies the soul's reality, keeps us from being in the present moment, blocks guidance, perpetuates fear and scarcity, causes illness and mistakes, and creates pain and suffering.

Is There Hope?

Is this long-term past conditioning something we can overcome and change in a reasonably short time? It certainly looks impossible from a logical point of view. But I think we can do it now. Because the frequency of the planet is accelerating and we are all accelerating with it, you have the chance to shoot past those ancient, collective, unconscious behaviors to be reborn as a nonsuffering being with an increasing memory of your true state— without having to die physically. Living in the present moment lets you make rapid changes to habits that have taken ages to form; you can reshape your brain and your reality. The times are empowering you.

To move forward, try questioning these accepted behaviors—these unhealthy perceptual habits—and actively seek to recognize them when they occur. Once you can see what you've been agreeing to, what's been influencing your choices and actions, and that it isn't what you want, you can make different choices about how to think and act. You can catch yourself midstream, pause, unplug, and choose anew, responding from your heart and soul instead. In the next chapter, we'll look at the exciting counterpoint to old, linear perception, and see what's possible.

> What is the most rigorous law of our being? Growth.
> No smallest atom of our moral, mental, or physical structure
> can stand still a year. It grows—it must grow; nothing can prevent it.
>
> Mark Twain

Just to Recap . . .

Old, linear perception gives rise to many unconscious reactionary habits. These behaviors have developed over thousands of years as a result of our fear-based reality and may have been passed from generation to generation in the womb, from mother to fetus. Old-perception habits have been generated by the reptile brain's survival instinct and the left brain's need to suppress painful memories or knowledge that might contain disruptive emotions.

A wide variety of old-perception habits contribute to keeping you in a contracted reality, slowing the progress of transformation. These habits pertain to the overuse of, or overdependence on, defensive behaviors related to adrenaline, security, helplessness, avoidance, submission, logic, isolation, ego-narcissism, willpower, and distraction. To move through the transformation process more easily, it helps to recognize these unhealthy behaviors, which lead to paralysis as well as hyperactivity, and ultimately, exhaustion. Then you can begin to change the habits and open yourself to a new kind of perception.

5

Recognize the New Perception

To attempt to change the world before we change our concept of ourselves is to struggle against the nature of things. . . . If we would become as emotionally aroused over our ideals as we do over our dislikes, we would ascend to the plane of our ideal as easily as we now descend to the level of our hates.

Neville Goddard

The new perception lies just beyond a door. It's there, all set to go, but we must leave the small, musty room we're in. Force of habit and allegiance to old perception keep us in the room, yet we're curious about what's outside. To leave what's been so familiar, we need a burning desire to change the old to the new—to shift what doesn't work to what fits and works perfectly. The old must feel bad, we must be sick of it, and bored by it. It must hold no advantages.

What do we *really* want? We need a sense of what we want to create next—what a new, better reality could feel like. And, we need a sense of how to make the transition between old and new. In this chapter, we'll explore the process of moving beyond old, limited, linear perception into the new, spherical-holographic perception of the Intuition Age. It's the new perception that will give you glimpses of what's possible to experience. We'll begin to build the habit of making it your main way of knowing.

Just Give Me a Minute!

Ingrid told me she has a hectic life, is uncomfortable, and knows she's probably damaging her health, yet she keeps going because she "owes it to other people"—though she knows she often shortchanges them. Her employer needs everyone to work fifty- to sixty-hour weeks. Her children need her at sporting events and to help with homework. Her husband, her house, her friends, her exercise, and her relaxation time—she wants to do it all. She is exhausted and running on adrenaline but "making it work," *sort of.* Ingrid wants to be more spiritual and intuitive, to improve herself, to meditate—but when? She said, "When I get a free minute, I'll think about it."

This is so many of us today. Ingrid can't stop her treadmill routine long enough to get a minute to think about stopping her treadmill routine! She's so preoccupied with external problems that she can't drop through the static they create to feel the core issues underneath and decide what to do. One of my entrepreneur friends told me that you have to make time to work "on" your business as well as "in" your business. You have to make time to be quiet so you can penetrate into real issues to find the most effective way to proceed. Ingrid is working "in" her life, not "on" her life. If she can take that minute and question her left-brain "shoulds" and "yes, buts," she'll discover that developing some right-brain habits like using intuition and meditating are not just extra things to add to the "To Do" list; they are the transformational means that can re-create her life as a win-win-win situation.

> Attain the climax of emptiness, preserve the utmost quiet:
> as myriad things act in concert, I thereby observe the return.
>
> Lao Tzu

First, Shift from Your Left Brain to Your Right Brain

Are you tolerating a rat-race lifestyle like Ingrid, or putting up with situations that detract from your natural joy or dampen your creativity? If so, your left brain is probably in control of your life. Remember that your left brain is the final resting place of each once-vibrant experience, after it's been analyzed, described in words, fit into a familiar pattern, preserved as a memory, and had judgments made about it. Your experience is no longer alive, no longer original, no longer connected to your soul.

When the left brain becomes dominant, it's easy to identify with it and think you are the way *it* is, that life functions the way *it* functions. You can fall into behaviors, like Ingrid, that exist to control reality, preserve safety, maintain familiarity, and prevent change. This is the small musty room. To leave your left brain is to leave the known physical world and enter the nonphysical world of free-flowing consciousness-and-energy—that's what's immediately beyond the door. It can be a scary shift, this step into the unknown of right-brain perception. You won't be able to recognize new perception in its entirety until you can make this first shift from the isolated, fixed, left-brain worldview to the bright, interactive, "anything's possible" right-brain experience. You need to recognize that your left brain doesn't know enough; you need a new leader!

> The left hemisphere denies the importance of what it does not understand, ignores what it cannot accommodate, ironizes what it doesn't accept, and generally pulls the rug from under the feet of those who would look to anything beyond what it has to offer.
>
> Iain McGilchrist

I spoke with a young man recently who had created a successful business designing software for smartphone apps. He wanted to develop his intuition and healing ability but didn't know how. I gave him tips like "use your senses and stop describing your reality" and "feel into an object, merge with it, and become it," and he said, poised with his pen to take notes, "How do I do that?" He was as sweet and sincere as could be, but it wasn't computing. We both had to laugh. He had developed a strong left-brain habit that made him an early success in a competitive technological field, and using his right brain—even *understanding* how to shift to his right brain—was like trying to paint a landscape with a keyboard.

To enter the right brain's world, it's best to pull out of the left brain's world in stages. Pause your engagement with language, and stop your internal self-talk and external speech. Give up interest in definitions and meaning in favor of the stimulation of your senses. Stop needing to know the steps to doing something and let the next urge come, then trust it and follow it. Allow for surprise. See what arises next to catch your attention. You're in the moment and don't need to be anywhere else. You don't need to know what will happen; just act and see what occurs.

Make sure to validate these free-flowing, inspirational experiences when they occur. Your left brain will surely put up a fight, protesting your disloyalty with many good reasons why right-brain perception is ridiculous, or how you'll fail or be rejected if you trust it: "But you can't ignore paying the rent! You can't risk losing your job! If you waste time, you'll fall even further behind! You don't know enough! You can't just stop and do nothing!" When the barrage of logic and fear begins, just say to your left brain, "Thank you for sharing; I'll get back to you later."

. . . .

Try This!
Shift from Your Left Brain to Your Right Brain

To shift from your left brain to your right brain, try any of the following things:

- Pretend you're a dog or a cat and see what you want to do next.
- Pretend you're five years old again and remember what it was like to play. How did it feel when you decided to make a painting? How did it feel when you wanted to use a red crayon instead of a brown one?
- Remember what it's like to stand in front of the pastry counter at a bakery or an ice cream store, anticipating what you're going to eat.
- Imagine a red rooster. Imagine a green rooster. Imagine a purple rooster! Imagine a snake made of shiny chrome. Imagine a snake made of fuzzy angora. Imagine a snake made of a slinky toy. Keep going!

- Put on some music and dance around the living room. Put on some music, sit in a chair, and let your hands dance with each other. Put on some music, sit in a chair, and let your feet dance with each other.
- Let your mind go blank. Ask your right brain to present you with an image of a place to go on vacation—not the name or a description in words but a little movie of a place.

• • • • • • • • • • •

Recognizing Right-Brain Perception

Right-brain perception is the beginning of Intuition Age perception. It renews you, as dreams do at night. It reminds you that there are other dimensions of consciousness and there's a vast territory in the nonphysical world to explore. Your right brain returns you to the realm of imagination, to the idea that anything is possible, to fun and joy, and to a deeper, integrated wisdom. Compare that to the left brain's stash of data bits and bytes!

Insights and urges come from your right brain, and you're in your right brain when you're in that in-between space just before you make a choice. Your right brain provides higher perspective, and it's where you go when you "space out." In her book, *My Stroke of Insight*, neuroscientist Jill Bolte Taylor, who experienced a stroke and lost her left-brain dominance for a while, describes her new life in her right brain like this: "[My right mind] is sensitive to nonverbal communication, empathic, and accurately decodes emotion. My right mind is open to the eternal flow whereby I exist at one with the universe.... My right mind is ever present and gets lost in time.... Consequently, my right mind is highly creative in its willingness to try something new. It appreciates that chaos is the first step in the creative process."[1]

Instead of being stuck in reptile-brain fight-or-flight behaviors, or in isolating, controlling left-brain behaviors, you are set free in a self-regulating world of direct experience where sensing, feeling, knowing, and decoding subtle vibratory energy information and emotion is second nature. Your intuition, or *direct knowing*, brings what you need to know just when you need to know it. There is no wasted effort, just profound relaxation. A more expansive life begins, with increased mystical experience and feelings of connection and communion. You relax your worry muscle, soften your need for control and willpower, and feel more supported in every way.

The great way has no impediments; it does not pick and choose.
When you abandon attachment and aversion, you see it plainly.
Make a thousandth of an inch distinction, Heaven and Earth swing apart.

Seng Ts'an

The right brain does not perceive in a linear way, so it has no sense of past, present, and future or cause-and-effect materialization. Instead, it lives in the present moment, which is as vast and inclusive as you want it to be. Within the present moment, you experience a deep sanity concerning the coordination of the Flow—of the creation and dissolution of the forms in your world. The Flow brings what you need and clears away what you don't need. It's awe-inspiring, and you learn to trust it implicitly. You realize there is a "right unfolding" to any process that is naturally win-win-win; everyone benefits and no willpower is required. In addition, when you're in your right brain, you remember how to play. You reconnect with imagination and the unlimited number of possible realities you can materialize. This "possibility awareness" makes for a positive attitude.

Your right brain *allows*. It allows the Flow, the unfamiliar, the surprising, the nonsensical, the ambiguous, the full range of emotion and human experience, and every frequency of consciousness. It even allows the unhealthy contractions of the reptile brain and left brain. It does not judge, and it does not speak. Instead of separating you from the world, it unifies you with others and finds similarities between things. The way you know what's true is by the way you feel—the more you merge with the soul's harmony and love, the more effective your choices, actions, and results become. This soul-influenced reality feels more *real* than any previous realities. By recognizing right-brain perception—and enjoying it—you generate a desire for it, strengthening your determination to transform your consciousness.

What must underlie successful (social) epidemics, in the end, is a bedrock belief that change is possible, that people can radically transform their behavior or beliefs in the face of the right kind of impetus.
Malcolm Gladwell

Next, Focus on Left-Right Brain Horizontal Integration

Right-brain perception becomes the new, larger context for re-creating your reality. You experience how the right brain gives you spot-on insight based on far-reaching wisdom, and you realize this kind of consciousness—not the left brain with its limited knowledge—is meant to be the CEO of your life.

It's not that somehow the right hemisphere has got it all right and the left hemisphere has got it all wrong. That's another either/or, black-and-white misconception which is typical of the left hemisphere's take on the world. The right hemisphere's take is broadly inclusive, as in the metaphor, the master (right brain) knows that he needs the emissary (left brain); it's the emissary that thinks it doesn't need the master.
Iain McGilchrist

At this point you naturally enter a process of balancing the two halves of your brain. The vast reservoirs of the right brain flood into the left brain, the wave rebounds back and forth, and the two sides begin to communicate. In effect, your right brain educates your left brain. A critical-mass point is reached and the hemispheres exchange roles. British psychiatrist Iain McGilchrist, author of *The Master and His Emissary*, maintains that the right brain's natural role is that of leader, or "master," and the left brain's natural role is as the "emissary," or (in my words) the servant or implementer.

· · · · · · · · · · ·

Try This!
Balance the Left and Right Sides of Your Brain

1. Sit quietly, with your back supported and your head level. Breathe in and out easily, slowly, deeply. Feel your brain inside your head.

2. Imagine the two hemispheres of your brain, and notice whether one side seems bigger than the other. Perhaps one side feels hard, one side soft. Or one feels darker, the other lighter. Just notice.

3. Imagine that between the two sides there is a partition. Reach in with your imaginary hand and pull out the partition. Now nothing is in the way, and the sides of your brain can communicate freely with each other.

4. Let the energy from the bigger, lighter, softer side flow into the smaller, darker, harder side and fill it, integrating and changing it in some way. Then do the reverse, letting the energy from the smaller, darker, harder side flow into its partner. Each time you do this exchange, let the two sides of your brain talk and give information to each other (you don't need to know what it is). Keep the back-and-forth exchange going until both sides feel equal and balanced.

5. Now notice your eyes and adjust them in your imagination until they, too, feel equally sensitive and unstrained. Do the same thing with your ears until they feel equally open and alert.

6. Smile, and feel the left and right sides of your mouth and facial muscles. Adjust them so they are equally relaxed and your smile feels even.

· · · · · · · · · · ·

When your brain balances and integrates horizontally, several things happen. Your left brain slowly relaxes its vigilance and remembers its true function as assistant to the right brain. It finds a new, healthier purpose in life, doing what it was meant to do as the organizer, communicator, and implementer of visions and wisdom. Relieved of its role as the boss, ego lessens. A process of vertical integration of the brain also occurs at this stage, where the flow from the higher, now-integrated hemispheres reorganizes and educates the midbrain and reptile brain, below. The ascending and descending processes of consciousness harmonize. I described this process in chapter 3. What's really happening here is the physical and nonphysical worlds are beginning to merge.

The phrase "mind over matter" certainly stands for something that does happen and is important. The principle is a simple one: each higher energy has the power of organizing the lower ones. . . . Consciousness can organize sensitivity.

J. G. Bennett

With Integration, You Experience Your Heart

Integration of the brain allows you to feel the intersection, or centerpoint, of the horizontal and vertical flows. *The experience of center is an evolutionary step beyond polarity.* This spot in the center of your head is a place where knowledge convenes from all directions and you have phenomenal clarity and perspective. You experience yourself as wisdom. You can recognize this integration experientially because it brings consciousness that is inspired and practical, matter-of-fact and obvious, expansive and motivating, peaceful and effortless, elegant and perfectly appropriate to situations at hand. When your consciousness balances like this, you enter a quietly powerful, nonconflicted state that frees you from the attack of others, and promotes harmony and unrestricted flow.

What's interesting is that once you're balanced and can center yourself and look out from behind your eyes with full presence, you almost immediately shift to the center of your heart, which opens and reveals a different experience of self. The heart is considered by mystics to be the center of the soul's unity, love, and compassion consciousness. Now, you experience yourself as compassion and love. *The powerful shift of locus from the center of the head to the center of the heart leads to all other self-in-the-center experiences.* It sets a powerful, oscillating resonance in motion—as though a great bell or gong has been struck—and all centers begin to vibrate in a subtle communion.

You can ride the resonance to other centers, regardless of size or location, and can understand, feel related to, and have compassion for everyone and everything—heart to heart. You might visit the heart of the earth, the center of a cell in your body, the hearts of people who have died, or the center of a creative masterpiece. Perhaps the heart is really a kind of magical spaceship, capable of effortlessly transporting us through time, space, and dimensions without actually going anywhere. It certainly is a key factor in Intuition Age perception.

You Discover Your Heart Is a Brain!

We commonly say things like, "I took it to heart," or "What does your heart say?" or "In my heart, I know. . . ." It's as if we've always known intuitively that our heart is in charge of the big decisions in life. Now, neurocardiologists have discovered that there is literally a brain in the heart—that the heart itself is a *brain*! They've found that an amazing 50 to 65 percent of heart cells are neural cells like those in your brain. These cells are clustered in groups, or ganglia, just like the neural groupings of the brain, and the same neurotransmitters function in both places. There is a nonstop, direct dialogue—or resonance— between your head and heart through these connections. In addition, the heart's ganglia connect to many other tiny ganglia, or "nonlocalized brains," scattered throughout the body.

It seems the heart resonates with the right brain in particular. When you shift from focusing on the physical organ to the nonphysical experience of "heart," you can feel how heart perception is open and feeling-oriented, but functions at a higher frequency than reptile-brain survival emotion or even the midbrain's affection—it resonates with the vibration of the *soul*. Your heart is the origin place for what I have called your home frequency, and it produces the experience of empathy and compassion—an unselfish, nonjudgmental, generous love experience that can range from personal to universal understanding. The heart also generates joy, bliss, and ecstasy—the emotional states that connect you to your soul, the unified field, and a sense of the sacred.

> Our brain, with its ganglia extensions throughout the body is, figuratively speaking, an instrument of the heart. Our heart, in turn, is an instrument or representative of the universal function of life itself. . . . Brain and body are fashioned to translate from the heart's frequency field the information for building our unique, individual world experience.
>
> **Joseph Chilton Pearce**

We might say your nonphysical heart center and its physical counterpart—your ever-beating heart—are expressions of the core qualities of your soul. Together they are the seat of the souls love in the body and serve to relay the soul's motivation for transformation and evolution to your earthly personality. *The heart is a place of transformation.* In meditation, I have always experienced the heart as being totally neutral. It brings understanding of what is fair, "just right," and in perfect harmony with universal laws and the soul's innate motives. It doesn't generate the mushy-gushy kind of love romantics associate with it. I've experienced how, when we let it, the heart quite innocently "eats pain" and transforms suffering into clear diamond light—because it doesn't actually *know* the experience of pain. Throw some pain into the heart—that cauldron of boiling diamond light and love—and the pain's a goner! Some might call this spiritual healing or forgiveness. The heart's love is about who loves and harmony.

But what about heartache, that common human experience, you say? My intuitive sense is that when we have heart problems like "broken hearts" or heart attacks, it's because we've blocked the flow of our soul and our deep desire to be loving. Old perception might say, "I have a broken heart because I lost a loved one." What's more true is that your left brain is fixated on what you're lacking rather than allowing your soul, via your heart, to keep experiencing and expressing the continuity of your unending love. Losing someone you love doesn't mean you have to stop loving them or anyone else. When consciousness-and-energy fixate in the left brain, you lose touch with soul and your heart hurts; perhaps heartache is simply the soul calling for attention: "Hello—remember me?" If the contracted condition of giving attention to lack-of-love ideas continues long enough—if we continue to invest attention in grief, anger, or resentment—the physical heart can develop serious problems.

> The true poet is a friendly person. He takes into his arms
> even cold and inanimate things and rejoices in his heart.
>
> William Wordsworth

Your Heart Opens Spherical-Holographic Perception

The heart is a vehicle for new, spherical-holographic perception. Remember how the experience of being in the centerpoint of the heart catalyzes the experience of being in other centerpoints simultaneously? By knowing one heart, you know all hearts: each heart center contains the experience of every other heart center, and they all contain the experience of the whole. Heart perception, then, has the capacity to expand you through the entire unified field—so you know what it's like to be any particle, any planet, any person, any object, any process, any field of consciousness or energy. *The heart's spherical-holographic perception means that each person, when centered in the heart, is the center of the universe.*

It also means you can become aware of your cellular consciousness, the cooperation among the many tiny centers of self that make up your physical body and contain the vibration of the heart. Jill Bolte Taylor mentions this in the description of her altered consciousness after her stroke: "Every cell in our bodies ... contains the exact same molecular genius as the original zygote cell. ... My right mind understands that I am the life force power of the fifty trillion molecular geniuses crafting my form!"[2]

When you can feel yourself as the consciousness of your cells, you can also feel yourself as the consciousness of any organ in your body—an experience that leads to truly "being in your body, as your body." *Whole-*

body consciousness can totally transform your experience of physical reality, making it personal and friendly. This is a huge key to new perception. You won't understand this by thinking about it with your left brain; you have to merge into your body's various centers to know these truths.

In addition, every center—or heart—is like a seed that contains an inner blueprint of what it's capable of radiating and materializing. The acorn contains the blueprint for the oak tree, the heart of the *Pietà* showed Michelangelo how to sculpt the masterpiece, and your heart contains the plans for your own magnificent fulfillment. Your heart receives this pattern from your own higher dimensions, then relays it accurately into the physical world. Why would we ever distrust or want to shut down the flow of wisdom from this opening?

$\bullet \quad \bullet \quad \bullet \quad \bullet \quad \bullet \quad \bullet \quad \bullet \quad \bullet \quad \bullet \quad \bullet$

Try This!
Feel Your Heart's Spherical-Holographic Nature

1. Calm yourself; breathe easily and regularly. Be fully present in your body and the moment. Then shift your attention to your heart center, the energetic space around your physical heart. Merge into it and be there, looking and feeling out in all directions from that viewpoint.

2. Notice that there is a calm wisdom in your heart. There is no agitation or negative emotion, just a clean connection to your soul and home frequency. There is no polarization, just compassionate understanding. Here, your destiny is encoded. This is the place of understanding where your most harmonious unfolding originates. Soak it in, and relax into the knowledge that there is a clear inner blueprint for you.

3. Now think about someone else's heart center. Go visit them in your imagination, and merge into their heart. Notice how similar it feels to yours. Now think of the heart of a tree. Go visit that heart center and merge into it—feel it. The tree's pattern is encoded there, and the tree's consciousness can be known there. You may feel great love for the tree and feel the tree's love for the world. Now think of the heart center of one of the cells in one

(Continued on next page)

89

of the organs in your body. Go visit it and merge with it. Let yourself feel the life force and perfect pattern of its functioning—the love it relays by living.

4. See if you can feel the highest frequency of consciousness-and-energy fueling, creating, and motivating all heart centers. Feel the experience of common love and compassion shared by all forms of life.

• • • • • • • • • • •

Joseph Chilton Pearce, in his book *The Biology of Transcendence*, describes many intriguing things about the functioning of the heart and the field of energy around it. I'll paraphrase some of it for you here. He describes how heart cells pulse. When a single heart cell is isolated, its regular pulse goes into fibrillation, and it dies. But when two heart cells are brought near each other, the pulse in both remains strong, and they move into a state of entrainment, or coherence—a synchronous resonance with each other—and they continue to live. Isn't this the essence of love? But there is more.

The heart of thee is the heart of all; not a valve, not a wall, not an intersection is there anywhere in nature, but one blood rolls uninterruptedly, an endless circulation through all men, as the water of the globe is all one sea, and truly seen, its tide is one.

Ralph Waldo Emerson

Heart cells not only pulse, they radiate a strong electromagnetic signal. They're like little generators, and when they work together, they produce a current that has an amplitude forty to sixty times greater than brain waves. The heart's frequency is strong enough to be measured as far as three feet out from the body, and it can form an electromagnetic field up to fifteen feet around the body—a field that's spherical and holographic, too. At every point within the heart's field, every frequency of the heart's vibration is present. Curiously, the earth's electromagnetic field operates the same way; it's a macrocosmic version of our own heart field. The whole of its functioning can be ascertained from any point on earth.

Finally, Focus on Feeling and Becoming the Field

Because of the heart's radiant electromagnetic field, you can naturally make the next shift in the integration of the new perception—the move beyond feeling yourself as a centerpoint to experiencing yourself as an expanded field of consciousness-and-energy. This is the "spherical" part of the new consciousness, because fields are spherical in nature. Place your attention on the energy that surrounds your body—your aura or personal field of vibration—and you can feel how it radiates equally in all directions, creating a ball of energy. You can feel how your heart center has actually blown up like a balloon, expanding to become the field of consciousness-and-energy that you occupy. You may also simultaneously experience how your field has coalesced your physical heart as its centerpoint. You are a ball of consciousness-and-energy with a particular vibratory frequency. Your tone, or your home frequency, patterns your life.

Biologist Rupert Sheldrake has posed the theory that there are morphic fields composed of the habits and life patterns of similar entities. These resonant fields live on, for example, after the plants of a particular species die, acting as a kind of memory repository. The memory preserved in the fields enables new plants to more easily form themselves and make adaptations, and thus morphic fields contribute to evolution. Morphic fields are similar to what Carl Jung called the *collective unconscious*, or what the Vedas call the *Akashic Records*, the library or memory bank of the planet composed of everything every individual or species has ever experienced. We might also think of morphic fields as inner blueprints that transmit their knowledge through subtle vibration, what Sheldrake calls *morphic resonance*.

When you personally occupy, merge with, and become the consciousness of a field, you can experience the many kinds of consciousness that contribute to the field's existence. Many individual beings come together to form a field, and you begin to understand concepts like collective consciousness and the mutual inclusiveness and cocreation of all beings and things. This is true whether you focus on your own individual field or on the field of a species, nation, or planet. You understand you're an individual *and* a collective consciousness simultaneously; you have ancestors, are influenced by teachers, have built your body from many kinds of food, and are even the result of your soul's many lifetimes. A plant is the result of generations of plants and many climate conditions, a nation is both itself and all its inhabitants, and a planet is an entity connected to all other celestial bodies and every form of life upon it.

This new, expanded perception derived from experiencing fields gives you a direct experience of why principles like the Golden Rule exist in every religion of the world, and why these principles are the hallmark of Intuition Age perception. When you realize how truly interconnected everything is, you can feel how denying or hurting any part of the unified field hurts every other part within the field—including you. A new system of refined ethics arises as a result, and a new, intimately interconnected cooperation becomes normal.

> The universe is built on a plan, the profound symmetry of which
> is somehow present in the inner structure of our intellect.
>
> Paul Valéry

The stages of new, Intuition Age perception progress sequentially from the most contracted consciousness to the most expanded. The process begins with the left brain and its erroneous sense of world-domination and moves to right-brain openness, then through the integration of the polarities in the brain to true centeredness and heart consciousness. Then, your perception grows to reveal multiple centeredness and the experience of being various fields of consciousness-and-energy. Eventually, you can experience unified-field consciousness. This whole process can happen in your lifetime, thanks to the world's acceleration and increasing frequency. In the next chapter, we'll refine the nuances of moving through the more difficult stages of the transformation process using new, skillful perception.

The Golden Rule Around the World

Buddhism: Hurt not others in ways that you yourself would find hurtful.

Christianity: All things whatsoever ye would that men should do to you, do ye even so to them.

Hinduism: This is the sum of duty: do naught unto others which would cause you pain if done to you.

Islam: No one of you is a believer until he desires for his brother that which he desires for himself.

Judaism: What is hateful to you, do not to your fellow man. That is the law; all the rest is commentary.

Native American: Respect for all life is the foundation.

Sikhism: Don't create enmity with anyone, as God is within everyone.

Fig. 5-1

Just to Recap . . .

To recognize and begin the shift into new, Intuition Age perception, you need to feel how limited you are by old perception and consciously decide to expand beyond what's been so familiar. To enter this new territory, you first need to shift from your left brain to your right brain—a shift that's easier if you understand the different kinds of experience the two hemispheres generate. The left brain is analytical and definitive, reducing experience to meanings that are separated into categories. The right brain is free-flowing, nonverbal, intuitive, and integrative. Once you shift to your right brain, then balance and integrate your two hemispheres, you experience greater clarity and stability. After that, you can feel and sense more, and ultimately, you open your heart and experience your soul's compassion.

The heart is really a kind of brain, and it generates an electromagnetic field of radiance that's spherical in nature. When you feel your heart, you begin to understand spherical-holographic perception. Your heart resonates with all other hearts, all other souls, and all other centerpoints. By being in your heart, you can know the core experience of any other being or reality—and, you can know yourself as the whole unified field.

With spherical-holographic perception, the heart spontaneously expands to become a spherical field of consciousness-and-energy around you. And as you experience spherical-holographic perception, you have insight into the workings of collective consciousness and an understanding of why the Golden Rule exists in all cultures.

6

Navigate the Transformation Narrows

Learning, unlearning, and relearning require cultivated distraction, because as long as we focus on the object we know, we will miss the new one we need to see. The process of unlearning in order to relearn demands a new concept of knowledge not as a thing but as a process, not as a noun but as a verb. . . . It requires refreshing your mental browser.

Cathy N. Davidson

Do you sometimes feel like a big tsunami is crashing in on you? That you're being carried down a flooded river filled with tree trunks, cars, and parts of broken houses? That's certainly how dangerous the transformation process can feel when the acceleration waves grow intense. In this chapter, I want to help you through the more challenging stages of transformation, showing you the problems and blockages that commonly arise and how to re-establish the Flow.

Unlearning and Relearning

The transformation process is largely about clearing the clutter that interferes with your soul coming all the way through into your body and life. Unlearning and dissolving old, ingrained perception habits is really the biggest part of this. But unlearning habits and establishing new ones is no more difficult than learning them in the first place. Here are some guidelines for freeing yourself from the automatic nature of your old-perception habits.

- **Decide what you want and don't want, and entitle yourself to have what you want—*now*.** Nothing can happen until you know what you want and set the process of change in motion by giving permission for it to occur. To know what you want, look at your old-perception habits to see how they're not working. Dissatisfaction is a huge motivator! How *could* it feel in the best of all possible worlds? *If you can dream it—and love it—it will come to you.*
- **Ask for help.** Everything in the nonphysical world is cooperative, service-oriented, and win-win-win by nature. With new perception, when you improve your reality you improve other people's realities as well, and they're happy to assist you. And there are many nonphysical beings standing by to help. *We don't do anything alone because we're connected to all beings and events through the unified field.* You only need to ask for help to receive it.
- **Keep your attention on what you want, without strain.** Keep your ideal reality—how it looks and feels—in your mind and all around you, like a living movie that hasn't quite solidified yet. Love it and massage it gently with soft attention. Don't try too hard. *Your inner blueprint creates your physical reality; the more you keep it in the present moment and feel it as real, the faster it materializes.*
- **Create a new set of criteria for making choices.** Notice that many of your old criteria relate to reptile-brain and left-brain perceptual habits. These old habits often contain words like "should," "can't," "have to," "never," and "always," and revolve around self-sacrifice, self-protection, and survival. Instead of deciding automatically, weigh each choice: Does this allow me to experience my home frequency? Does this keep my intuition open? Does this let me be more loving? Does this create a win-win-win situation for everyone? *These new criteria validate the Golden Rule and the idea that the soul's truth sets you free.*

Chapter 6: Navigate the Transformation Narrows

I find the notion of voluntary simplicity (doing one thing at a time with full presence) keeps me mindful of what is important, of an ecology of mind and body and world in which everything is interconnected and every choice has far-reaching consequences.

Jon Kabat-Zinn

- **Determine to notice yourself in action.** Intend to catch yourself when you're in an old, negative tape loop, or when you react (past experience) rather than respond (present moment insight). Witnessing yourself on- and off-purpose helps you measure your actions against your ideal. *Honesty leads to freedom.*
- **Choose the way you want to feel—then choose again, and again.** The mind moves; it strays and gets trapped in eddies and whirlpools. However, you are now a self-correcting organism. You can simply return to your home frequency instead of staying stuck. *What you pay attention to comes alive.*

  Choosing is really about placing your attention on something, so pay attention to what you love instead of what drags you down. Imagine you've plugged your headphones into the wrong headphone jack. Just pull the plug out and plug it into the jack that's transmitting your home frequency. You may need a brief moment—a pause that refreshes—where you give yourself the space to remember the choice you truly want to make.
- **Monitor your inner and outer speech.** Notice the tone of your self-talk. Is it negative or positive? Are you complaining? Or are you telling yourself how interesting your current activity is? What are you saying out loud? Are you making negative declarative statements, like "I'll never try *that* again!"? What you say in thought and spoken words can lock in and ground a pattern. Language, one of the functions of the left brain, can hinder—or help—your unlearning and relearning process significantly. Remember that *your word is law in your world.*
- **Validate your successes.** Notice when you shift your thoughts and actions successfully. Pat yourself on the shoulder, and thank your body. Say out loud, "Congratulations, we did it! This feels good." Use

What Choice Will You Make?

Old Perception
(Based in FEAR)

New Perception
(Based in LOVE)

Old Perception (Based in FEAR)	New Perception (Based in LOVE)
Reactive	Responsive
Protective	Explorative
Confrontational, avoiding	Communicative, engaging
Willful	Willing
In denial, judgmental	Receptive, open-minded
Worried, doubtful	Lucky, optimistic
Stressed, depressed	Excited, peaceful
Restless, bored	Patient, interested
Feels limited, hoards	Feels abundant, generous
Separate	Connected
Partial, incomplete	Whole, complete
Unconscious, wandering	Alert, attentive
Attached	Detached
Stuck (can't stop or start), inflexible	Fluid, adaptable
Blaming, punishing	Understanding, forgiving
Martyr, tyrant	Able to receive and give support
Focused in the past or the future	Focused in the present moment
"It should be this way"	"It's OK the way it is; it's OK if it changes"
"I can't do, can't have . . ."	"I'm entitled to do and have anything"
No time, no space	All the space and time needed
They agree with me, I agree with them	There's room for all opinions

Fig. 6-1

positive self-talk: "I turned my mood around!" "I saw I wasn't getting anything from feeling vindictive, and I let it go." "It's easy for me to notice what I want to do." *Physical acts of validation make the new habit real to your body.*

- **Repeat the steps as often as possible.** Be patient. Relearning isn't difficult; it just takes repetition to form the new behavior. As the oracle of the I Ching often recommends, "Perseverance furthers." Sometimes it really does take repeating something three times before it registers as real. *The more you make the process conscious, the faster it stabilizes.*
- **Remember who's directing the unlearning and relearning.** It's you—the soul! You're in charge of your personality, mind, and reality. *Know thyself!*

It is a question of the right silence in the mind and the right openness to the Word that is trying to express itself—for the Word is there, ready formed in those inner planes where all artistic forms take birth.

Sri Aurobindo

Easing the Challenges of Transformation

I sketched the stages and symptoms of the transformation process loosely in chapter 1. Now, I'd like us to move through the process to see how we can ease the difficult parts.

You Become Ultrasensitive

In the earliest phases of the process, you may feel irritated, overly electrical, or even physically overheated. You can become ultrasensitive to environmental disturbances and emotions, feeling that things are out of control or that you're under pressure that won't let up. You might feel continually overwhelmed and exhausted, develop aches and pains, get sick more than usual, or be unable to sleep.

Problems arise when you define the increased vibration as unfamiliar, and thus dangerous and threatening. This happens when you're not centered and mindful, and it's easy then to resist the Flow of the accelerating

Guidelines for Unlearning and Relearning: A Summary

- Determine what you really want by feeling what you don't want, then imagine your best possible scenario. Be excited about it, and entitle yourself to have it now. Give permission for it to occur.

- Ask for help from others, in both the physical and nonphysical worlds.

- Keep your ideal vision alive with attention; live it in your imagination, in the present moment.

- Create a new set of criteria for making choices that align with your home frequency.

- Determine to notice yourself in action. Make it a game to catch yourself in an old-perception habit. When you do catch yourself, don't beat yourself up. Unplug from giving attention to the old-perception habit, then pause and be in-between. Let yourself remember what you really want.

- Choose what you really want again. Realign with the feeling state of your home frequency. You're placing attention on what you want; you're plugging into the correct headphone jack.

- Monitor your inner and outer speech so it aligns with your desire, rather than blocking it.

- Validate yourself for choosing correctly—for rejecting old-perception habits—and acting from the new, expanded perception.

- Keep at it patiently. Repeat the steps often, until the new reality becomes second nature.

- Remember that you are your soul! Be careful not to disempower yourself by identifying with just one of your parts, like your personality, your reptile brain, your left brain, or your physical reality.

Fig. 6-2

energy. If you react to these symptoms with old-perception habits, you'll try to distance yourself from the discomfort or try to control it. But remember: if you push against it, it pushes back with doubled force.

For example, Joan became ultrasensitive and was overwhelmed by the negativity in the news, the rudeness at the market and gas station, and the chaotic level of noise pollution she encountered everywhere. She developed mild environmental allergies and a subtle phobia about driving. When she was forced to deal with the public, she often flew into rages and returned home exhausted. She didn't understand that she was experiencing the early stages of transformation.

> There will be many times when we won't look good—to ourselves
> or anyone else. We need to stop demanding that we do.
> It is impossible to get better and look good at the same time.
>
> Julia Cameron

On the other hand, without resistance, the high-frequency energy and ultrasensitivity can carry you to a new level of functioning. Jake is a good example. His work situation was coming apart at the seams. Scores of people were laid off, and he was carrying twice his normal workload. The pressure was terrible, and it seemed everyone around him was complaining and getting sick. One day he, too, was laid off. Instead of worrying, he felt a great sense of relief. He took it as a sign that he didn't fit in at that job, that he needed to be around people who were on his wavelength. He thought about what he really wanted to do next and proceeded to create a freelance consulting business on his own terms, which proved successful.

· · · · · · · · · · ·

Try This!
Dissolve Anxiety and Depression Energy

1. When you notice you're caught in an anxiety attack, depression, or a kind of energy that makes you want to jump out of your skin, pause before you

(Continued on next page)

(Dissolve Anxiety and Depression Energy, continued)

do anything rash. Sit with the vibration and breathe fully and slowly for at least ten counts, pausing between the in-breath and out-breath.

2. Close your eyes and move your attention inside your skin, into your body. Feel the buzzing, or the dull vibration, occupying the same space as your body. Notice if the vibration is located in any areas of your body in particular.

3. Move your attention into the vibration and let yourself merge with it. Become the vibration; role-play it. Give the frequency permission to go where it wants to go and do what it wants to do. You may feel it spread out into other parts of your body, or perhaps it will focus in one area and act like a jackhammer, breaking up a block. Notice if it's trying to say something; is there a message for you?

4. From within the vibration, imagine you are increasing its frequency to a higher octave, letting the vibration become more refined and smooth. Or you may see it move from opacity to transparency, or darkness to radiance. Let the frequency increase until it feels supremely comfortable and soothing. Let your body, emotions, and mind acclimate to this ideal vibration, and soak up as much of the good energy as needed.

• • • • • • • • • • •

Subconscious Fears Surface

As you accelerate, negative memories, old fears, and limiting beliefs— things you thought you had successfully eliminated—pop back into your conscious mind and your daily reality. They tend to reenact, presenting you with worst-possible-scenario dramas and traumas. You can experience extreme emotions and a destabilization of things that used to be in balance. Scandals, taboos, abuse, and skeletons in the closet can be revealed in public, and you can't tell whether what you're feeling is your own problem or someone else's.

Everything in your life is there as a vehicle for your transformation. Use it!

Ram Dass

Chapter 6: Navigate the Transformation Narrows

If you react with old-perception habits, it's easy to become paralyzed or explosive. Conflicts and polarities intensify, patience and tolerance are at low ebb, and judgment is at an all-time high. Graham's behavior epitomizes this. In his childhood his mother left his father—and him—for another man. He suppressed the pain of the abandonment, then as an adult, his own wife left him in a similar situation. He found a new relationship, and it lasted only six months before she, too, left him for someone else. He began bad-mouthing women to his friends and colleagues, and became intensely bitter. His negative memories seemed to be locking Graham into a chronic pattern.

> We cannot escape fear. We can only transform it into a companion that accompanies us on all our exciting adventures. . . . Take a risk a day— one small or bold stroke that will make you feel great once you have done it.
>
> Susan Jeffers

If you embrace this opening of Pandora's box as an opportunity to clear negative patterns, you interpret situations differently. When Kelley gossiped about a friend and it got back to the friend, a drama erupted. Her friend wrote her off and said she didn't want to see her again. Kelley felt chastised and ashamed, but she didn't stay in that contracted state. Instead, she used the experience as a growth opportunity, asking herself, "Why would I feel so threatened by my friend that I'd need to belittle her?" The answer came: her friend was stylish and beautiful, and Kelley envied her. But, in truth, her friend never had time for Kelley. Kelley realized she was angry because she felt hurt and unappreciated. She saw she'd engineered the whole rejection scenario as a way to end what wasn't really a friendship to begin with. The relationship had been one-sided, and it had been dragging her down for a long time. She sent a note to her friend, apologizing and wishing her the best. Then she let it go.

This stage of transformation emphasizes oppositions. You can move through the impasses by understanding that "What's in you is also in me in some way." Find the underlying issue that's the same in yourself and the other person you judge or resist. For example, you may be handling an issue by controlling it, while the other person is avoiding it, yet you're both dealing with the same issue underneath. With Kelley and her friend, the issue was a lack of confidence. Kelley was playing the more passive role, doubting herself because she wasn't receiving attention, while her friend was acting overconfidently, not admitting her doubts and demanding attention. By finding the common underlying issue, conflict dissolves and backed-up energy can move again. Every problem is an opportunity to create greater clarity and love.

> The meeting of two personalities is like the contact of two
> chemical substances: if there is any reaction, both are transformed.
>
> Carl Jung

Old Structures Malfunction and Fail

Toward the end of the clearing process, you reach some of the big beliefs and attachments at the core of your worldview that are out of alignment with new perception. These might relate to how you think society should function; or what you believe is right and wrong, good and bad; or what you think you must do to survive. At this point, many things you thought were important and meaningful become useless or boring in comparison to what's "real" at a deeper level, and you let them go. Old methods fail to produce results. Old institutions collapse. You notice lies and hollow stories, or feel disillusioned. You may have little certainty left about who you are, why you're here, and what you can rely on. You may be forced to stop, perhaps by failing, or by having losses or an injury.

> We always know it's transformation because it surprises us. . . .
> When you throw yourself open by asking empowering questions and
> by being willing to be more than you've ever thought you could be,
> you get surprised by the depth of what's inside of you!
> It's so potent. It's like free fall.
>
> Michael Bernard Beckwith

Marina is an example of how many of us tend to spiral down due to negative thinking during this phase of transformation. She had reached a point where she felt suffocated by her work. As a stockbroker, she had analyzed the pros and cons of quitting and moving, but she would lose a large sum of money by selling her home in the bad housing market— if it even *would* sell. Plus she didn't know where to go; everywhere she thought of had some flaw. And how would she start a new business in a new place, at *her* age?

Marina's world had narrowed, she was exhausted, and she was thinking herself down the drain. Since she wouldn't voluntarily change any variable in her situation, she was not far from having one, or several, of her basic structures—job, financial security, home, health—break down and *force* a change.

If you allow the dissolution of things you don't need during this time, you find that external security, structure, and rules aren't so necessary—you're being directed by inner wisdom to discover a better way. You naturally shift from left brain to right brain, and serendipitous occurrences materialize to magically free you from stuckness. Then new forms appear naturally that bring a sense of expanded self-expression.

Clare's situation was similar to Marina's, but she handled the challenges by embracing the changes. She realized her boredom with her advertising career was a sign that she was finished with that sort of work. She'd learned enough and wanted to move on, but to what, she wasn't quite sure. She decided to sell her house, in spite of the down market, and got enough money to move to a state where she could buy a comparable place for less. She gave herself some downtime, took art classes, wrote a book for women in transition in their fifties, and ended up with a viable seminar business. Her decision to flow with the new energy allowed her shifts to occur without friction or struggle.

You Stop, Be Still, and Find Your Soul

When nothing seems to work, you eventually hit bottom or have a mystical, enlightening moment; either can reveal truth. Doing more is not the answer because there's nothing to achieve. You enter the present moment and experience simplicity, spaciousness, quiet, freedom, and peace—though as you first encounter this state, it may feel like emptiness. As you let things *be*, you experience your own *being*—the real sense of your soul's vibration—and you feel full. Suddenly you know who you are with your entire body!

> When I dare to be powerful—to use my strength in the service of my vision—then it becomes less and less important whether I am afraid.
>
> Audre Lorde

If you remain in this mode, your brain integrates. You focus on acceptance and trust and feel fine—fantastic, even—just as you are, no matter what comes. You soon find you have shifted to the center of your head and heart. Now you saturate with the frequency of your soul and receive clear yet subtle signals directly from your core. You feel connected to the world and have compassion for all living beings. You remember truths about yourself and gain great understanding, often all at once. As the experience of being "at home in the center" becomes routine, you entitle yourself to prefer your new self and new reality. This is the crucial turning point where it dawns on you that you really are the soul. You intentionally choose that identity and the kind of world you want to live in, knowing your home frequency is what filters your reality into form. The tide turns and your life, health, and happiness improve.

Believe it or not, it's still possible at this stage to resist the Flow and leave your direct experience of the truth! Your left brain may retreat into skeptical, "yes, but" mode, citing the thousand reasons why you are deluded by wishful thinking, why the world is really so much more powerful and negative than you, or why you are missing important information that will disprove your direct experience. You may need to watch for these small derailments.

Lyme disease forced Lillian into the present moment to confront her deeper issues and be her inner self, yet she didn't get the message. She lost muscle strength, and her mind became extremely fuzzy. She could barely work or keep up with friends. She listened to her doctors and took antibiotics, but after an initial period of success, the symptoms came back. The doctors had no further solutions, so she resigned herself to her limited reality and missed finding her home frequency and soul.

On the other hand, Craig, who also had Lyme disease, realized it was his chance to deal with the domination and abuse he'd suffered as a child; he saw the disease as a symbol of his subconscious belief that he was always going to be invaded by hostile forces. He worked diligently on centering and feeling his home frequency, on displacing the invading bacteria with his own energy, and raising his vibration beyond the vibration of the illness. He made a gradual but amazing recovery—aided by allopathic medicine, diet, and other means. Because he engaged with the moment and his own soul, and let energy flow through him instead of interpreting it negatively and pushing it away, he had a much different outcome than Lillian.

Once you move through these challenging phases of the transformation process, you'll have established a positive behavior of welcoming and embracing what the Flow brings you. You'll demonstrate to yourself how something that seems negative at first really contains a gift tailor-made for you, and that everything occurs so you can move into full-on, conscious evolution.

A Few More Tips for Smoothing Your Way

Listed below are several mistakes of perception we all tend to make when we're shifting our perceptual habits. Noticing them can help you avoid unnecessary snags.

- **Interpreting causes and solutions too superficially.** It's easy to look at the idea at the forefront of your mind and think it's the cause of—or the solution to—your discomfort. It's important to feel into things more deeply. For example, you may think making a lot of money is the solution to your problem of feeling insecure, but the real problem may be that you're afraid to be alone, and the real solution may be learning to meditate.

- **Rushing to judgment.** When you don't sit still with a problematic situation long enough, it's easy to react emotionally and backtrack into subconscious memories of what worked in the past. The left brain has previous experiences and lessons catalogued, ready to assign them logically to any similar new situation. However, the situations that arise in each present moment are unique, and it's your right brain that really knows what to do. If you go too fast in your mental processing, you'll likely end up with a reapplication of old knowledge that may be totally inappropriate.

- **Blaming others or taking things personally.** When a fear surfaces and you feel contracted, hurt, or anxious, there's a tendency to disown the feeling by attributing it to another person. "*You* made me feel this way. *You* caused my pain." It's just as easy to identify with the pain or the problem and say, "I am a terrible person because I'm intolerant of others." Or "I am defective because I can't feel intimacy." Either way, you don't engage with the pattern that's trying to clear and you block the Flow.

- **Wanting life to be just one way.** It's easy to forget about the oscillating nature of consciousness—how sometimes you're clear and sometimes you're confused, how sometimes your love radiates and sometimes your fear radiates. When you backslide or have a negative experience, you can blame and judge things, create a contraction of consciousness-and-energy, and lock it in with negative declarative statements. This is your left brain caught in a defensive, limiting, old-perception habit. Remember that you are a jewel with many facets, and you contain the full range of humanity's behavior, from the slimy to the sublime. You're entitled to experience all of it! Don't let your left brain become a tyrant.

- **Letting fear-flooding overwhelm and paralyze you.** Your subconscious mind is opening like Pandora's box and freeing your little "demons." In fact, every individual's subconscious mind is opening, and so are the collective subconscious minds of countries, governments, churches, corporations, banks, militaries, and populations of people with similar experiences and morphic fields (e.g., abused women and children, soldiers, disrespected and mistreated elders, and so on). You are swimming in a vast cesspool of negative emotions, and when you're not centered and alert, it's easy to mistake other people's negativity for your own.

- **Letting the ego fool you.** During the phase where your left and right brain are balancing and integrating, you'll feel tossed around by your left brain in its ego mode, which is resisting the idea of relinquishing control. The ego can flash through a veritable strobe-light movie of clever behaviors to get its way, from seduction to reasoning, to domination, to intimidation, to direct attack, to abandonment, and back to charm and self-effacement. It will aim these narcissistic behaviors at you and others, but don't make the mistake of believing it or identifying with its point of view.

- **Not letting the ego "die."** As your ego relinquishes control, you may enter a period marked by a strange flatness. You might feel you're in Limboland—that not much matters anymore and perhaps *you* are going to die soon, and that's OK. You're not depressed or sad, just flat. You're not even apathetic. In effect, you're "detoxing," or coming down from a life lived via willpower. Without willpower, who are you? Without superiority and specialness, who are you? Without cleverness and emotional manipulation, who are you? This is another trick of the ego. Just keep on *being*, and see what emerges from each new moment. As you let your right brain be the master and your left brain be the assistant, your world lights up in a new way.

> Penetrative insight joined with calm abiding
> utterly eradicates afflicted states.
>
> Shantideva

You Can Be a Radiant Sun!

We are all becoming ultrasensitive now, and our level of telepathy is increasing. Without realizing it, you may frequency-match the low vibrations and troubled thoughts floating around just below the surface in the nonphysical world—and wonder why your mood suddenly changes from cheerful to somber. You can read people better than ever before, and even feel their feelings. That means it's easier to match someone's bad mood or worried or agitated state when you pass him or her on the street. You can sense negative dramas about to happen and feel other people's lives about to crack open, often without realizing what you're noticing. You can also feel the "high road" and connect with the potential in everyone and everything. Good moods are contagious too. You have a choice, constantly, about which frequency to match.

It's helpful to practice centering throughout the day, returning to your home frequency and checking in with your best self often. Your new criteria are meant to help you sort your experiences: How do you prefer to feel? Does a behavior or feeling allow your energy to flow in an optimal direction? In spite of the massive amount of negativity surfacing in the world, your place in the center of yourself can turn you into a sun radiating bright light. You can be a force for good—a field that clears pain by not engaging with it.

Once you can see through the emotional confusion of the current shift in consciousness and become an expert in navigating the tricky disentanglement from old perceptual habits, you'll be ready to stabilize the new Intuition Age reality. The chapters in the next section examine specific attention skills that will be normal in the transformed reality, and which can help you integrate your new way of being.

> The pressure becomes so great, the intensity of the question so strong, that something in the consciousness shifts. Instead of being outside looking in, you are inside; and the moment you are inside, absolutely everything changes completely.
>
> Sri Aurobindo

Just to Recap . . .

Unlearning old-perception habits is really no more difficult than learning them in the first place. There are guidelines you can practice to help you stay motivated, work with positive imagination and speech, and focus attention on what you really want. With each challenging stage in the transformation process, you can either resist it by using old-perception habits to try to preserve your old reality, or you can embrace the process, clear the clutter you don't need anymore, and become more open to your soul's guidance. When you become clear and loving, the new, transformed perception unfolds in you, step by step, naturally.

Part 3

New Attention Skills
for the Intuition Age

7

Practice Direct Knowing

*Knowledge is singularly replaced by something that has nothing
to do with thought and less and less with vision, something of a
higher order which is a new type of perception: you simply know. . . .
It's a perception, yes, which is global: simultaneously vision, sound,
and knowledge   It replaces knowledge. A perception so much truer
but so new that you don't know how to express it.*

Mirra Alfassa, "The Mother"

You've stepped through the doorway! The Intuition Age welcomes you with its new worldview and way of functioning. There are different ways of thinking and doing things now. On the other side of the door, there is an immediate experience of heightened sensitivity and intuition. You're learning to let your right brain lead and left brain follow; you're not so stuck in ego and fixations. You're more able to communicate without words and to read energy information directly from the environment. The first new attention skill in Intuition Age perception is *working with direct knowing*, an expanded version of intuition.

Rising to a New Speed of Perception

When your consciousness transforms, you don't *poof*, dissolve in a burst of light, and ascend! You're still here in this world, but it's a different physical world, and you're a different kind of human being. You perceive every physical thing to be teeming with consciousness-and-energy and responsive to thought. You're able to know about anything by placing attention on it and penetrating into it.

In the Intuition Age, knowing is direct and immediate. Your process of learning and finding meaning streamlines into something that occurs in a millisecond, sourced from all centers in the unified field and transmitted telepathically into all the centers within your personal self. You *know* in every particle of your being at once—via ultrasensitivity and feeling—in such a heightened and refined way that you instantly sense whether something is able to occur or why not, or if something is about to occur and its probability for a complex array of outcomes and repercussions.

You're able to grasp the inner blueprint of a reality and the mechanics of its materialization process and lifespan, adjusting its variables in your mind to shape it perfectly for any need at hand. You feel the subtle impression of a friend thinking about you or of someone who needs something, and know you're the one to give it—and you swing into action. When you're supposed to know something, the knowledge just shows up. You discover that life responds most rapidly and accurately to love and compassion. And this is just a glimpse of the way direct knowing works. There is more to be revealed as you evolve!

> In ordinary consciousness there is a sort of axis, and everything revolves around the axis. . . . And if it moves a little, we feel lost. . . . Now, for me, there is no more axis. . . . The consciousness can move here or there, it can go backwards or forwards, it can go anywhere—the axis is gone.
>
> Mirra Alfassa, "The Mother"

Getting Your Own Attention: It Starts with Intuition

Instinct and intuition are the first levels of direct knowing—they both help you perceive the consciousness-and-energy world—instinct is concerned with physical survival (you might think of it as a lower-frequency kind of intuition focused in the reptile brain), while intuition brings guidance from the soul. Intuition registers in one segment of your awareness at a time—your hearing, or vision, or tactile sensitivity, for example. Direct knowing, in comparison, is a heightened intuition that brings inspiration, guidance, and wisdom via all your channels and centers at once. There is no need to go through a process of decoding it; you know immediately. Let's examine intuition first, so you understand how it functions and what it can do, then we'll explore the expanded attention skill of direct knowing.

Intuition is nonlinear, nonfragmented, and fluidly spontaneous. It opens naturally the minute you shift attention from your left to your right brain, and becomes normal (and preferred) when your brain integrates and you perceive yourself as a center connected via resonance to nameless other centers everywhere throughout the unified field. It's like leaving that musty room I mentioned previously, and stepping through the door to roam free amidst a vast, stunning landscape.

You use intuition, or right-brain perception, every day but aren't often aware of it. "Why did I wear red today?" "Why did I leave the house for a meeting a bit early, then encounter a traffic jam and still manage to be on time?" "Why did I suddenly decide I don't want to drink alcohol?" "Why did I call my mother right after she'd had a bad fall?" These choices are not random; they're based on data from your inner, nonphysical world. When you first notice intuition, it's often about mundane things. Intuition greases the wheels of the daily round, helping you solve problems, be more creative, and feel your inner, spiritual life. When you make the small uses of intuition conscious by noticing them, you naturally progress to seeing intuition at work with larger, more complex issues. How do you know if you're being intuitive? Perhaps it's easier to see what a lack of intuition is like.

• If you think you're not being intuitive, you're right! You're in your left brain, thinking and analyzing rather than feeling. The right brain—the home of intuition—doesn't experience what doesn't exist.

- If you're saying "I don't know," "I'll have to think about it," or "Explain yourself!" you're in your left brain; otherwise, you'd already know the answers.
- If you're aware of talking, with inner or outer speech, you're in your left brain. Intuition works in the pause, in silence and spaciousness.
- If you think you told yourself to wear red, or to leave early for your meeting, you're in your left brain. With intuition, the Flow guides your choices and actions, and you simply engage, without marching orders.
- Postponing knowing, needing excuses and reasons for knowing, or feigning ignorance are all signs that you're in the left brain and out of touch with intuition. Intuition is fearless.
- If there is security but no fun, joy, or real creativity, it's not intuition. Intuition is inspired and totally positive and growth-enhancing.

> The boy was beginning to understand that intuition is really
> a sudden immersion of the soul into the universal current of life,
> where the histories of all people are connected, and we
> are able to know everything, because it's all written down.
>
> Paulo Coelho

Intuitive Perception Is Fluid and Generous

Intuition has no agenda or goals, no need to change anything or improve anything. All is well; there is plenty. Life is functioning and you are functioning, in perfect alignment with what's best for everyone. You are immersed directly in the Flow of the collective consciousness and in feeling and sensation. You're living in a bigger, more harmonious and peaceful world. You understand how higher dimensions function.

Question and answer exist together in each moment, and all is freely given—nothing is held back. There is no fear, there are no blockages. Perfect guidance exists as soon as you realize you need or want it. You attune to imagination and the unlimited possibilities for creativity. You can make the shift from the left brain to intuition by affirming and feeling the truth in each of the following statements:

- What I want to know or have is available to me as soon as I ask.
- I already know something about the answer to my question.
- I don't need to fix or change anything.
- The Flow brings whatever I need, to do the next thing.
- I trust whatever comes because it is always "just right."
- I can relax and enjoy. I can smile, be amused, and feel entertained.
- I notice what I'm noticing and act when the Flow moves me.

Intuitive Perception Is Right Now

When you're focused in the hard-edged, goal- and action-oriented consciousness of your left brain, you're tied to the past and future via your privately owned memories and goals. As soon as you open the softer, being-oriented consciousness of your right brain, you're in present time. All memory, all possibilities, and all wisdom are accessible because everything is in the now with you.

While in your left brain, you may feel that solving a problem is confusing and difficult—that it's going to take a long time to do the research, analyze all the options, take everyone else's agendas into account, and weigh the projected outcomes against the liabilities. There's nothing direct about this kind of knowing! With intuition, all this is done for you instantly by the great "computer" of the present moment and the unified field. Ask a question, and ding! You have your answer. Question and answer always exist together and draw each other forth. If you want to know more, ask another question. Even the questions come via intuition—it's the way your soul seeds guidance into your conscious mind.

· · · · · · · · · · ·

Try This!
What Do You Already Know?

1. Think of a problem, question, or issue you've been preoccupied with for a while. Close your eyes, center yourself, and breathe easily and deeply.

(Continued on next page)

(What Do You Already Know?, continued)

2. Bring the situation or question to the front of your mind, then feel your desire for an answer, insight, and understanding. Ask yourself: "What do I already know about this situation?" Remember that your question and answer exist together at the same time and are tied together.

3. Write what comes to you in your journal, without thinking it over or monitoring your answer. If the writing stops, ask about it again: "What else do I already know about this? What wants to happen so everyone wins? What is the best timing? Who else might need to be involved? What do I need to know before things will progress? What am I learning from this experience?"

• • • • • • • • • • •

Intuitive Perception Is Quiet and Appreciative

In your left brain, it's noisy. There are multiple conversations, like several radio stations playing simultaneously, and the conversations are often conflicting. Various internal experts are competing for prominence, and underneath there's static, like the sound that accompanies the "snow" on your television.

> The realest thing was the thick darkness at night. . . .
> Night, in which everything was lost,
> went reaching out, beyond the stars and sun.
>
> D. H. Lawrence

With intuition, it's peaceful and quiet. There's a velvety feeling of silence that allows you to expand without end, that lets you rest and fill up with the truth of who you are as a high-frequency being. With intuition there is one clear perception at a time, and that perception can miraculously integrate all your senses, other people's realities, and the understanding of a variety of probable paths for outcomes. To shift into the right brain and intuition, silence is required. Still the "monkey mind"—your overactive, talkative left brain. As you settle into the moment and the simplicity, turn your attention to appreciation and the experience of being with what is, and enjoying life the way it is. It's as if you bless things by being with them this way. And as you do this, what you need to know is effortlessly and graciously transmitted.

Intuitive Perception Leads to Communion

Intuition is perception based on unity and connectedness—on communion. When your intuition is open and you place your attention on a tree, or a problem, or the cells in your lungs, you immediately merge with the object of your attention and know it from inside its own reality. You feel connected through the simplicity of your noticing, and through this you can directly *experience*—not think about—its life pattern and potentials. Through this communion, you know the consciousness of your body, your cells, your heart, and the life force inside every form and field in your reality. You are those various foci of consciousness. You're in each cell, perceiving as the cell.

Mirra Alfassa (1878–1973), known as "The Mother," was Sri Aurobindo's spiritual partner, and in the latter part of her life she undertook an amazing inner journey into her body that she called the "yoga of the cells"—a journey that led her to an experience she called "the great passage," the discovery of what it means to become a new species of human. One of my favorite books, *The Mind of the Cells*, by Satprem, who was her secretary, documents her observations as she learned to live directly in her cellular consciousness and in a kind of perception she called "the Other State," or simply "That." She sought to dissolve fear and the left-brain control of her body and the cells themselves, to be merged with the higher vibrational mind that ran through everything.

She describes the Other State, what we might call direct knowing: "The consciousness floats in this (undulation) with a sensation of eternal peace. But it is not an expanse, the word is wrong: it is a limitless movement with a very quiet, vast, and harmonious rhythm. And this movement is life itself. I walk about my room, and that is what's walking. And it is very silent, like a movement of waves, with no beginning and no end; it has a condensation like this (*vertical gesture*), and a condensation like that (*horizontal gesture*), and it moves by expansion (*gesture of a pulsating ocean*). That is, it contracts and concentrates, then expands and spreads out."[1]

• • • • • • • • • • •

Try This!
Know Directly As Your Cells

1. Shift your attention into the cells of your body and imagine them as a community, a group consciousness. They all work together, communicate vibrationally, and support each other by being authentically themselves, giving and receiving freely, and staying healthy. You *are* the cells.

2. Imagine visiting and merging into various clusters of cells throughout your body: brain cells, heart cells, muscle cells, bone cells, blood cells. Feel yourself becoming part of those various clusters, living and working together—you are inside the consciousness field, or group mind, of those cells. What do you notice about the cohesion, functioning, flow, and nurturing within that cluster? Between that cluster and other kinds of cell clusters?

3. From your vantage point within cellular consciousness, what do you know about (a) how cells stay healthy; (b) why some cells become cancerous; (c) how cells remember to function properly? Make your intuitive insights conscious by describing them in first person plural in your journal; speak as the cells (e.g., "We stay healthy by . . .").

• • • • • • • • • • •

What I especially like about The Mother's personal experiment with using herself as a kind of lab rat, is that she journeyed straight into the density, infused her body with high-frequency consciousness, and transformed the very nature of cellular consciousness and matter. She demonstrated the transformation process that occurs as the immersion phase changes to the evolution phase of consciousness. And while she lived in her right-brain, intuitive state, she articulately described the various progressions in her process of increasing consciousness with her

Open Your Intuitive, Direct Knowing

- Pause what you're thinking about and shift from your left brain to your right brain.

- Stop what you're doing and drop from your head into your body to *become* your body. Know as your body knows, the way a simple animal follows its instinct.

- Bring your full attention into the present moment. You can say to yourself: "I am here, and I am 100 percent present and alert."

- Stop your internal dialogue and actively feel the silence; imagine it as a texture and sink into it—merge with it.

- In the quiet stillness, notice what you're noticing. Notice yourself just being, and notice everything else just being in the same moment.

- Be with everything in your environment without needing to do or change anything. All is well as it is.

- Appreciate each thing, each quality. Feel grateful for its unique life form and knowledge.

- Find similarities between yourself and anything or anyone you notice. Feel into objects, people, and places, and sense their energy and inner blueprint. Notice it's the same presence and consciousness that's in you.

- Focus on entering your heart and experiencing the world directly from your core. Feel your home frequency. You might focus on the resonance you now have with all other heart centers. Notice that when you love anything else, it loves you. Let that communion be the vehicle for direct knowing.

Fig. 7-1

left brain; she worked simultaneously in an enlightened way with her entire brain, heart, body, and personal field. She was a good example of someone moving into direct knowing.

Trusting Your Inner Perceiver

There is a part of your consciousness that causes you to notice what you notice, and it exists only in the here and now. It is the revealer, the teacher, the messenger part of your mind—your "inner voice." You might call it the Holy Spirit, the higher self, the master teacher, or your spiritual guide; I call it the *Inner Perceiver*. Perhaps it lives on the bridge between your right brain and left brain. This function of consciousness relays the soul's intent, direction, and plan to the personality—in effect, it doles out perceptions in a perfect sequence so a message or lesson can be made conscious, learned, and integrated.

You and a friend could walk the same path through the woods and you'd each notice different things, in a different sequence, making the walk meaningful to yourselves in your own way—and you'd each receive what you needed from the experience. So, in any given moment, you might ask yourself, "What is my Inner Perceiver teaching me? What does it want me to notice right now, and why?"

I made a choice years ago to have an active relationship with my Inner Perceiver. I talk to it as though it's a wise person, I ask it questions and receive insights. I trust my noticings implicitly—the order in which they appear, and their groupings and parallels—and I interpret these noticings the same way I interpret dreams. For example, I noticed a colorful variety of birds suddenly came into my yard after a lull, then I had a rash of clients from foreign countries, then some people sent me little gifts in the mail. The sequence had a buoying effect, showing me that I was connected through the unified field globally, and that abundance and generosity were free-flowing. It was like my soul was saying, "See? All is well. Just remember how connected everything is, how things come just at the right moment, and how entertaining life can be."

Working with your Inner Perceiver can be a simple way to keep your intuition open and active. If you practice checking in with your Inner Perceiver upon waking, throughout the day, and just before sleep, you build a habit of shifting to your right brain to feel what the message is, then to your left brain to make the insight conscious, then back into intuition to sense the pattern in what's occurring, and so forth. Soon the process becomes rapid and second nature. It's also a way to develop a mindfulness practice—that process of bringing full attention into whatever you're doing in the present moment.

Questions to Ask Your Inner Perceiver

- What am I trying to show or tell myself by noticing this?

- In noticing this, what experience does my soul want me to have that I've been missing?

- Am I trying to show myself a way or a place where my energy isn't flowing?

- What do I already know about this idea, situation, or person?

- Am I showing myself something that relates to an action I need to take?

- Does this situation pertain to the next step toward my destiny?

- What feeling or energy state does noticing this generate in me?

- Does noticing this feed into a creative process I'm involved in? Should it?

- What is the higher teaching connected with this situation I'm noticing?

Fig. 7-2

By dialoguing with your Inner Perceiver, you become even more aware of what's going on around you. You might ask it, "Why am I noticing that the music seems too loud in this restaurant?" Right away you may understand how conflicted and disturbed you've been feeling due to too much fragmenting external stimuli—how you're out of touch with your core. Maybe you need to meditate more or go for a walk in nature. But then you continue paying attention to the restaurant and notice a couple young girls chatting animatedly at a nearby table. "Why am I noticing these girls?" you ask. You drop into your feeling place, and an insight comes to you: here is a quality of enthusiastic bonding with a friend, a feeling of mutual validation with another, a real experience of the flow of ideas and energy between people—and this is something you'd like to cultivate in your own life. The more you notice, the more you learn.

> The feeling state of trust is important to cultivate in mindfulness practice, for if we do not trust in our ability to observe, to be open and attentive, to reflect upon experience, to grow and learn from observing and attending, to know something deeply, we will hardly persevere in cultivating any of these abilities, and they will only wither or lie dormant.
>
> Jon Kabat-Zinn

Moving from Intuition to Direct Knowing

As your body increases its frequency, you're able to pick up more information about what's going on around you and what your soul wants to do. These insights come in the form of energy information, directly through vibration. Guidance is no longer cloaked in words; it is understood in the present moment through your highly attuned felt sense. The energy information registers in all parts of your brain at once, in all parts of your body—in your cells, organs, and tissues, as well as in your personal energy field, or aura. Intuition, which is already fast on its own, becomes direct knowing, which is *instantaneous*.

Direct knowing allows you to use your ultrasensitivity as a vehicle of perception. You perceive yourself as a vibrating being of consciousness-and-energy in a sea of frequencies, with no boundaries anywhere. All knowing is available in this experience of immersion and communion, and the issue becomes how to discern what you need to know without being flooded with unnecessary information. How do you understand the pertinent energy information at the earliest point so you can translate it into action while staying in the Flow?

Fortunately, your Inner Perceiver regulates the flow of pertinent information from the huge unified field into your personal field, then into your body and right brain, and eventually into your left brain to become officially conscious. If you practice centeredness and dialoguing with your Inner Perceiver, you'll build the habit of knowing what you need to know just when you need to know it. As to understanding energy information at the earliest point, this begins to happen as your left and right brain balance and achieve horizontal integration. The two sides of your brain then act in harmonious partnership, accessing, registering, and understanding all at once.

This is all about making your perceptual process conscious and more instantaneous. As you learn to live in the Intuition Age, it's important that you think of yourself as a person who is consciously intuitive and blooming into the fullness of everything direct knowing offers. You are now consciously evolving. Direct knowing brings the insights for monitoring your evolution process by making you conscious of what's blocking you, how well your energy flows, how and why you know things, and what wants to happen most naturally in any moment.

Understanding Energy Information

The first key to working with energy information is being able to recognize the feeling of a surfacing or incoming flow. Is there something to know or not? You can use your increasing sensitivity to tune in to the subtle states of your body to find out. Do you feel relaxed, open, spacious, and at peace? There may be nothing urgent you need to know right now. Or do you feel antsy, slightly distracted, or mildly pressured? This is often the sign of an insight knocking on the door, asking to come in. An incoming flow of energy information can feel like a subtle tactile impression, like something pushing on you gently. It's also common to have an incoming flow activate one of your other senses. You might hear a voice, a knock, or a tinkling sound; feel hot, cold, or buzzy; see a glow or the ghostly image of something; or even smell something that's not physically in the space with you.

When you don't notice the incoming flow of energy information, pressure builds up and more information is added to the Flow, like a sky choked with planes waiting to land. It's easy then to feel overwhelmed, irritable, or even sad. Sometimes the energy information you're receiving is emotional and you'll match the vibration, thinking it's about you feeling despondent, or frustrated, or ebullient. You can also pick up information about physical states, as when your niece breaks her arm, your friend has her baby, or your grandfather dies. Until you process it, you may have similar, though more symbolic, symptoms and not know why. Perhaps your arm or belly begins to ache, or you feel like you might be close to having a dangerous accident.

When you don't translate this preverbal, energy information into understanding, and the pressure builds behind the incoming flow, you may protest against your growing empathic ability, saying, "It's all too much!" and withdraw into your cave. You may unconsciously decide you don't want to know anything. Hiding your head in the sand won't help, though, because the information just keeps coming. It's best to accept the messages and discover what your Inner Perceiver is trying to show you. If you unconsciously fear being overwhelmed by things you don't want to feel, you may want to change your attitude by welcoming the information and understanding that you only notice what you need to notice. *Think of ultrasensitivity as a way of getting smarter.* Resistance only blocks you from learning.

Control of consciousness determines the quality of life.

Mihaly Csikszentmihalyi

The next idea to try on is: *There's no such thing as bad energy information. It's all in service to your transformation and evolution.* Let your Inner Perceiver help you find the underlying messages and meanings in what you notice—even if what you notice is dreadful and difficult to look at. Your Inner Perceiver can reveal the positive purpose of that information and why you're noticing it right now. The more you practice letting inner meanings pop to the surface and become conscious, the more you'll be able to decipher energy information in the moment, on the fly, and without wasting time mulling it over and second-guessing it. Soon you'll be knowing things directly.

Imagine you're at the market, in a good mood, when you're suddenly hit with a wave of anxiety. What is it? Did you forget to lock your car? Is someone you know hurt? You scan the environment and notice a mother and small child. The mother is short-tempered and has just punished the child for taking an attractive item from a shelf. You realize you're feeling them both! Tension is relieved as you decide your action is not required.

As you become more practiced, you'll notice more sophisticated kinds of insights. It could be information from the ripple-wave of a past or coming event; a warning about a hidden pattern in another person's emotional body that could sabotage a process or be dangerous; an understanding of the consequences of a certain path of choices and actions; or the sense of what you need to do (or not do) to intersect with a person or an event that you require for your growth.

What the new consciousness wants: no more divisions. Being able to understand the extreme spiritual nature, as well as the extreme material nature, and to find their meeting point, where . . . they become a real force.

Mirra Alfassa, "The Mother"

As you work intentionally with direct knowing you gain understanding of multiple, simultaneous meanings and insights from each thing your Inner Perceiver notices. Your perception is integrating various points of view. The highest forms of direct knowing are akin to revelation and inspiration—they take you to a level of sophistication and holism you could hardly imagine before. You may have sudden insights that seem to have no trigger. Here are some examples:

- a past-life memory that explains and clears a long-standing behavior
- a vision of a possible reality that you know will occur and how it will do so
- an understanding of how a complex energy process works and how it can be applied to innovation in science and technology
- a revelation of how a societal trend will effect the economy and politics
- the changes that need to be made—and in what order—to affect immediate physical healing
- an understanding of your growth process through time, and your present life purpose and lessons

> A person experiences life as something separated from
> the rest—a kind of optical delusion of consciousness.
> Our task must be to free ourselves from this self-imposed prison,
> and through compassion, to find the reality of Oneness.
>
> Albert Einstein

Managing Your Empathic Ability

Your intuition and ultrasensitivity eventually lead to *empathy*, the ability to "feel with" someone or something else, to know another life form by becoming it experientially. With empathy you know the heart experience of another by being fully centered in your own heart. Far from causing you to feel overwhelmed, empathy leads to compassion, the soul's way of knowing. It allows you to experience more unity and simplicity, instead of fragmentation and chaos.

As long as you give attention to difficulty, pain, and suffering, you feed those states and help make them real. Of course we hurt sometimes, but it's not our natural state as souls. We don't need to put so much effort into avoiding pain; it's much more effective to invest attention in remaining in the openhearted, home-frequency state. If we unconsciously validate the awfulness of pain and suffering, or only feel into the surface of physical reality, we can erroneously think that being empathic is overwhelming and debilitating. But if we choose to validate the soul-in-the-body state, and feel all the way to the core of people, things, and situations, empathy becomes an extremely high form of direct knowing.

With empathy, decoding energy information is simple. First place your attention on the feeling of the vibration, then temporarily merge with the vibration, and ask your Inner Perceiver what's being conveyed. Remain quietly in the intuitive state as the impression registers in your field, body, heart, and integrated brain. As the meaning takes shape, like fog burning off to reveal a gorgeous view, allow your left brain to describe it while you maintain connection with the living state of direct knowing.

People often ask, "Don't I need boundaries?" Until you develop the habit of living in your center and home frequency, it's easy to be flooded with the fearful contents of individual and collective subconscious minds as they empty. You can be confused by the multitude of conflicting messages, and disoriented by other people's dramas. Putting up a fence or wall might seem like a good idea to protect yourself but this just adds to the reality of separation, and reinforces the idea that the world is outside, bigger than you, and dangerous. Holding this worldview forces you back into left-brain perception and immediately blocks direct knowing.

Here are a few tips to help you manage your direct knowing, empathic ability, and ultrasensitivity:

- **Direct knowing functions in the present moment, and in each moment there is just one thing to know.** The moment itself becomes a regulating force, bringing you bite-size insights that you are absolutely capable of processing one by one. They say, "Life never brings you more than you can handle," and this is why.
- **Your Inner Perceiver knows what it's doing.** If you notice something distasteful or upsetting, you might be tempted to react from an old-perception habit and lose your neutrality. But then you lose the lesson your soul wants you to learn. If you stay centered and ask your Inner Perceiver what it's trying to show you, you can put the perception in its proper perspective. Even if you react negatively, there's always a useful lesson.

- **You can visit other centerpoints, and gain other points of view, but between each foray, come back to your own.** By placing your attention on someone or something—by "feeling into" objects, ideas, places, and fields—you become one with them and know them from their point of view. This is valuable data only if you return to your own center and allow your left brain to make sense of the information: *How useful is this to me? Do I want to do something with this insight?* If you stay enmeshed with what you're exploring and forget to come back to your center, you lose touch with your soul's guidance and will feel drained.
- **No one, and no thing, can occupy your space if you're fully present.** When you remain fully centered in your body and personal field, saturating the entire thing with your home frequency, nothing can displace you or prevent you from staying connected with your soul. You don't need shields to protect yourself; you are your own safety.
- **Remember that empathy involves compassion, not necessarily emotion.** When you involve your heart center in the direct knowing process, you gain a much higher perspective about anything you notice. You feel how what you're perceiving fits into the scheme of things—how it both receives and transmits consciousness-and-energy, and evolves in the process. Things aren't good or bad, they just are what they are.

> The smokescreen of the world is lifted. Everything is interconnected
> within a great, joyous vibration. Life becomes vaster, truer, more alive;
> little truths twinkle everywhere, wordlessly, as if each thing held
> a secret, a special sense, a special life. One bathes in an indescribable
> *state of truth*, without understanding anything about it—it just *is*.
> And it is, marvelously. It is light, alive, loving.
>
> Sri Aurobindo

Try this: Stop reading when you finish this chapter, and notice what your body was previously processing and what it's noticing right now. Check all your senses. Check your intuition. Let the feel of the chapter's content slosh around in you and make connections on its own. Hold still for it. Notice when it feels right to move on to the next thing.

Just to Recap . . .

Direct knowing is a heightened form of intuition that results from the integration of your brain and other centers of perception. It uses your growing ultrasensitivity as a vehicle of perception to find insight in energy information that comes directly via vibration. It helps to recognize and use intuition, first on small things and gradually on more complex issues. Intuition is fluid, open, in the present moment, quiet, appreciative, and interconnective. When you practice validating your intuition, direct knowing increases.

There is a function in your consciousness that I call the Inner Perceiver—some call it the "inner voice." It helps you notice what you notice and understand why you're noticing it. When you dialogue with your Inner Perceiver, you more easily understand your intuitive insights and can understand the energy information that's coming straight from the field around you.

As transformation occurs, your intuition deepens to direct knowing, and you rapidly perceive all at once, all over your body. Your left and right brain operate in a cooperative partnership. But being able to pick up energy information can be overwhelming if you don't recognize when a flow of information is surfacing, or if you resist experiencing certain kinds of insights that your left brain has categorized as bad. Your ultrasensitivity leads you to become empathic, which then leads you to compassion, the knowing of the soul. Far from being a negative thing, empathy is a sophisticated kind of direct knowing that allows you to experience great love and oneness.

8

Practice the Spherical-Holographic Reality

I've dreamed of heaven—the full and perfect bliss
That waits the spirit in a larger sphere
And, looking up, have found enough in this
To realize the rapturous vision here!

Alice Cary

One of the biggest adjustments we need to make in the Intuition Age is to change our fundamental *geometry of perception*. The way we perceive follows an inner blueprint or pattern based on a particular geometry. This underlying geometry determines the way consciousness-and-energy can flow, and this, in turn, influences the way we see reality. Until now, our geometry of perception has been linear. With this pattern, we understand the inner workings of the brain as linear (the ascending and descending flows of consciousness), and also see the outer functioning of reality as linear; time and space are organized in lines. We perceive along "lines of thought" and "timelines," and move across the shortest distance between two points in space. Dimensionality and potentiality are limited in this view.

In this chapter, we'll discuss the next new attention skill in the Intuition Age: *your ability to recognize and to begin to live in the reality*

135

created by spherical-holographic perception. I see spherical-holographic perception as composed of two related experiences. The first experience is "spherical perception." It begins when you experience yourself as the centerpoint in a spherical field of consciousness-and-energy, and feel yourself to be both the centerpoint and the field simultaneously. With spherical perception, you never leave the center; the sphere—which is your reality—simply expands and contracts around you like a balloon, blowing up or contracting depending on your frequency, focus, and desire.

When your sphere expands, you encompass more of the body of knowledge that is the unified field—you vibrate at a higher frequency (which is not necessarily better). When your sphere contracts, you focus on less of the field, or vibrate at a lower frequency (which is not necessarily worse). Your reality is always inside the sphere, and you cannot get outside the sphere. We intuitively know this kind of perception; we often speak of one's "sphere of influence" or "sphere of interest."

The second experience is the holographic part of the new perception. It comes when you realize that, as a centerpoint, or the heart of your sphere, you are naturally connected to every other centerpoint—every other heart—in the universe via resonance. Every point is inside your sphere, available to you. That means you can shift your attention into any other centerpoint and know any other reality as though it's yours. What's more, from any centerpoint, you can know yourself as the entire unified field of consciousness-and-energy, because with holograms, each tiny bit of the whole contains the entirety of the whole. So the sphere and the hologram are slightly different experiences, but they blend together seamlessly.

In chapter 5, I outlined a series of shifts of consciousness in the brain and body that help take you from old, linear perception to new, spherical-holographic perception. I also described many effects of the two different kinds of perception. In this chapter, I want to go into this shift in more detail to help you understand how to work with, and live within, the resulting spherical-holographic reality.

The Linear Thought Process and Reality

Since it's useful to be able to clearly compare the old and new, let's dip back into linear perception briefly to refresh our memory about the effect it has on us and reality. Linear perception has many limitations that cause you to perceive at a fairly low frequency. This can generate fear and make life seem to operate in slow motion. Linear perception can also interfere with your ability to experience nonphysical reality. Take a closer look and you'll see why, as we begin to transform, linear reality now seems so antiquated and sluggish. Here's how we think in a linear world:

- **There's a boundary between me and life. I feel isolated and at the effect of the big world "out there."** I always feel an imaginary line around myself—the experience of where "I" end—and there's empty space beyond that. I'm separated from the rest of life spatially and temporally. The world can seem so huge, so uncaring, so dangerous, so against me in every way—I fear being overcome or swallowed up by the vastness. I'm small and terrified of losing my individual identity. I can't remember who I *really* am either, because my soul is in some distant space far above me called "heaven."
- **I want it, but I can't have it or know it right now.** I am here and you are "over there." My best-possible-scenario-dream-reality is "out there" as well. The solutions to problems are in the future, so I can't know them now. The people, places, and possessions I want to have, and the ideas I want to understand, are elsewhere, postponing my satisfaction. The carrot is forever suspended in front of the donkey, never to be reached.
- **To attain and maintain what I want, I must use willpower.** To get to what I want, I must cross the boundary and empty space (the gaps) between me and what I desire. To be successful, I must use willpower and cleverness; I must have a plan. I start an action (cause), and it must go through steps to occur (effect). It takes time and progress is slow. I must maintain my motivation, keep my energy "up," and have

ambition and a positive attitude—it's all up to me! Life is hard, and no one really wants to help me; if I relax, things fall apart. When I get a result, I have to use willpower to keep it.

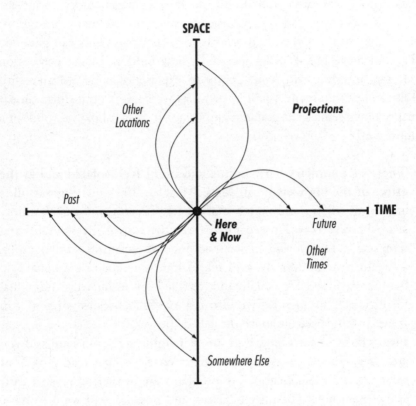

Fig. 8-1: With linear perception, your mind projects along lines into the future or past, or into other locations. By doing this, you create imaginary gaps between you and your objectives.

- **The empty gaps I perceive limit my speed. The lines I must adhere to limit my dimensionality and possibilities.** I'm an expert at project-ing back and forth with my mind along the timelines and tracks in space. When I do this, I inadvertently create empty gaps between where I am and what I want to have; my mind always sees blank space between point A and point B. Because I define the gaps as empty, I don't experience the information that resides in the gaps, and I can't experience the part of myself that lives in those spaces. Therefore, the gaps create big holes in the Flow of my consciousness-and-energy, and slow me and life down.

I must stay on the line of past, present, and future and do things in that order. And I must travel from here to there along a logical line; I can't jump over any steps if I want the process to work. Life is so physical! Uncontrolled bursts of intuition and wild, imaginative creativity are frowned upon. I check out probabilities before they occur, thinking how they will be, drawing on experience from the past, and projecting those ideas into the future. I don't understand why the present seems to have its own agenda, and why I can't control life with my mind and willpower

> Let us not look back in anger or forward
> in fear, but around in awareness.
>
> James Thurber

- **I fall into negative thinking easily.** The slowness, blank spots, exhaustion (from overuse of willpower), and loneliness (from thinking I have to do everything myself), lead me to make erroneous assumptions about life and who I am. I validate negative emotional states and think I must be flawed, undeserving, unlovable, ignorant, incompetent, weak, and not disciplined enough to have a better life. I can easily feel frustrated, angry, bitter, overwhelmed, drained, depressed, unmotivated, fatalistic, and dull. I define myself by what I'm *not*.

You can see from this little progression of thinking how linear perception creates a world based on the experience of separation, fear, willpower, difficulty, and suffering. It's not a pretty picture! In the next section, I'll give you a model that can help you imagine and feel the shift to Intuition Age consciousness.

Linear Reality Is Like a Donut and Its Empty Hole

With linear perception, we tend to project away from center—the here-and-now and our body—looking at and feeling into other times or other locations (including other people's realities), and we neglect our own core. If you remember from chapter 5, it is the experience of centeredness that begins the transformation to spherical-holographic perception. With linear perception, however, we are everywhere else except "at home" in our center and in our home frequency. Life seems outside us, surrounding us, and what we want is out of reach or postponed. In many ways, linear reality begins to resemble a donut and its empty hole.

On the next page in Figure 8-2, you see the donut and its empty hole centered on the axis of time and space. The intersection, or center-point, in the here-and-now (the center dot), is where you are with your body, personality, and access to your soul and the nonphysical world. That centerpoint is like a doorway to higher frequency dimensions of consciousness.

The donut represents where most of your attention resides—somewhere else, or in the past or future. If your attention is absorbed in the donut, you're unable to perceive what's happening in the hole at the center, and therefore, you cannot access that magical centerpoint that opens you to your soul, nonphysical life, and the Intuition Age reality.

Because you're looking elsewhere for what you want, for validation of who you are, and for the meaning of life, you don't experience your true self in the center. You can feel "mindless," or "out of your mind." Your consciousness has "left your body" to occupy other points in time and space—and in effect, "nobody's home." You yourself have become a gap! It's not easy, then, to feel your body, emotions, or true motivations, or to have a clear sense of what's real and what you want or need. When your conscious mind is not in the here and now, you can't notice what you need to notice or recognize the intuitive guidance that's constantly pouring into your reality via your Inner Perceiver. To connect with your soul, your truth, and your destiny, your consciousness-and-energy must be fully centered in the present moment, in your body.

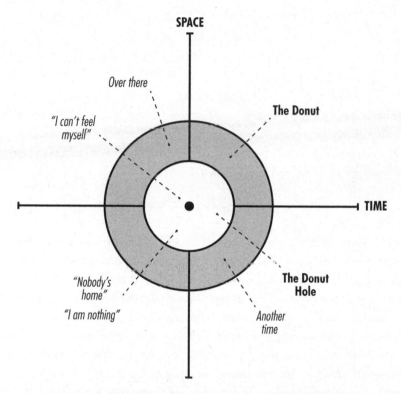

Fig. 8-2: By projecting your mind into other times and spaces,
and by seeing the world as separate from you, life becomes like a donut,
out of reach. Your body, personality, and soul exist in the empty hole.
It's easy to think you are "nothing" because you can't feel yourself.

• • • • • • • • • • •

Try This!
What Do You Project or Postpone?

Quiet yourself, and with your journal, make a list of answers to the following
questions. We'll do more with each answer in the next exercise.

1. What have I postponed doing? Postponed thinking about? Postponed having? Postponed experiencing?

(Continued on next page)

(What Do You Project or Postpone?, continued)

2. What goals do I have that I've placed in the future?
3. What ideas from the past limit how I might do or know something today?
4. What am I nostalgic for?
5. What other places do I imagine visiting?
6. Who do I focus on so strongly that I can feel what it's like to live their life?
7. What problems can't I solve because I think the solution is too distant?
8. Where in my life do I feel I must use willpower? Or that I can't stop without everything falling apart?

. . . .

When you live in the hollow center of the donut, it's easy to associate emptiness or negativity with who you are—to think you are nothing, or not good. Many of my clients who were abused as children tell me they feel they have a psychic hole in the middle of their body. They try to fill it in various ways—with food, sex, fame, or explosive emotion, for exam- ple—but it always empties again. When you've been scared out of your body, or "out of your wits," especially repeatedly, this empty-hole phe- nomenon often occurs. *So much of what psychologists call lack of self-esteem is simply lack of self-experience.* How can you experience your true self when your attention is creating a reality that's outside and separate from you?

> There is no need to run outside for better seeing, nor to peer
> from a window. Rather, abide at the center of your being,
> for the moment you leave it, the less you learn.
>
> Lao Tzu

Turning the Donut into the Sphere

To transform and find Intuition Age perception, you need to take up your rightful place in the center of the here and now and in your body—starting with the centerpoints in your head and heart. You need to feel your home frequency—your soul in your body and personality—

as your normal state of being, and connect deeply with whatever is occurring in the present moment. As these conditions align, you become acutely aware of the aliveness of your personal field, noticing how it extends out around you spherically in all directions, and how what's in the sphere is your present-moment reality. If you could see yourself energetically, you'd be a glowing ball of light.

In Figure 8-3 below, you can see how, to transform, you withdraw all your projections from the donut and retreat to the center to be still

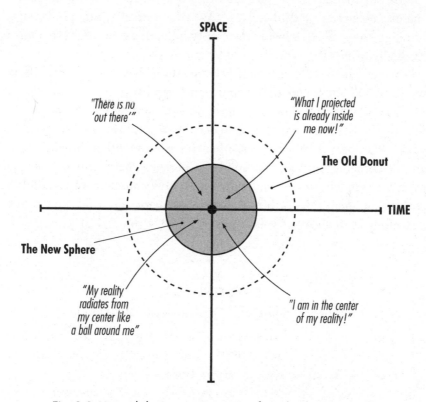

Fig. 8-3: You withdraw your projections from the donut and pull everything inside yourself. Now all your dreams, goals, and solutions exist inside your present moment and there is no outside world! The sphere is your reality.

and silent—to experience unity in the present moment. It's as if you've cast thousands of fishing lines out into the world and now you're reeling them back in to your core. This is when you take the "pause that refreshes," reach the end of progress, let go of willpower, and be with yourself and your reality the way it is. Remember, though, that when you first stop and center yourself, life may seem quite empty. You may go stir crazy. But as you continue "just being," your experience shifts magically and you feel full.

In our model, as you pull attention out of the donut, it drains of energy, collapses, and dissolves. As you retract your projections, bringing them all back inside the empty hole, this centering experience gradually brings the experience of your true self back into reality, back into focus. The once-empty hole becomes an active, living center, filling with consciousness-and-energy and transforming into a radiant sphere.

You now expand slowly, like a round fruit getting ripe, through and beyond the space the donut used to occupy. You realize your knowledge, goals, other people, other places, other times—even other dimensions— are all contained inside your spherical personal field, which is also a greatly expanded present moment. You're now conscious of effortlessly containing many ideas, things, and frequencies, all while you reside peacefully in the heart of your big reality-ball.

. . . .

Try This!
Reabsorb What Was Previously In Your Donut

1. Quiet yourself, bring your attention inside your skin, then focus your attention in your heart center. Let a ball of light radiate from your heart until it becomes a large sphere around your body.

2. Let this personal heart field resonate to the vibration of your home frequency or preferred state—the way you really like to feel. Let it expand until everything you're aware of is inside the sphere.

3. With your journal, review your answers to the questions from the previous exercise, *What Do You Project or Postpone?*. Bring each question back

inside your sphere so you feel it as part of your present moment, your living reality. Write about how doing this changes your perception of each answer and what you now want to do about each thing.

• • • • • • • • • • •

How Reality Functions When You're a Sphere

After changing from linear to spherical perception (the first part of spherical-holographic perception), reality functions differently. For starters, *there is no outside world!* Everything is inside your sphere with you, interconnected by a field of consciousness-and-energy with no separating boundaries. And everything is personal, highly efficient, and lovingly supportive. What was important in your life previously is still there, but it has a quality of heightened reality.

You experience being a multifaceted, multidimensional self who never leaves your home frequency. You don't have to go anywhere to know and have what you want. You only have to place your attention fully on an idea and it shows up in your personal field, materializing miraculously with help given freely and generously by others. The process is lightning fast because everything is in the present moment. You are no longer hollow but joyfully "full of yourself," and you're able to know anything because the answers are in you, right now. You are the newborn, risen phoenix.

> When we engage in a creativity recovery, we enter into a withdrawal process from life as we know it. . . . We ourselves are the substance we withdraw to, not from, as we pull our overextended and misplaced creative energy back into our own core.
>
> Julia Cameron

Your Spherical Field *Is* Your Reality

As a sphere, you always experience your reality from the inside. You cannot get outside yourself. Your spherical field is your present moment, your conscious mind, your reality, and your sense of self—but it's not static; it can expand and contract in frequency to access more or less of the unified field, depending on the scope of your attention. You can be a small, tight focus of consciousness or a large, expansive focus of consciousness. You can know the reality of a particle, or of the whole unified field. When you're focused in the physical world, this gives you the sense of encompassing more or less time and space. When you're focused in the nonphysical world you can attune yourself to higher and lower frequencies—and dimensions—of consciousness-and-energy. You have freedom to move anywhere in the unified field and experience it all. And yet, there's nothing outside your sphere of experience. I know this isn't easy to understand when we're using linear perception!

Here's the tricky part: In spherical perception, when you have a new thought, it's not coming from outside your sphere, but from a new frequency within your sphere. The activation of frequencies and the movement of consciousness-and-energy within your sphere is a function of the Flow, your soul, and your Inner Perceiver. Higher frequency thoughts produce the experience of living in a larger, more expansive sphere. When you think there is more to know, do, or have, your sphere has already focused the new thoughts at a frequency where you can access them and make them conscious. If you're tempted to see "more" as beyond you in time, space, or dimension—you've regressed into linear perception.

Inside Your Sphere Are Limitless Frequencies

When you live from the center of your sphere, you become conscious of a vast array of frequencies that coexist within you. You experience how different frequencies correspond to different realities—that there are many dimensions of experience available to you. And you play with changing your personal vibration to change your reality, discovering how your sphere expands or contracts to match the vibration.

Shifting frequencies is as easy as focusing your attention differently. If you focus on changing a watch battery, for example, your sphere is relatively small. If, in the midst of that activity, you think of your dream vacation and how enthusiastic you'd feel if you were there, your frequency increases; your sphere has expanded to encompass the vision and make you conscious of it. If you meditate on compassion and feel how your heart connects to all other hearts, your sphere expands in frequency even more.

Inside Your Sphere, Life Is Naturally Safe

If what you perceive is inside you, it's familiar. You know about it intimately—and it knows you. *Everything inside you is cooperative because it's all the same self with one goal—evolution.* There is no opposition; that collapsed with the dissolution of the outside world. If you have a desire, it materializes easily because it wants to materialize—because it's "you" in another form. When your world is familiar, and you're focused in your home frequency, your reality becomes supportive and win-win-win, and your consciousness-and-energy produces safety, love, and joy instead of fear and danger.

"But isn't that naïve?" you say. "What if, while I'm blithely going along, someone mugs me? What if my boss fires me? What if I see a spider and my phobia is triggered?" First, if something seems oppositional and external, you've fallen back into linear perception. Instead of relating to the spider as kin and seeing the world through its eyes, it becomes the enemy; you're back in the empty donut hole, feeling helpless and out of touch. It can happen in an instant—but you can correct yourself in an instant too, by recentering. Then you might see that your boss isn't working against you; she's bringing an important insight you need. Perhaps the spider is a messenger for your Inner Perceiver.

You soon recognize the kinds of subtle contractions that flip you into the empty donut hole, and eventually you stop reacting that way, because it's a needless bother, and you have a clear preference for feeling better. When you stabilize your new worldview, you will be safe; you simply won't be drawn to the time and place where you might be mugged. You won't have a need for that type of fear-based "lesson," and will trust your intuition and Inner Perceiver to direct you down the path to greater creativity and growth instead.

You Can Visit Many Dimensions in Your Expandable Sphere

With spherical perception, you see how your physical, emotional, mental, and soul realities are connected smoothly in a continuum. Just as you might play a scale of music, you can slide through a similar "scale" of the different "frequencies of self." Because it's all connected so fluidly via resonance, there are no more lines of demarcation—changing dimensions is just a matter of changing vibration, of shifting your attention, which can happen instantly.

When you meditate, work with imagination, or dream at night, your sphere expands and includes higher dimensions of consciousness: the etheric, emotional/astral, mental, and causal realms. With each expansion, you know more—are more—of your totality. When you return to daily reality, your sphere contracts; it contracts even more when you focus on a task. What's so much fun is that you have total freedom to activate any frequency and scope you desire, at any time, in any order. It's possible to feel that you include the whole planet, solar system, or galaxy inside your sphere. Match the size and vibration of your sphere to the sphere of the earth, and you can know the earth as yourself. Contract your sphere to the size and vibration of an atom, and you can know that atom as yourself. As spiritual teacher Neville Goddard said, "We become that with which we are *en rapport*."[1]

When you expand your sphere, you may also experience having a greater amount of time. This occurs because you include more of the past and the future inside yourself. You have the odd sense that the present has swallowed up what used to be the past and the future, giving you access to information you used to think of as memory, or as precognitive insight. You also have a more leisurely sense of having "plenty of time," and you see how things that used to take a lot of time happen in an instant. *What used to be the future is now your potential self.*

Perhaps you receive a vision concerning your destiny—something you used to define as in the distant future and thus barely perceptible—but now, because your destiny is inside your sphere, it's close and much more real. It's a possible you, within reach. *Your destiny is in you, at a higher frequency of your current reality.* To materialize it, you only need to raise your personal vibration to match the frequency of the destiny pattern, and allow the scope of your sphere to adjust and match the new vibration. Eventually, when you can shift your vibration skillfully, you'll be able to materialize a new reality instantly. No cause-and-effect, gradual process of creation required! The "future," you will discover, is becoming an outdated concept.

• • • • • • • • • • •

Try This!
Expand Your Sphere by 50 Percent

1. Quiet yourself, and feel the scope of your present life as though everything you're aware of is inside a spherical reality. Notice that there is space and time included in your sphere; you have a routine, projects in progress, relationships, movement and flows, repetitive thought patterns.

2. Now imagine adding 50 percent more energy to your sphere, raising the frequency of your reality by 50 percent and expanding the scope of your life by 50 percent. Do this until that new level of consciousness and activity seems comfortable and normal.

3. What new developments might be occurring in your expanded sphere? What do you know about now that you didn't know before? How do you feel about yourself, others, and life's possibilities now?

4. Write about your observations in your journal.

• • • • • • • • • • •

How Reality Functions When You're a Hologram

Now that you have a sense about how spherical perception works, let's add in the second part of the new perceptual geometry—holographic perception. Then you can begin to feel how they effortlessly merge to create a transformed reality.

Remember that any part of a hologram reveals the totality. The microcosm perfectly symbolizes the macrocosm, or to paraphrase an old metaphysical truth: "As below, so above." As your spherical field of consciousness-and-energy expands and contracts, you learn to see how any focus—any reality—no matter how tiny, acts as a hologram. And you experience how the universe itself is the superhologram.

Michael Talbot, author of *The Holographic Universe*, says, "Just as every portion of a hologram contains the image of the whole, every portion of the universe enfolds the whole. This means that if we knew how to access it, we could find the Andromeda galaxy in the thumbnail of our left hand. We could also find Cleopatra meeting Caesar for the first time, for in principle, the whole past and implications for the whole future are also enfolded in each small region of space and time. Every cell in our body enfolds the entire cosmos."[2] Your sphere contains the whole of the universal mind and unified field. With spherical-holographic perception you don't have to go anywhere to know everything; it's all enfolded—*encoded*—in your heart center and in every center in your body.

You Have Access to Any Center and Any Reality

As you begin to experience life holographically, you discover you have access to universal wisdom from any point in the unified field. All centerpoints become available to you, because they're in you—just as the many-worlds theory in physics says. You can slide into other centerpoints via resonance: they're not separated in space, but in frequency. You don't leave your center to go to another center, you just imagine it and you're there—you just shift your vibration.

Think lovingly of the heart of an ancient tree, and you're there, feeling the experiences that occurred throughout history as each ring of your trunk grew, knowing the world from that point of view. Attune to the heart of a spiritual teacher, and you're there, feeling what that person feels and knowing the world from their enlightened perspective. Think of a potential reality, like getting a great new job with twice the salary, and you can feel yourself as that new person. You can joyfully explore this game of *shape-shifting*—of merging into various centers to experience aspects of your larger self.

Any centerpoint is the seed of a unique reality and each reality simultaneously contains the experience of the entire unified field of consciousness-and-energy. All centerpoints, or points of view, are legitimate paths into oneness. I am the center of the universe, and so are you. There is an inner blueprint in each centerpoint. When you place attention in any center, you can know its full potential form—its perfect, optimal expression. You can become one with anything and know it personally from within. This gives you the capacity for deep respect and compassion because when you know something this way, you see the importance, magnificence, and beauty of every form of life. When you perceive with respect and compassion, you can magically shift into the experience of the universal, superhologram—from anywhere.

The ability to see the universe from different perspectives may be a reflection of the different vantage points of perception of our subtle energetic vehicles of expression, such as the astral, mental, and causal bodies.

Richard Gerber

Memories and Visions Are Alive, Each in Their Own Sphere

In the spherical-holographic reality, every memory, lifetime, imagination, and vision—every experience ever fantasized or lived by any person throughout all time—still exists as a unique frequency, readily available as a reality for you to experience. I've often seen these realities in my dreams as transparent bubbles floating in space, filled with tiny, living movies that grow larger and more real the more I merge into them. When you move your attention into one of these spherical bubble-realities, you'll notice it has its own center. Merge with that centerpoint, match the vibration of the sphere, and you'll be in that reality, living that memory or vision in your present time.

This is an example of how the spherical and the holographic join. One centerpoint can commune easily with any other centerpoint; anyone else's experience or spherical field can be your experience, and vice versa. And, you can know the self, the world, and the totality from any point of view.

I've been describing how spherical-holographic perception works in your inner world, but remember that transformation involves the merger of the nonphysical and physical realities. In the Intuition Age, they won't be separate like they are today. Therefore, it's feasible that as you become adept at shifting your frequency, centerpoint, and sphere in the nonphysical world, you'll eventually be able to do this physically. For instance, time travel, teleportation, and bilocation may become more normal after transformation. We'll discuss this in chapter 14.

You Can Merge with Any Group Mind or Pool of Knowledge

In the spherical-holographic reality you can move into communion with other souls, groups of souls, and the huge "soul of the world," to know what these kinds of collective consciousness know. In my early years of developing intuition, I regularly felt a council of beings sitting at a round table some distance, or frequency, above my head. In meditation I attuned myself to that reality by picturing and feeling it in detail, and I'd be in the room with them, sitting at my place at the round table. During these "conferences," knowledge was transmitted telepathically among all the beings via direct knowing. When the transfer was complete, I returned to my physical reality by imagining it again and dropping my vibration. There are endless kinds of group minds you can join via *frequency-matching*, and each is a sphere where the participants' knowledge is equally available to all.

You are beginning to experience life as a sphere and a hologram because the earth's frequency now allows you to understand this high-vibration way of functioning. It's interesting that as the geometry of our perceptual model is shifting, science has also been seeing the holographic nature of the way the brain and body function. Our process of learning and creating is going to accelerate greatly—in fact, photographic memory may well be one of the byproducts of the spherical-holographic reality. We may access existing and yet-to-be-documented data directly from the unified field—a search engine that's faster and more accurate than anything on the internet today. Our technology may be something we soon leapfrog over into a much more efficient "new human" technology that's built right into the fabric of our being.

> To see a world in a grain of sand
> And a heaven in a wild flower,
> Hold infinity in the palm of your hand
> And eternity in an hour.
>
> William Blake

Just to Recap . . .

We are changing our underlying "geometry of perception" from a linear to a spherical-holographic model and this changes our reality. Linear perception, which we know so well, causes many forms of limitation and contributes to the existence of pain and suffering. Shifting to the new spherical-holographic perception, and its resulting transformed reality, begins with attaining spherical perception, then adding on the second part, holographic perception.

Spherical perception begins with centering, and learning to live in the here and now, inside your body. A simple model for understanding how this shift takes place is to imagine that linear reality is like a donut with its empty hole. The mind constantly projects away from the center along lines to times in the past or the future, and other locations in space. The center is neglected, which makes you feel empty, while "reality" seems like a donut, outside and separate from you. It's difficult to feel your body and soul.

You need to reel in all the projections and pull attention out of the donut, then take up residence in your center, allowing the hollow "hole" to fill up again like a fruit getting ripe. Then you regain a sense of your truth. The donut disappears and reality becomes a radiant sphere with you always in its center. Once you've made this shift, you can expand or contract your sphere in frequency to encompass any amount of the unified field. Your reality becomes extremely fluid.

Holographic perception begins when you realize you can resonate with any center or heart within your field—because your sphere contains all the hearts of every form that's ever been or will be; they're all in the present moment with you. Any center can lead you to an experience of the totality of the universe. You gain infinite freedom, wisdom, and respect for every form of life in this new spherical-holographic reality.

9

Practice Undivided Attention

My experience is what I agree to attend to.

William James

Being on the cusp of the Intuition Age, life is sloshing with waves of fear, confusion, and yes, excitement too. We gleefully embrace new technologies, while processing mountains of data, juggling the multiplying components of our lives, and avoiding the negative consciousness permeating the ethers. We distract ourselves from overstimulation with new types of stimulation, trapping our consciousness in a shallow layer on the surface of reality. We're ripe for the development of the next attention skill—*the conscious use of attention itself.* In this chapter we'll examine just what undivided attention can do.

Attention: A Valuable Commodity

It's interesting to think about the origins of the phrases we use to talk about attention. So many of them sound like we're speaking of money.

We say, "*Pay* attention, please!" Or "I'm *investing* attention in (or *withdrawing* attention from) this idea." Or "He just wants to get attention." Or "Can I *have* your attention?" We have a deficit of attention these days just as we have a national budget deficit. Attention is obviously a highly valued commodity! The origin of the word actually comes from the idea of "stretching toward" something with your consciousness-and-energy. To *attend* an event is to bring your self to it, to be present at it. To *tend* your garden is to bring consciousness to it by caring for it.

Attention is valuable because it's not just an act of focusing your mind on a single point, it is the bringing of your very essence, your soul—the most valuable thing you have—fully into the moment, to perceive with clarity. In the military the command, "At-ten-*tion!*" is a call to full alertness and presence for safety's sake. Jon Kabat-Zinn, a leading teacher of mindfulness practice—a key method for developing undivided attention—says, "Mindfulness means paying attention in a particular way: on purpose, in the present moment, nonjudgmentally. . . . [It] is an appreciation for the present moment and the cultivation of an intimate relationship with it through a continual attending to it with care and discernment. [Mindfulness] is the direct opposite of taking life for granted."[1] When used properly, attention is life promoting and soul revealing, and it leads to conscious evolution.

Attention Reveals Presence in the Present

Note the repetition in the ideas of *presence*, being *present*, and the *present* moment. Attention only functions in the present moment; in fact, if you pay attention, the very act *brings you into the present*. When you're present, you have presence—and presence is the experience of the soul. You can invest attention superficially or deeply, unconsciously or consciously, reaping benefits to the extent it is focused. When attention is focused by the left brain, only a small amount of the soul's presence filters through, and what is revealed only fits the left brain's limited understanding. But when attention is focused fully by the soul, you discover pure consciousness-and-energy wherever it is placed, invested, granted, given, directed, or turned. This kind of undivided attention creates a live connection to the world and opens you to seeing through the surface of life into the nonphysical world.

When the soul sees, everything you attend to enhances evolution and inspired creativity; the more deeply you pay attention, the more truth and spirit you find. When you realize it is you, the soul, who is paying attention, you experience more purposefulness and power. You may even wonder: "Am I creating life by perceiving it?" What's interesting is that the soul only sees *itself* wherever it focuses attention because it is undivided and has no concept of "other." So if you pay attention as the soul, you recognize a kinship connection between yourself and whatever you notice.

You might ask yourself, "Who is paying attention right now?" Is it your left brain or your soul? Seeing as the soul activates presence, which is more valuable than money because when you're saturated with it, everything is saturated with it, and life's mysteries unfold; wisdom is transmitted on its frequency. When the viewer and the viewed become the same, nothing can be hidden. You see the light inside life, and life becomes sacred.

People and places with presence have energy that makes you feel more conscious. I'm sure you've noticed that whoever or whatever has real presence is authentic, trustworthy, convincing, vital, magnetic, universal in some way, and naturally attention-getting and attention-giving. Think about people like the His Holiness the Dalai Lama, or structures like the Great Pyramid and the Taj Mahal, or places like the Grand Canyon and Mount Everest, or beings like the oldest trees on the planet. How enlightening it is to be in their presence!

· · · · · · · · · · ·

Try This!
Activate Presence with Attention

1. With the next person you have an exchange with, bring your attention fully into your body and the present moment. Remember that you are the soul,

(Continued on next page)

(Activate Presence with Attention, continued)

perceiving through the eyes of your personality, and really notice the other person, without labels or judgment. To do this, find quietness inside yourself. Being a neutral yet compassionate observer is the beginning of presence.

2. Place your attention on, around, and in the other person, softly and gently, as though it is golden or diamond light. Pay close attention to the way the other person speaks and moves, to their personal vibration, to any intuitive clues you pick up. Don't match the other person's vibration. Stay in your own home frequency.

3. Notice what they're saying and why it's important to them. Validate what they're saying by acknowledging that you understand. While you're attending to them, open your heart and appreciate them for who they are; feel the soul quality inside them.

4. Notice if there is something you'd like to say to them that comes from your appreciation, and say it. Be mindful that this isn't about you making an impression or being validated; it's about finding the soul everywhere in the moment, generated by both of you equally.

5. Is there a subtle shift in the other person during this process? You might notice if they relax and open up a bit, or smile. Perhaps they reciprocate your appreciation in some way.

6. Try practicing this with an animal, a tree, or your car, and write about what you notice.

• • • • • • • • • • •

Measuring Attention in Time

Attention is most often measured in terms of time. How long can you hold your focus or concentration on the object of your attention? What is your *attention span*? This is a linear way of seeing attention that can cause you to experience attention as a function of the left brain. Linear attention can reveal different amounts of information depending on how long you maintain focus. The longer you maintain focus and connection, the better chance you have of experiencing presence, but all too often, our attention spans are narrow and short.

Quick, glancing attention brings quick recognition: "So that's where I left my glasses!" Maintain attention longer and you gain understanding: "This houseplant isn't happy in this spot; it wants more light." Continue with a more penetrating, undivided attention, and you find rapport and communion with what you're observing: "Now I feel why my rescue dog is so anxious; he was abused and abandoned by his owners. I can sense when his panic will occur and what he needs to feel safe." Short attention spans can lead to experiencing life as a string of brief, often unrelated perceptions, which inadvertently validates linear reality and separation.

Attention Is Guided by Your Inner Perceiver

You invest attention in what you find valuable. What your Inner Perceiver causes you to notice draws your interest, and you focus on that to create or learn. Maintaining attention long enough to experience presence can be challenging when you're not interested in what you're attending to.

When I first studied meditation, we were to breathe in and count slowly, "One, two," then exhale and count slowly, "three, four." And, repeat! What could be easier? Ha! No one in our class lasted long. We learned firsthand about what meditators call "rising mind," where you become restless and thoughts jump crazily from thing to thing, and "sinking mind," where you space out, lose focus, and almost fall asleep until a myoclonic jerk in your body snaps you back to present time. I chalk this up to "One, two, three, four" being a fairly boring focus, and since we hadn't yet experienced the interesting shifts that come when the mind quiets, balances, and deepens, there was little motivation.

But plant the spring garden, play on social networking sites, or read a murder mystery, and you're oblivious to counting the minutes. You fall into the present moment—into the Flow—and upon reentry, or "coming to" into ordinary self-consciousness again, you may discover an amazing amount of time has passed. You've been involved in something that has presence.

It is this immersion in the moment that marks the beginning of experiencing attention from the spherical-holographic point of view. Interest, curiosity, and harmony with your home frequency can transform your experience of attention into something that supersedes physical reality and ushers you into the more mystical experience that comes when you perceive from your entire personal field. We'll explore this more a little later.

> I wasn't losing my focus, but I was getting tired of focusing.
> What I was focusing on was becoming too routine, too ritual,
> not something that was interesting, new, and exciting.
>
> Picabo Street

Attention Blindness and Deficit

Brain experts (looking through the linear perception filter) agree that a basic structuring principle of your brain is the exclusivity called *attention blindness*, where concentrating on one thing causes you to miss other things. This ability to focus the lens or flashlight beam of your consciousness can be quite helpful in the physical world. The world is a place teeming with an infinite number of things to perceive, ways to be impressed by stimuli, meanings to understand, and actions to take. If you couldn't narrow your focus, you'd be awash in a flood of sensation, paralyzed and unable to choose, act, or know yourself as an individual. So when it comes to life on earth, concentration can be a positive thing.

Yet single-pointed focus can also be dangerous and misleading, especially with the increasing amount of stimuli battling for your attention these days. By listening to music through your noise-canceling earbuds, you may miss the sirens of the approaching fire trucks. Focus too long on one belief system or methodology, and you risk becoming righteous and calcified as your understanding and creativity decrease. One-pointed focus, when applied too long to one thing, can overemphasize the left brain and stop the Flow. There is a proverb in Zen Buddhism that says, "This is it, but if you fixate on it, then it isn't anymore." It implies that one-pointed attention can disrupt direct experience and direct knowing, both components of the spherical-holographic reality.

Spirit is the master of mind. Spirit is within, and employs mind outwardly. The mind also directs energy. Employing energy, mind goes outside in service of spirit. When the mind lingers in one place, efficiency is lost. Therefore it is essential to make sure to not keep the mind on one point.

Yagyu

The Left Brain Can't Keep Up

Much of society's current Information Age stress is a symptom of linear perception. Experts generally see attention as a function of the left brain, and from that perspective, we have a limited reality, a limited amount of time, a limited concept of how much can be included in an attention span, and a limited sense of our capacity as individuals. It seems like an insurmountable challenge to deal with the amount of data to be processed today—and it creates great pressure. To perceive one thing at a time seems woefully inadequate.

The left brain's logical conclusions about how to solve the problem of time acceleration and data proliferation are also limited: *Go faster! Do more things at the same time!* In its penchant for the negative view, the left brain has created limiting labels that hinder the evolutionary Flow: *attention blindness, attention deficit disorder, attention deficit hyperactivity disorder.* Treating nonorderly attention "dis-orders" is, in fact, becoming a big part of psychology and education because so many "executive functions" are affected—like inhibition, task initiation, sustaining effort, memory retrieval, planning and organization, and self-monitoring. If we described these so-called disorders more positively and holistically, not seeing "disorder" but new, larger, right-brain patterns, we might have some innovative breakthroughs.

Speed and Multitasking Cause Shallowness and Mistakes

Trying to keep up by perceiving one thing at a time *faster and faster* causes you to understand less about each thing, because you spend less time with it and focus in a shallower way. Cramming more activity into each moment splits your attention and creates perceptual gaps that *really* cause attention blindness. It's easy to jump to the wrong conclusion or act on insufficient information. Now we combine hundreds of functions in a single gadget—multitasking phones, for example, are so addictive they have spawned the "app" industry, which produces even more stimulation and activity for our already-divided attention to process.

I'm not saying information technology is bad, because it is certainly expanding what we previously knew to be possible. I am saying that one-pointed focus on technology is contributing to a dependency that is causing important natural human abilities to atrophy—and these are skills we need for transformation. Our capacity for deep attention with presence is being undermined by speed and fragmentation. Remember when television programs began running ads on the screen while a program was in progress? It was jarring even when it was just text! But now explosions burst behind animated words as little people walk across the full bottom third of the screen. Just when I'm deeply engrossed in a great performance by an actor, up pops a flashing ad for a cheesy reality show. This splitting of attention causes subliminal stress, and even anger: "Which thing am I supposed to focus on? And why was my deep perception interrupted?"

These assaults on our nervous system continually stimulate and foster desire and agitation rather than contentedness and calmness. They foster reaction rather than communion, discord rather than accord or concord, acquisitiveness rather than feeling whole and complete as we are. . . . We are entrained into being more and more in our heads, trying to figure things out and stay on top of things rather than sensing how they really are.

Jon Kabat-Zinn

Are Respect and Intimacy Suffering?

At a restaurant recently, I saw six people meeting for dinner, all with their smartphones ritually laid beside their silverware like napkins. Boundaries between the intimate and the professional are blurring, and it seems intimacy and the inner world are suffering for it. Take calls from "strangers" who seem more important than the friends at hand, and what love message is sent? Perhaps this is why many people don't have a strong, clear experience of the inner, nonphysical world; they seem to be finding a facsimile of it by projecting into computers, televisions, and screens of every size. We seek programming and content as if *it* were the key to experiencing soul.

Thanks to texting, chatting, and video teleconferencing, our friends and family are inside the screens too. And though this is helping us understand more about the interconnectedness of the collective consciousness, our social lives are more disembodied. Perhaps screen addiction shows our hunger for intimacy and the inner reality, but the left brain sees the machines and gives them the credit. Meanwhile, programming replaces real, live relationship skills. Where is the deep experience of presence in all this? Where is the time to just feel your own core?

• • • • • • • • • • •

Try This!
Be the Spoke of a Wheel

1. Quiet yourself and be centered, inside your skin, in the present moment.

2. Place your attention on the projects or growth themes you're engaged with at this time. Feel the Flow of these creative ventures having its own momentum and intelligence.

3. Expand your mind through the field of consciousness-and-energy around you in every direction, imagining that you're the hub of a wheel with many spokes converging into you from a larger reality.

4. Each of those spokes is an idea or resource that wants to be part of your creative, expressive process and your learning. Let your attention include your right brain, heart, body, and personal field, and let these incoming ideas and resources make themselves known to you. Out of everything you could notice, what wants to be noticed? What's registering?

5. Use your journal to list the ideas you receive.

• • • • • • • • • • •

Distraction: The Pro and the Con

Distraction, when you're centered, can be part of your Flow. It can be an interjection of an insight you need, something you might have been missing that needs to be known right now. But the distraction that occurs as a result of multitasking and overstimulation becomes a sort of addiction—an old-perception habit—that keeps you fairly unconscious. Anxiety about not getting enough done causes restlessness, and when you're restless and superactive long enough, your body can create chronic electromagnetic habits and addictions to certain neurotransmitters that perpetuate the unhealthy behavior.

We're drugging ourselves with stimulation, and so much of it isn't worth paying attention to. We are trying to do too many things at once and aren't setting priorities. The teenager steps blindly into a crosswalk, texting while walking, not noticing she's about to be hit by a car. A woman applies makeup, drinks coffee, and talks on her speaker-phone in the commuter lane on the highway, steering with her knees. An executive disrupts the Flow in a meeting with an important client because he can't stop taking incoming calls.

> To pay attention, this is our endless and proper work.
>
> Mary Oliver

Every multitasking, distracted behavior masks a reason why you obsess over certain activities and ignore others. By examining your underlying motivations and priorities, you can discover emotional blocks, and this helps you find the cause of dysfunctional attention behaviors and clear them. For example, deep down the texting teen doesn't want to feel alone and is most interested in belonging to her tribe—at the expense of her own life, it seems. The hurried woman applying makeup at seventy miles an hour needs approval by looking good and isn't concerned about the danger she poses to others. The distracted executive is so interested in being important and sought after by others that he jeopardizes his relationship with the client who's actually in the room with him. If these three people were more conscious of their fear-based motives, they could use their attention to find more productive ways to experience what they really want: (1) close friendships with healthy boundaries, (2) a sense of inner beauty and calm, and (3) high self-esteem and good working relationships based on mutual respect.

. . . .

Try This!
Understand Your Distraction Habits

1. In your journal, list the ways you allow your attention to be distracted, especially when a task you want to finish suffers as a result.

2. List your most common ways of multitasking. Which of them are actually dangerous to you and/or to others? Which ones are disrespectful to others? Which ones cause you to miss important information? Which ones reinforce passivity and lack of creativity? List any other ways your distraction habits may detract from or handicap your overall health, wellness, happiness, and success.

3. For each of your distraction and multitasking behaviors, what is your deep, core motivation for wanting to do it—for preferring it to another activity? What feeling or insight might you be avoiding?

4. Of all the things you routinely do, what is most useful to invest the most undivided attention in? What activities will you commit to choosing over others to maintain safety and health?

. . . .

A Positive Spin

Cathy N. Davidson, author of *Now You See It*, has been studying attention and our accelerating Information Age consciousness. She thinks attention blindness, multitasking, and distraction are not such big problems; she says attention blindness offers an opportunity to develop our ability to perceive collectively in collaborative ventures. If we perceive selectively, then put our minds together, we might see more of the picture. She points out that old perception taught us to complete one task before starting another, and that lends itself to perpetuating attention blindness. But now, we're discovering a new pattern of attention.

According to Davidson, "Multitasking is the ideal mode of the twenty-first century, not just because of our information overload but because our digital age was structured without anything like a central node broadcasting one stream of information that we pay attention to at a given moment. On the internet, everything links to everything and all of it is available all the time, at any time."[2] This is an interesting insight that hints at how we're going to perceive in the Intuition Age, when our center can simultaneously be in any other center of the holographic universe.

I think Davidson's ideas are headed in the right direction—toward a new, more comprehensive vision of our mental capacity and brain potential—though I still think multitasking and distraction can prevent us from feeling deeply, experiencing our soul, and developing our own expanded, "new human" abilities. Yet these new tendencies can also help break old-perception habits. Davidson says, "In the end, distraction is one of the best tools for innovation we have at our disposal. . . . Without distraction, without being forced into an awareness of disruption and difference, we might not ever realize that we are paying attention in a certain way."[3]

We are in a muddled process today where many innovations in technology are helping us break through the hypnosis of linear perception, yet in other ways they're hindering our transformation. The key is not to vilify technology but to discover our innate human abilities and develop them equally—so we can use technology without being limited by it.

. . . .

Try This!
Do One Thing at a Time with Full Attention

1. For thirty minutes, focus on doing just one thing at a time. Don't brush your teeth while listening to the radio. Don't talk on the phone while having lunch

with your friend. Don't drive and drink coffee, or walk and text. Pay full attention to one task alone, then let it flow into the next thing.

2. Notice the beginning and end of each task, and how, within the task, each small segment flows into the next without gaps.

3. Notice how your mind might interrupt the task with thoughts about it being too slow or boring, or about how many other things you have to do or want to do. Brush those thoughts aside and maintain your focus of attention.

4. While you're focused on one task, soften your attention slightly and notice what also is going on simultaneously in the background. The clock is ticking, traffic is driving by on the street, the sun is partly covered by clouds, your heart is beating, and you're breathing. Let other things happen without turning your attention to them. Feel the background activity with your body and simultaneously stay focused on the task at hand.

. . . .

Spherical-Holographic Perception and Attention

I believe the attention practices we're resorting to in these last years of the Information Age—multitasking, hyperactivity, attention blindness, attention-splitting, subliminal attention-getting, and planned distraction—are frantic yet transitional. They *are* loosening us up and readying us for the shift to a new, calmer, more elegant, spherical-holographic way of working with perception and attention. And, as transformation occurs more globally, they will be superseded, outmoded, and revised appropriately.

Linear perception is hard-focus; it uses attention to zero in on one thing at a time, seeing the object of attention as external. Spherical-holographic perception is soft-focus; attention focused this way is like the radiant sun, shedding light on many things simultaneously because they're all in the present moment, within your personal field. What you perceive with spherical-holographic perception, you know directly. Your left and right brain are integrated and you perceive with your whole self, trusting the Flow and your Inner Perceiver to guide your attention and reveal what you need to know. It's easy, then, to attend to something as long as is necessary—with full presence. Attention is effortless and continuous. There is no unconsciousness.

> If you don't put your mind anywhere, it will pervade your whole body
> fully, spreading through your whole being, so that when you need hands
> it works your hands, when you need feet it works your feet, when you need
> eyes it works your eyes. Since it is present whenever you need it,
> it makes the functions you need possible. If you fix the mind in one place,
> it will be taken up by that place and thus deficient in function.
>
> Takuan

The New Attention Span Is about Scope

Think of Intuition Age attention as something that fills the present moment fully, encompassing the entirety of your sphere. It allows you to perceive any amount of time and space, any frequency or dimension, and any depth of understanding you need. Your attention matches the scope of your sphere and brings you the understanding of a complex, holistic pattern of information all at once via direct knowing.

With spherical-holographic perception, everything you need to know is with you already, at some frequency of yourself. There is no struggle to know, so relaxation, trust, and enjoyment blossom. You aren't in a hurry because there is no future to reach, in which you will know more, so cramming multiple activities into one moment to know more, faster, seems silly—an artifact of a less dimensional era. Rather than becoming attached to one object of attention and experiencing blindness to other things, you renew your attention continually, choosing what is most real and necessary each time, in a natural, matter-of-fact way. The kind of concentration we now think of as hard work—focus maintained with willpower and intent—is a thing of the past. Zeroing in is unnecessary; understanding simply *occurs*. And yet, you can vary the scope of your attention whenever you want.

When I was learning to speed-read, I couldn't move past a certain speed without losing comprehension, no matter how I tried. Then someone told me to pretend there was a ball about the size of a tangerine slightly above and behind my head, and to imagine that my point of view was inside the tangerine. When I tried reading from there, I could take in more of the page at once. Now I understand that using willpower to make myself read faster in a linear way simply jammed my circuits. Comprehending from the "tangerine" helped me increase the size of my sphere and allowed my attention to adjust to that scope. Though I could comprehend more at once from the expanded scope, the experience was less physical and personal. Deciding on the scope of your sphere is up to you—a smaller, slightly slower focus can give you a deeper, felt sense of something, while a larger, faster focus lets you understand greater complexity all at once.

> Seeing with the heart and mind is fundamental.
> It is only when you see from the heart and mind that your eyes catch on.
> So seeing with the eyes comes after seeing with the heart and mind.
>
> Yagyu

Soft Attention vs. Intention

With spherical-holographic perception, measuring attention isn't important. You're more interested in being responsive to the Flow, in allowing your focus to shift on its own while staying fully engaged in the experience of presence. You don't need to focus a long time since full awareness occurs in each moment. Therefore, you don't need to use intention. *Intention is attention with willpower added.* It is left-brained and unnecessary. With spherical-holographic attention, you notice an idea you want to understand or materialize without having to attach special force to it. Instead of the hard focus of intent, you simply "be with" the idea softly. Include it. Keep it company. Entertain it.

When an idea is on your wavelength, it remains alive in your field without you having to grip it to keep it in place. The idea can shift if it wants to change. As you continue focusing on it with soft, loving attention, it reveals its knowledge pattern or shows up physically; you don't have to make yourself or the idea *do* anything. With a softer, more expansive focus, you notice that your personal field itself is paying attention, that your soul is continually paying attention to creating your reality in the best possible way.

Try softening and rounding out your attention so it's spread evenly through space in all directions. Feel your core consciousness permeating your body, feelings, mind, and personal field; let it be broad, direct, unclouded, open, neither tense nor slack, no part of it over- or under-active. Let yourself feel simultaneous attraction toward and repulsion from objects and directions. Where does the movement want to go? Release self-consciousness, and as the Zen saying goes, "Soften your light to harmonize with the world." *As you use more of your sensing capacity, attention becomes direct experience and direct knowing.* You walk around in your soft, spherical, personal field, taking it with you wherever you go, and everything inside your sphere is conscious and you are conscious of it.

When your attention fills your present moment, it may seem that time stops. "Speed" becomes a magical kind of no-speed in which everything is instantaneous, coordinated, and synchronous. Zen warriors knew that success was based on fluidity in action and spontaneous responsiveness—but that this was not a function of speed. Their success was possible through immediacy of attention and freedom of mind, where attention didn't stop and linger on any one thing, because that would cause a gap in the Flow, which would lead to defeat.

Transforming Information Age Stress

The solution to healing the societal stress caused by time acceleration and the end of the Information Age is found in spherical-holographic perception—in attention focused in the present moment, in our bodies, and inside us. When you fill your sphere with attention, you notice many things occurring simultaneously and you also experience one continuous, inspired action.

If your attention is focused in a linear way, you experience one small action in one small moment. If this involves a process, your left brain breaks it down, sees and labels the separate actions that "have to be done" to reach your goal, then triggers willpower and adrenaline. Your left brain projects the goal into the future, and the gap between your present, small action and the end result causes you to rush.

On the other hand, if you keep your attention saturated evenly throughout your sphere, and let your goal be in you at a higher frequency, you engage in a pleasurable dance with the Flow, trusting the sequence of ideas and urges that come, and responding naturally with perfect timing. You can already feel the result existing. You can feel how the outcome is actually creating itself while you do your happy part. You know the result has its own perfect moment that is a win-win-win for all involved.

• • • • • • • • • • •

Try This!
Attend to Many Things as Part of One Flow

(Note: you can do this exercise in one place or you can walk around.)

1. Relax and stop your internal dialogue. Let your attention fall on an object, or be drawn to a sound, texture, or physical sensation. Perhaps it's a table. Connect with the table fully, feeling it existing entirely inside your sphere; you might even imagine that it can talk to you telepathically. Dwell on its characteristics lovingly and consciously for ten to twenty seconds.

2. Let your attention move smoothly to another thing, perhaps to the sound of birdsong outside. Engage with the auditory sensation fully and appreciatively, again for ten to twenty seconds, then shift your attention to the next thing that wants to be known. Notice that shifting itself is also something you can be with fully.

3. Continue moving your attention from thing to thing, experience to experience, and each time you engage, drop in fully to the live connection, keeping what is observed totally inside your sphere, and personal.

4. Any time your left brain tries to insert a gap or break between items, fill the gap with more attention to continuity. Keep the Flow going without breaking your attention. The movement between "things" is also a "thing."

(Continued on next page)

(Attend to Many Things as Part of One Flow, continued)

5. Notice that it is really your body, heart, and right brain that are attending to the Flow and the items in the Flow. Continue for ten minutes or more.

· · · · · · · · · · ·

When I'm writing, if I pay attention with a tight, flashlight-beam focus, I might notice that my finger pushes a key and a single letter appears on the screen. Even that minor action is composed of tinier acts that could be separated and labeled as well. If I enlarge the radius of my beam, a word appears. When I expand it again, multiple words arrange themselves into a sentence. If, suddenly, my left brain jumps ahead in time, thinking about meeting my writing "dead"-line (don't you love that left-brain term?), I've created a gap between making words and publishing an entire, finished book. Suddenly there are a million tasks to finish, and I am multitasking under pressure. My left brain is projecting a potentially disastrous future, and I'm not enjoying the Flow.

The alternative: I keep my attention open and soft, with everything in my present moment and I feel one continuous Flow. Typing letters, spelling words, making sentences, arranging points in paragraphs, making chapters that tie together into an overarching theme, handing in the manuscript, working with the production team, and holding the finished book are all one movement. There are no gaps, as each action flows into the next. There is no stress, since everything is in the moment and materializes rapidly—*magically*—without willpower. I don't run out of attention and energy because I have plenty. My sphere is *made of consciousness-and-energy*!

The more the left brain interferes with and divides the soul's naturally seamless attention, the more you experience difficulty, pressure, limitation, lack, and overwhelming stimuli. The more the right brain, heart, and personal field guide your attention, the more nurtured you feel in the continuous process of being, living, thinking, doing, creating, and dissolving. You drop into the pleasure of "playing with" attention instead of "paying" attention. You choose to do less and enjoy it more, to love the surprise and fullness of each moment. Ironically, in spite of doing less, you actually accomplish *more*.

Invisible Factors Relieve the Pressure

With your new, naturally undivided attention, you have a stronger experience of how other people are part of you, and it fosters a sense that mutual support, cooperation, and collaboration are the norm. So, people help you more and you help them—and we all do it voluntarily by doing what we love. Ask, and you do receive. With help, results and solutions occur faster.

As the nonphysical and physical worlds merge, you understand that the unified field is doing a big part of the work you used to think you had to do alone—work like the logistics of making things happen, or the coordination of the sequencing of learning. This is because the unified field is full of conscious life. When you work nonphysically, you experience beings just as you do when you work physically. On earth, beings have dense physical bodies, and in the nonphysical world, their bodies are less dense "energy bodies."

There are many kinds of nonphysical beings, from souls that are between lifetimes, to angels, to intergalactic beings, to the spirits of animals. Just as your sense of mutual support increases with physical people, so does your experience of cocreating with nonphysical beings. We often pray to saints, masters, and angels, asking for help—and we do this because these beings do exist. They provide much help in smoothing the processes of creativity, learning, and spiritual growth—and until now, their assistance has not been much acknowledged. By experiencing nonphysical reality, you see how what you thought was given coincidentally by life's circumstances is really the work of many beings, behind the scenes, helping you.

As synchronicity increases, the pressure to multitask decreases, because things are lining up and materializing without snags. Results materialize as soon as a clearly focused inner blueprint registers in the ethers. Everything is smoother and faster because subterranean fears have been dissolved and can no longer interfere with the soul materializing its destiny. By not "trying" to know, attention blindness is no longer a problem. You experience knowing a vast amount all at once, and whatever wants to become physical registers in your sphere in progressively descending vibrations.

> There is no limit to my sight—my skull is
> one great eye, seeing everywhere at once.
>
> Charles Lindbergh

One Great Eye

A friend of mine just died after a lingering illness, and a few days later, I spoke to another friend who is telepathic. He said he could talk to her if I wanted, and I accepted his offer. He relayed a few platitudes, then said, "She has moved into superconsciousness and can see everything all at once. She says it's fantastic!" It had the ring of truth, and I shivered. Somewhere in me, I know this state too—we *all* do. But we have temporarily forgotten it, so distracted are we by our absorption in physical reality.

About the same time, I read a story about young Charles Lindbergh's experience in 1927 when he made his three-thousand-mile, solo flight to Paris. As he passed the halfway point, he was sleep deprived and began to drift into unusual states of consciousness. He first noted that he couldn't distinguish between his real life and his dream life—that a barrier between the two had broken down. He had to remain vigilant, so he began to doze off with his eyes open. He said, "When I fall asleep this way, my eyes are cut off from my ordinary mind as though they were shut, but they become directly connected to this new, extraordinary mind, which grows increasingly competent to deal with their impressions. . . ."[4]

He began to feel and see friendly, "ghostly presences" riding along with him, and felt no surprise. He reports that he could see them in the back of the plane without turning his head, and that they could pass in and out through the walls of the fuselage as if nothing were there. Then Lindbergh says, "I'm not conscious of time's direction. . . . All sense of substance leaves; there is no longer weight to my body, no longer hardness to the stick. The feeling of flesh is gone. . . . I live in the past, present, and future, here and in different places all at once. I'm flying in a plane over the Atlantic Ocean, but I'm also living in years now far away."[5]

Lindbergh isn't the only person to describe this shift to spherical-holographic perception. Ralph Waldo Emerson had a similar experience that he described like this: "I become a transparent eyeball; I am nothing; I see all. . . ."[6] And the poet Baudelaire, while listening to music, felt released from gravity as he entered a long daydream in which space was "a solitude with an *immense horizon*, and widely diffused light; in other words, immensity with no other setting than itself."[7] Neurologist and Zen practitioner James H. Austin says of this new kind of attention, "We do seem to require a big uncluttered *volume* free of sticky mental cobwebs whenever we need to process many operations at high speed. When such a mental space *expands* . . . the awareness within its vacancy almost tingles with all its preparations for imminent sensate experience. The visual result, in its simpler forms, is a realm glittering with potentials and infused with enchantment to the nth degree."[8]

• • • • • • • • • • •

Try This!
The Great Eye of the Diamond Light Dome

1. Imagine an open space somewhere in nature. In the center is a transparent, glistening crystal dome. Walk up and place your hands on the crystalline wall. Feel the vibration of the crystal and raise your body's vibration to match its frequency. When you reach the same vibration, your hands, arms, and body will pass through the wall as though it wasn't there. Step inside.

2. Inside, feel the quality of the ultra-fresh air and clean energy, and notice the pure quality of the diamond light. Everything inside this dome matches your

(Continued on next page)

(The Great Eye of the Diamond Light Dome, continued)

soul vibration—your home frequency. Move to the center of the dome, and either sit in a chair or stand. Relax. Let the diamond light enter and fill you, clearing any fixations or blockages. Connect to the heavens, the earth, and everything around you. Sense the other half of the dome that lies beneath the ground and also vibrates at the frequency of diamond light.

3. No one else can enter your space unless they match the dome's vibration, and anything you need to know will be filtered by this powerful vibration before you become conscious of it. Any visions you receive will thus be compatible with your highest vibration and truth.

4. Imagine closing your eyes inside the dome; feel the exquisite consciousness in the diamond light that fills you and the whole spherical space around you. Feel what it's like to pay attention spherically, without a hard focus, trusting the light to bring any insights you need. If you feel comfortable, imagine that your body dissolves into an energy body that matches the vibration inside your dome, then imagine that the walls of the dome dissolve.

5. Let yourself experience being made entirely of the diamond light of your soul, radiating a field of the same light. You are one great eye, seeing in all directions simultaneously.

• • • • • • • • • • •

By entertaining the thought of walking around inside your highly conscious, diamond-light sphere during the day, and being in it at night when you dream, you give yourself the message that you can pay attention undividedly, with full presence. You begin to practice consciously receiving information with your entire self.

> To concentrate your mind on something is not the true purpose
> of Zen. The true purpose is to see things as they are, to observe
> things as they are, and to let everything go as it goes.
>
> Shunryu Suzuki

Just to Recap . . .

Attention can be focused on things from the point of view of linear perception or spherical-holographic perception. From the linear view, we measure attention by its span, see one thing at a time, which causes us to experience divided, fragmented attention. With spherical-holograhic perception, we see many things at once and understand the interconnections without effort. Today, at the end of the Information Age, we're trying to use linear perception to process an expanding amount of data, and are developing attention problems that cause stress and mistakes. Often, our patterns of multitasking, distraction, and speeding cover underlying emotional patterns that need clearing.

With spherical-holographic perception, our attention becomes refined, revealing consciousness-and-energy—and the soul—in everything. It is unified in a way that relieves the pressures of the Information Age; we see that the unified field and nonphysical beings are helping do much of the work we used to do as individuals. Undivided attention helps us begin to develop the skills technology is trying to do *for* us, and we learn we're actually far more effective than machines in the long run.

10

Practice Flow Attention

Self-forgetting is inherent in self-knowing. Consciousness and unconsciousness are aspects of one life. They coexist. To know the world, you forget the self—to know the self, you forget the world. . . . By itself, nothing has existence. Everything needs its own absence.

Sri Nisargadatta

Sandy was treading water. She'd been working at an insurance company for ten years, but was chafing at the bit; she was bored and going through her days on the surface of life. She had studied photojournalism in school but had let her photography and writing slip in the face of her many adult responsibilities. She now saw these things as a possible new direction, but wasn't sure she had any talent, had never made money with the skills, and wouldn't know where to start. Yet it was the only thing she could think of as an alternative to her desk job. Sandy wanted some lost part of herself back, but if she left her job she couldn't live for long on her savings. She spent hours worrying, telling herself why nothing was working, and feeling trapped and incompetent; her choice to work in insurance had surely been all wrong.

Sandy had been using her left brain almost exclusively in her work and was a fantastic analyst. But she'd overstrengthened that part of her consciousness to the point where it was limiting her ability to make changes and stay in the Flow. Her left brain was projecting ideas from the past onto her future, using her familiar, analytical, problem-solving method to find the next thing. Her geometry of perception was decidedly linear: she saw her future as a distant point on a line, as a goal to set and achieve. To Sandy, the Flow was "forward" and it was going to require cleverness, willpower, and a lot of energy, which she wasn't sure she had.

Many of us are reaching turning points like Sandy, and it is at these times that we come face to face with the need to develop the next attention skill of the Intuition Age: *understanding the principles of the Flow*, and staying engaged with the Flow so shifts and turns come naturally. The experience of stuckness is an indication that we're missing the mark on this and need to pay deeper attention.

> It is the full involvement with flow, rather than happiness, that makes for excellence in life.
>
> Mihaly Csikszentmihalyi

The Flow Doesn't Really Go Anywhere

If you perceive along lines, you experience the Flow as going somewhere, like a sine wave moving through space; you experience your Flow moving into the future or to another location. But if you shift to spherical-holographic perception, your experience of the Flow changes. Now you're at the center of a sphere of consciousness-and-energy, and that sphere is oscillating. Sometimes it collapses to a point; then it becomes large and mental; then it contracts to become tight and physical; then it expands and becomes vast, collective, and universal. You're alternating among many frequencies, dimensions, and realities—in no particular, set order—learning to access more and more variations of consciousness. You might think of the Flow as "breathing" in the unified field, taking in the wide-angle view, then the close-up focus.

When you're practicing new perception, the Flow doesn't really take you anywhere; you're always at home in the center of your sphere—in your heart—no matter what reality you're attuning to. *In spherical-holographic perception, the Flow is the rocking between the centerpoint and the spherical field, the particle and the wave, the physical and nonphysical reality.*

The Flow is the movement between what physicist David Bohm called the *implicate (enfolded/nonphysical) order* and the *explicate (unfolded/physical) order*. Bohm proposed that matter and consciousness are both holographic, in that they both enfold the structure of the whole within each part, and both are involved in a continuous process of enfoldment and unfoldment. He said, "There is the germ of a new notion of order here . . . that each moment of time is a projection from the total implicate order."[1] Bohm said consciousness is a process, and in each moment the content that was previously implicate (nonphysical) is presently explicate (physical), and the content that was previously explicate has become implicate.

It's helpful to realize that there are two main frequencies of this rocking Flow. There are long cycles that pertain to your growth and creative processes, and there is the very vibration of matter itself. The creative cycles in our lives occur in varying lengths, from taking a full breath or making dinner, to knitting a sweater or taking a trip to a foreign country, to studying to become a doctor, working ten years at an insurance company, or even living a single lifetime. All the while, in a concurrent, microscopic cycle, we're blinking on and off, or in and out, of physical reality like an extremely fast strobe light that never stops. Our reality, which only exists in our now, is coming and going with us—it's as though the present moment itself is breathing!

The Flow Is Entirely in the Present Moment

The experience of the Flow never leaves the moment. It's not headed toward the future or another location, because the future and other places are not "out there" anymore. Instead, you and your reality dissolve into the nonphysical world, where you realign and repattern yourself to be in harmony with the collective consciousness. Then you re-project or unfold back into the physical world with a different configuration of variables to create a slightly revised reality—and you're free to choose any frequency you want. If you're focusing on knitting a sweater, you'll probably re-project your reality in a consistent way to allow that process to unfold smoothly, moment by moment. If you're making a big life change, you might re-project your reality from such a different vibration that you'll feel like an entirely new person.

The movement of the Flow is a great, coordinated force. It's really the wisdom of the collective consciousness, which is you and everyone else, at your highest level of identity. This force makes all our individual worlds appear, disappear, and reappear in their varying sequences and frequencies. It might seem random in its oscillating motion, but it is perfectly coordinated to help every individual evolve in the most effective way. It is *so* wise!

You probably already know what this fluidity of consciousness, with its rapid changes, feels like because you make similar shifts in your dream world all the time. In dreams, it's easy to change realities on a dime and think nothing of it. You're visiting your dead aunt, then you're piloting a jet plane to an emergency landing on a narrow airstrip. The next thing you know, you're in your living room watering a dry plant, then you wake up in your bedroom. Between each scene, there's been a rapid blinking out into the nonphysical world, and a rapid unfolding back to a new reality—it's just that in dreams, you accept the fact that realities can change dramatically in a millisecond. When the Flow shifts your reality, you may not be aware of blinking out and back in; you may just notice the next thought and skip over the turn in the Flow. Yet if you focus your attention into the Flow and stay fully in the moment, you'll feel how you're rocking between realities.

. . . .

Try This!
Feel the Turn in the Flow

1. Pay attention to something you're in the middle of doing. Notice when your attention wanes and a new thought of what you want to do next pops into

your mind. Notice yourself getting ready to finish the current task and start the new activity.

2. Before you begin the new activity, notice what's in the space between the activities. Are you giving yourself time to feel complete? Did you actually finish the previous activity? Are you giving yourself time to notice how you want the next activity to feel or how you want to do it? Are you letting yourself have a conscious pause to recenter and be still?

3. What are you doing between the two activities? Are you walking between rooms? Turning on your computer? Getting a cup of coffee? Talking to someone? Be totally present in these activities and feel how one flows into the next, and the next.

4. Are there any parts of this transition that you weren't aware of? Where was your consciousness? Repeat this process with the next turn between tasks and see if you can be present for the entire flow.

·   ·   ·   ·   ·   ·   ·   ·   ·   ·   ·

At the end of a phase, like being finished with knitting the sweater or working at the insurance company, life doesn't just stop and shut off. There is no gaping Void waiting. You don't follow a zigzagging line, with sharp, shocking, directional changes between phases of the Flow. Therefore, there is no need to fear the shifting of scene. If you pay attention, you'll find that endings and between-states are full of experiences. Instead of a shocking end, there is a curving turn that gently ushers consciousness from the physical to the consciousness-and-energy world, then back to the physical or to another dimensional focus, as in your dreams. There's a reason we call it a "turning point"—to turn, you must flow. The entire process is full of consciousness, and there is no emptiness, ever!

The web of life is a beautiful and meaningless dance. The web of life is a process with a moving goal. The web of life is a perfectly finished work of art right where I am sitting now.

Robert Anton Wilson

The Feeling of the Flow

To pay better attention to the feeling of the Flow, it helps to merge into a rhythm of rocking and enjoying the phases of the life's creative cycles. Perhaps the experience of Flow has something to do with taking the path of least resistance. By this, I don't mean the lazy way, but the path that's inviting you, the path that already feels like it has your kind of frequency and momentum. It helps to ask your Inner Perceiver, "What's immediately next? What's new? What's real? What's most honest? What's rising into consciousness right now? What do I most need?" Sometimes you need space and time to recenter, sometimes action and industrious creativity. Then you may need space again to enjoy what you created.

A cycle of creativity and growth doesn't flow from one form directly to another form but from form to spaciousness, where you can experience consciousness-and-energy and repattern yourself appropriately. From consciousness-and-energy, it flows into action, *then* to form. Then the cycle continues through release and dissolution, back to spaciousness again. Think of several ideas and activities in your life. Are you resting in peaceful silence, contemplating how and when to begin? Are you in action? Have you finished materializing some results? Do you need to "stop and drop" into the stillness?

> Secretly we spoke, that wise one and me.
> I said, "Tell me the secrets of the world."
> He said, "Shhhh, let silence tell you the secrets of the world."
>
> Rumi

Flowing Through Stuckness

Let's go back to Sandy and her stuckness. Sandy's consciousness became fixated in her "explicate order," in the physical world. She saw the solution to her problem—being out of touch with her purpose—as finding another form to replace the one she currently had. She wasn't allowing the real Flow to occur—wasn't allowing the next experience of spaciousness—because she was afraid it would be a huge Void that could somehow destroy her. Her left brain was using willpower to maintain her reality as physical, to give her "security" by moving from form to form. Sandy was at a turning point but wasn't allowing herself to experience what the turn actually felt like.

Any turn of the Flow is full of presence as soon as you enter it and bring attention to it. At the end of a creative phase, investing full attention in the turn brings the remembrance of truth and peace, the joyful return to home frequency and soul. You merge into the nurturing "family" of the collective consciousness, feel childlike glee in fantastic surprises and new ideas, and experience the renewal of heartfelt motivation to do and create new things.

Sandy can find the solution to her stuckness by shifting to her right brain, into her nonlinear, sensory, artistic, nonverbal self, where she can practice direct knowing in the present moment. It is the spaciousness of the unknown—the inner realm of imagination and limitless consciousness-and-energy—that offers the solution. Sandy's next step is not to find "the" answer right away; it's to feel *herself.* By moving into intuition and empathy, Sandy can understand and appreciate the inner dynamics and lessons of the reality she's been living, then let herself subside back into her center and inner stillness, so she can rest deeply and rejuvenate. Her left brain gets to take a nap.

After resting and recentering, Sandy's childlike desires can re-emerge, and she can allow a new moment with a new reality to unfold—one that's closer to her heart's desire and destiny. Perhaps she'll want to take a photography refresher course or attend a creative writing workshop—not because her left brain thinks it's a strategically "good idea," but because she *feels* it will be fun and she *wants* to do it! Maybe her next new moment will appear with a new thought about working virtually from a motor home as she travels around the country with her camera and laptop. When she relaxes again, the next moment might contain a person who has done this very thing, so Sandy can feel more about how it might work for her. Momentum and motivation grow.

If Sandy allows herself to "not know" and let go—if she can stop holding the old reality in place by resisting it, and if she can drop into her body and the present moment to feel what her Inner Perceiver is trying to show her, she can zero in on what to do, step by step, to change her reality without shock or self-sacrifice. She may need to let herself expand and contract between the physical and nonphysical world many times, each time bringing a new feeling and frequency back with her that is incrementally closer to the next higher expression of her destiny. As she allows the Flow to inform her new moments, she may find that the change from an analytical desk job to a more creative life is loaded with synchronous meetings, leads, opportunities, and surprise successes. Better yet, she may not have to think up the idea for a new career; someone may offer it to her out of the blue.

Becoming Transparent Empowers the Flow

To know what the Flow wants to do for you and with you, you have to stay loose—be able to change mid-stride. That means clearing fixations, embracing the work of "ego death," and surrendering any part of your life that's become too static, paralyzed, precious, or protected. *This loosening and clearing of clutter is the process of becoming transparent.*

Transparency doesn't mean that people can see through you, or vice versa, it means that we can easily perceive each other's true nature. There are no cover-ups or smokescreens; there is nothing in the way. To become transparent, you release old perception, negative thinking, and other people's ideas you've unconsciously agreed to live by. You stop clenching and contracting your consciousness-and-energy by holding back, holding on, holding forth, or holding out, so the Flow can be free to go where it needs to go. Let the Flow show *you* where to go, rather than you trying to control *it*. Rigidity of thought and emotion—attachment—interferes with the Flow. With attachment, you may successfully blink out to the nonphysical world, but when you blink back, your left brain reasserts its defined reality structure and you're right back where you were when you left. Your reality doesn't have much chance to change.

Qualities of Stuckness vs. Flow

Stuckness	Flow
anxiety, distrust	relaxation, trust
frustration, anger, blame	peace, happiness, enthusiasm
obsession, pressure	feel supported, supportive of others
resistance to change	
complaint, worry, criticism	openness to new ideas, surprises
rigidity, judgment	exploration, experimentation
poor choices, delusion	
willpower, effort	positive inner and outer speech
lack of imagination and vision	flexibility, allowing
focus on physical world and security	creativity, clear thinking
	faith and engagement in each moment
divisive and isolated	high visionary ability
focus on past, future, somewhere else	not invested in outcomes, receives easily
limitation-scarcity thinking	synergistic and cooperative
disappointment and difficulty	focus on present, energy, consciousness
logical, proven solutions	abundance and freedom thinking
	synchronicity, luck, ease
	home frequency solutions

Fig. 10-1

My research has shown me that when emotions are expressed—which is to say that the biochemicals that are the substrate of emotion are flowing freely—all systems are united and made whole. When emotions are repressed, denied, not allowed to be whatever they may be, our network pathways get blocked, stopping the flow of the vital feel-good, unifying chemicals that run both our biology and our behavior.

Candace Pert

In one of my meditations, I heard a voice say, "Don't get in the way of life with thoughts that don't move." Not too long ago, we didn't give much credence to the power of our thoughts to create one sort of reality or another. But now, as life vibrates closer to the level of consciousness-and-energy, thoughts take on new importance and we understand the old adage that "thoughts are things." Thoughts can be as solid and interfering as concrete walls, or as porous and permissive as sunlight. We may reach a point where we don't even form thoughts because they're too slow. For now, as we're just shifting into conscious evolution, we're learning to feel the impact of thoughts, their role in materialization, and their ability to block or free the Flow.

I have a good friend, who I have to chuckle about, who has an odd array of intense opinions that she regularly announces enthusiastically: "I hate velvet! I hate shrimp! I hate Jack Russell terriers! I love crossword puzzles! I love zucchini relish! I love Harry Potter!" Though this seems innocuous, it's still a habit that prevents growth to some degree. When my friend blinks out and comes back, she maintains a negative relationship with velvet that prevents her from experiencing any parts of life connected with that texture. By staying open and loose mentally and emotionally, your flexibility allows the Flow to bring your next "just right" experience. There is less distortion of your soul's plan for materializing your destiny.

Being transparent also means you develop a strong agreement to trust your Inner Perceiver, the part of your consciousness that reveals where the Flow wants to go next. You lose the need to monitor every incoming stimulus or expressive urge for potential danger. In fact, when you're really transparent, the soul's desires slide through from the nonphysical world to the physical with such ease and immediacy that the left brain doesn't have the slightest sense that it has anything to do with the process.

When you're transparent, you don't have to remember any rules or formulas; you make creative choices to shape the Flow as the Flow shapes your choices. Synchromesh! And one other thing: As life continues to accelerate, if you attach yourself to any projection, form, definition, or thought for too long, you become progressively drained—and eventually the Flow forces you to change anyway, but with more drama and trauma. So, embrace what's coming and release what's going! The Flow is doing the rest of the logistics for you.

• • • • • • • • • • •

Try This!
Become Transparent

1. Quiet yourself; be in your center. Feel your spherical reality around you, containing everything in your present life experience. Feel it all moving and not moving.

2. Place your attention on the areas of your life where movement is easy and the Flow feels unrestricted by rules and edicts. Notice how this rhythm makes you feel, then list these areas in your journal.

3. Place your attention on the areas of your life where you experience stuckness. Where are there repeating behaviors and storylines? What habits do you find hard to break? What issues trigger avoidance, resistance, refusal, or hostility? What roles, beliefs, styles, or possessions do you identify with so strongly that losing them would feel threatening? What do you "hate" or "love" adamantly? List these things in your journal.

4. For each thing you resist or attach special meaning to, your energy slows and blocks the Flow. Imagine dissolving the solidity of those thoughts until there's clear space all around you.

5. With each item from your lists in steps 2 and 3, feel what the Flow would like to do next. Would it like to shift the outcomes, the processes, the depth

(Continued on next page)

(Become Transparent, continued)

of your experience? Imagine you've given total permission for the Flow to do what it wants to do, and you have faith in what comes next. Follow each path: blink out and let go, then let the reality be re-created from the soul's point of view. Make notes in your journal.

. . . .

The Flow Itself Evolves

The Flow is coordinating your perfect pathway through a variety of life lessons and situations designed to help you evolve into the consciousness of who you really are. And it's doing the same thing for every other person. In any given moment, each of us is having a thought, making a choice, and taking an action. *By the way we think and act, we affect what others think and do, though each of us has free will.* The composite of all those choices and movements changes the pattern of the whole—every millisecond—and it changes what you might need as your next experience.

If in one moment, you think you want to start a nonprofit organization to help small businesswomen but someone else actually does it, your action may not be needed by the whole, and in the next moment you change your mind, because a nonprofit now feels boring. Going back to school to get your masters degree feels more interesting—the collective of all beings needs you to get your masters degree, and you respond by wanting to do it. As each individual within the collective evolves, so does the totality, and the totality then influences the way the Flow affects each individual.

The Akashic Records, the earth's evolutionary "plan," and the resulting Flow are constantly adapting and evolving. This is why it's a good idea not to fixate on goals and outcomes. The inner blueprint of the planet and humanity is not fixed, so why would you want to lock down an idea and its process of materialization when something better and more appropriate for everyone might be given to you instead?

190

By trusting the Flow to blink you out of form and back in to the next reality you need, you stay in alignment with the collective consciousness, and your next new ideas and urges come from the highest truth of the moment. What you achieve occurs more and more easily. Every good, generous thought you think, wise action you take, and form you materialize in a skillful, beautiful, conscious way adds to the momentum of the Flow, easing the paths of countless others. You can be much more aware of your role in influencing and assisting the Flow—right now. If you watch, you can witness the effects of your "anonymous" thoughts and actions on the lives of others—and on your own evolution, too.

A person in flow is completely focused. There is no space in consciousness for distracting thoughts, irrelevant feelings. Self-consciousness disappears, yet one feels stronger than usual. The sense of time is distorted: hours seem to pass by in minutes. When a person's entire being is stretched in the full functioning of body and mind, whatever one does becomes worth doing for its own sake; living becomes its own justification.

Mihaly Csikszentmihalyi

Mindfulness in Motion

There is another sense of Flow, where we say we are "in the zone" or "in the groove"— where body, feelings, mind, and soul merge and the doing of an act feels charmed, as though the motion is actually moving *you*. It might be the athlete hitting a perfect home run; or a speaker mesmerizing the audience with unplanned material that spontaneously emerges from her; or the artist painting a canvas with paint that simply occurs in the right place, in the right order, in the right shape. While you're in that state, you are as one possessed, and there is usually a moment where you "snap out of it," and feel like you've just been deposited back on earth after a ride in a spaceship. In the Intuition Age, this sort of oneness perception or Flow attention becomes more common; in fact, we may never leave it.

I watched a friend of mine, a skilled martial artist, gather his energy and awareness and pull into a poised stance, hands up and slightly separated in front of him, balanced perfectly on one foot, the other foot raised and resting easily in the air. He paused this way for an amount of time known only to him, then the raised foot led the way and he stepped into a river of energy. I could almost see it, this stream of fluidity, this current of liquid fire. It enveloped him, moving through his body with lightning speed and guiding him through a complex sequence of silky smooth, mercurial movements. He was a tiger, then a water bird, then a snake. The Flow consumed him entirely, and when it finally released him and moved off in another direction, he sat on the ground, almost dizzy, as his personality slowly reformed itself.

My formula for greatness in a human being is *amor fati* [love of fate]:
That one wants nothing to be different, not forward,
not backward, not in all eternity.
Not merely [to] bear with what is necessary . . . but [to] love it.

Friedrich Nietzsche

Later that evening, as we walked past a gnarled cherry tree, he stopped. Silently, he stared at the forked trunk and twisted branches. Then his hands and arms began to snake their way up through the air, turning gracefully and sensually. "I often do this as part of my practice," he said. "I enter the flow of the tree and follow the path of its growth." After feeling the power of his focus and almost seeing the real currents of energy my friend was tapping into, I have been more conscious of streams of action and the flowing of any process I step into.

Wherever you are right now, you're in a stream, too. The current of your Flow is carrying you into new experiences—moving through you, possessing you, informing you. By staying present and trusting the wisdom of each moment, your expression can be inspired, beautiful, and effortless. And yet, you're not going anywhere. I've often had the sensation when I'm on a trip that I'm actually standing still and the reality I'm moving through is actually passing through me.

If you've practiced a walking meditation, as in Buddhism, you know that you focus on "Lift, Place, Step, Lift, Place, Step," feeling your heel come off the ground, then your toes, then your foot lifts and bends as the heel reaches to find a new spot to land, and the rest of the foot follows, in tiny increments. One phase melts into the next. Then you become aware of how both feet are doing different phases of the cycle to empower each other, and how your knees help your feet, your hips help your legs, and so on. The Flow absorbs you, and everything is working so intimately together that it can't be separated into parts anymore. You are walking, but what's walking you? Even when you stop the meditation, you feel yourself flowing seamlessly into the next action, and the next—like drinking a glass of water, then flowing into washing the glass. Where's the demarcation line between the tasks? It's only the left brain's labels that fragment the Flow.

• • • • • • • • • • •

Try This!
Continuity Meditation

1. Try this for ten minutes (you might set a timer to free your mind for the task): Begin moving somewhere or begin doing a task. Feel the parts of your body working together in sequence to assist you. Concentrate on your fingers and hands cooperating with each other; your feet, legs, and hips cooperating with each other. Notice, as you move into a task that your mind defines as a single thing, like putting a dish away or washing your face, that there are actually many components to each task. Feel each one and how it blends into the next motion, then the next task. Where did one end and the next begin? Where did the thought that started the motion begin and end?

2. Let your body go where it wants to go in the manner it wants to go, without your left brain telling it what to do. Notice the Flow moving your thoughts and urges—and how thoughts can come and go without you acting on them. When you do decide to act on an urge, how does that happen?

(Continued on next page)

(Continuity Meditation, continued)

3. Notice the spaces; if you move something or put something away, feel the space it occupied and the new space now holding the object. When your thoughts dissolve, who are you?
4. When do you notice individual moments? When you're in a Flow, do you notice them? Note your observations in your journal.

• • • • • • • • • • • •

Interruptions to Your Flow

So, what happens, when you're merged in that Flow state and your mind suddenly jumps or spaces out and derails the train you're on? Imagine you're creating your fantastic new website, full steam ahead, engrossed in the Flow. Before you realize what's happened, you're standing in front of the open refrigerator, hunting for a satisfying snack. Something caused you to deflect from your experience of absorption, and it might be interesting to find out what it was. A sudden dissociation can be caused by hitting a subliminal fear, for example.

Think back. What were you just doing moments before? Ahhh, yes. You were writing your bio and thinking about the photo you'd use. Pay closer attention to what was happening in that part of the Flow. You encountered a "yes, but" "I could say I'm an expert in this area, *but* am I? Am I being egotistical?" And, "I could use that photo, but it doesn't make me look engaging enough; I don't want people to get the wrong impression. Maybe I'm not that attractive." If you pay closer attention, you may discover an underlying feeling of shaky confidence. Instead of covering over the fear by eating something, return to your home frequency. Ask your Inner Perceiver to help you decide what to do to recover your true sense of self.

Your ultrasensitive self may also be picking up on subtle energy information. Perhaps there's a traumatic personal or world event looming. I remember how distracted I was the day my father died unexpectedly, three thousand miles away. My mind absolutely would not stay focused on my writing. In retrospect, I see that my Inner Perceiver was trying to get my attention, but the idea that my distraction might be caused by my father dying—well, it was so far from what I thought might be possible that it literally couldn't enter my mind. Interruptions can be caused by more innocent things, too, like a friend thinking about you intensely, which then makes you think about him; it's like a telepathic phone call ringing just below the surface of your consciousness.

Interruptions to your Flow are part of the Flow. Cathy N. Davidson, author and Duke University professor, says, "When we feel distracted, something's up. Distraction is really another word for saying that something is new, strange, or different. We should pay attention to that feeling. Distraction can help us pinpoint areas where we need to pay more attention, where there is a mismatch between your kneejerk reactions and what is called for in the situation at hand."[2]

If you make an agreement to trust your Inner Perceiver and pay attention to the good reasons for noticing what you notice, you can allow distractions and interruptions to add to your creative and growth processes. It has happened many times as I'm writing: I think I know what goes in the paragraph I'm working on, when suddenly, I stand up, in a blurry state of mind, and think maybe I should look for a quote in a reference book. I pick up the book and skim through it only to find an important point that needs to be made in my paragraph to better connect it to other points. Distractions can simply be your sphere shifting to a new scope that contains something you need.

O! the one Life within us and abroad,
Which meets all motion and becomes its soul,
A light in sound, a sound-like power in light,
Rhythm in all thought, and joyance everywhere.
Samuel Taylor Coleridge

The Flow has its attention on you constantly. It adjusts itself to you moment by moment, trying to keep you attuned to humanity's and the planet's most efficient mode of evolution. In effect, it's choosing a recommended path of thought, motivation, and action for you, and it knows what it's doing! So, it behooves you to be alert and responsive to your incoming instructions, which can come in the form of the thing that fascinates you, a thought you keep thinking, a situation that keeps repeating, or the most obvious thing in your field of vision. *Choose what's choosing you!* Meet the Flow with a smile on your face. Join it. There is something of significance waiting to be made conscious.

Just to Recap . . .

When using linear perception, the Flow appears to be going somewhere, through space or into the future, the way a sine wave moves. By using spherical-holographic perception, you see that the Flow doesn't really go anywhere. It simply oscillates between the physical (the explicate, unfolded order) and nonphysical reality (the implicate, enfolded order), dissolving and reforming again and again. When you "go with the Flow," you blink out and can reform yourself from a new imagination and frequency, if you want, then you blink back in again and resume your physical life. You're not locked into a cause-and-effect process of creation. The Flow never catapults you sharply into the Void but turns gradually in cycles, revealing life at every stage.

The Flow is the constantly evolving consciousness of all souls and all forms of life. It sources you with ideas and gives your creations to others who need them, so we all evolve in the most efficient, loving way. Flow can also be an experience of alignment and unification of your body, emotion, mind, and soul with an action—to the point where you can't tell if you're doing the moving or if something bigger is moving you. Interruptions and distractions are also part of the Flow; they can help break through the fixations of the left brain, bringing creative discoveries and sudden insights, as well as pointing out underlying, suppressed, fear-based blockages.

11

Practice Unified Field Attention

Quantum physics has established that physical existence is also
hierarchically structured in "layers," from the gross level . . .
through more abstract molecular, atomic, and subatomic levels
to underlying quantum fields. Although physical objects appear
as discrete . . . quantum field theory has shown that . . .
[they] may be more appropriately understood
as fluctuations of underlying fields.

Charles N. Alexander

Imagine that you could shift your perception a hair to the left or right
and the world of form would dissolve into a world of light and
energy. You'd be walking around encountering varying densities of
energy and levels of light that you would recognize as your car, or a
happy person, or a sick dog, or rain. You'd be walking on energy a little
denser than you, which you'd recognize as ground, through a porous
energy you'd know as air. You'd feel the waves of an upcoming meeting
or event long before you became involved in it.

If you placed attention on an idea, it would dance and develop and
interact with you, right in front of you, like an animated cartoon
becoming real. If you felt love for someone or something, the sun would
shine through the field in an extraordinary way, for all to see. The light
would spread farther than you'd think reasonable, affecting other areas
in the field so they, too, would vibrate faster, and radiate more brightly

and intensely. If someone thought about you, you'd feel it immediately as a soft prickling—a call to a certain kind of directness of attention.

If you can imagine this reality, you're on your way to activating the next Intuition Age attention skill: *practicing unified field attention*. In this chapter, we'll explore the experience of finding the truth of unity, first in the nonphysical, then in the physical world. When you center yourself in, and live in, this kind of communion as your natural state, many more aspects of the transformed reality open to you.

Your Worlds Are Merging

We're at the "turn" of a flow; involution has turned to immersion, and is now turning to evolution. You are remembering your identity as a soul—as pure consciousness-and-energy—and this is not just for a few people; it's a planetary process. The higher spiritual frequencies are saturating matter, and the inner and outer realities are matching each other in vibration and merging. The more you realize there is no separation between the worlds, the faster your transformation and evolution can be.

The scenario I described of living in an energy-and-light world is actually happening now, at a frequency slightly above the frequency you recognize as "real life." As the worlds merge and integrate, it becomes easier for you to see the light (or consciousness) in matter and feel energy information via vibration. When you perceive the consciousness-and-energy world, you experience openness—there are no boundaries around and between us, others, and things. It is one unified field of consciousness-and-energy. And as the metaphor goes, we are waves in the sea, never leaving the sea. We are energy beings moving around in a sea of energy, with our physical reality appearing out of the sea and disappearing back into the sea—the sea of the unified field. There are no lines between inner and outer, personal and impersonal, life and death. The physical reality only appears separate because we haven't been able to feel and see the energy-and-consciousness inside it.

Outer space is wide open and unimpeded, just as the inner space of rigpa *(innate consciousness) is also wide open and unimpeded.*

Chökyi Nyima Rinpoche

Bodies and Fields

Physicists are coming to conclusions that validate what mystics have directly experienced for thousands of years—that the inner world is really a unified field of consciousness-and-energy. And the physical world of matter coalesces out of that unified field via subfields or intermediary entities (consciousness-and-energy patterns), that are all still part of the unified field. Rupert Sheldrake calls these *morphic fields*, and I call them *inner blueprints*. Physicists also know that forces are not transmitted directly between objects but move through these mediating fields first. Norman Friedman says, "*All* gestalts [patterns] of matter are actually manifest portions of quantum matter fields.... All matter, biological or not, is a manifestation of its own field. The implications of this are startling. Not only is an electron an explication of its own field, but a human cell can be viewed in a similar manner and, in principle, so can human beings. Our whole body is a manifestation of its own matter field."[1]

Many mystics have known that living things are surrounded by a field of energy that can be seen as light, heard as a tone, or felt as varying textures or temperatures. In recent years, these fields have been able to be photographed. While it looks as if the physical organism may be emitting the field, it's more true that the field is emitting its physical counterpart. *We are not so much bodies with fields but fields with bodies.* Your personal field is actually the creative medium for your soul, much as clay is for the potter. Working with your own personal energy field, or inner blueprint, is the first step to understanding your expanded nature as the whole unified field. *Your personal field is your interface with the unified field.*

Everyone with any perception or sensitivity at all can sense an aura, even when they do not actually see it.

T. Lobsang Rampa

Your Personal Field Is Your Inner Blueprint

All possible worlds and creations already exist in the unified field, waiting to be called forth. For example, your soul holds the ideal destiny pattern for your life as a resonating spiritual field of consciousness-and-energy. Mental patterns with corresponding thoughts drop down in frequency from that to create the mental field—the mental body; then those patterns drop down in frequency creating the emotional field—the emotional body; and on to the next slower field that closely models the physical form—the *etheric (energy) body*. Clairvoyants often see this electromagnetic energy body as a subtle body-double made of light, or etheric energy. This is also your aura, personal field, or inner blueprint, and your physical body, life, and destiny coalesce out of it. The same process is true for any project, situation, or object you want to materialize and have.

What you do while you're a physical being—the thoughts you think, choices you make, emotions you feel, actions you take—feeds back into your system of resonating fields, or "bodies." Any contractions of consciousness-and-energy based on fearful thoughts and emotions can act as clutter and distort the Flow through this system of fields, impeding the ability of your soul to transmit your destiny pattern into form.

I often think of this system of fields as a sieve: The holes are where you have cleared fear and are practicing love and unity; at these places, your soul's truth easily passes through. The solid areas are where you hold fear or create perceptual gaps, so you experience blind spots, distortion, and negativity in these places. When you clear—or add—contractions or fixations, your system of fields changes frequency to match, and your physical body and life rapidly adjust to match the inner blueprint.

Every physical ailment, for example, precipitates in your body from a counterpart in your mental, emotional, and etheric fields. Perhaps you had an inordinate number of loved ones die over a sustained period. The contraction we call "grief" lodges in your emotional field, and contracted beliefs of the same frequency ("I'll never see these people again." "Life is unfair, and I, too, may be doomed.") lodge in your mental field. Your etheric and physical bodies then resonate to that frequency and lung and heart problems may precipitate, as these are the corresponding target areas for grief in the body. However, if you clear the blocked emotion and fixed beliefs by expanding your view to reveal the fallacies in your perception, the physical ailments can heal, often spontaneously. More of your soul's truth can now flow through the expanded holes in the sieve.

The more you choose to vibrate at the level of your home frequency, the clearer your field becomes. It's also easier to trust that your life is coalescing out of your soul's highest vision or destiny pattern, that you as an individual don't have to make everything happen. When your field is transparent, accurate intuition just comes, visions and creations just materialize, and you just intersect with the opportunities you need. You empower your field and let it grow you, like the sprout finds its natural path to its specific, adult-plant form.

> [Professor Harold Burr's research found that] the electrical field
> around a sprout was not the shape of the original seed.
> Instead the surrounding electrical field resembled the adult plant.
> Richard Gerber

Sensing Personal Fields

You can easily feel the quality of other people's personal fields. You, like everybody, tend to frequency-match the people you're near, and this lets you pick up the quality of their field in your own body and field, as though you're a tuning fork resonating to another tuning fork. Around a disturbed person, you may feel nervous and antsy. Around a clear, warm-hearted person, you may feel like laughing and being generous. You may fear a fearful person, or get angry with an angry person. Around a perfectionist, you may lack confidence or make silly mistakes, because that's what they themselves are most afraid of. Other people will do the same thing with you. If people aren't acknowledging you, you may be withholding your energy. If you're being repeatedly misunderstood, you may be sending mixed messages about what you want. If you're clear and openhearted, those around you feel more empowered and accepted for who they are. We're all reading each other's fields constantly.

• • • • • • • • • • •

Try This!
Read Personal Fields

1. As you move around in the world, be extra attentive to the people you encounter—children, adults, and elders alike. Notice your first impressions, first from a distance and again as you come closer. Notice how your body feels, without reading facial expressions or interpreting body language. Do you feel certain intensities, emotional qualities, or levels of light? Do you hear tones? Sense colors?

2. Pay attention when you walk through other people's fields and when they walk through yours. Is subtle information exchanged? Is their field cluttered or clear? Are they in their body or spaced out?

3. Experiment with adjusting the vibration of your field as you interact with others. Sometimes you can affect other people's fields with your own; try "lightening up" and see if other people match you.

4. Now, see if you can feel the fields of plants and trees. Do some feel really healthy and others, not so vibrant?

• • • • • • • • • • •

The more you match other people's varying frequencies without returning to your own center and home frequency, the more confused—and confusing to others—you become, because you aren't being coherent. Your energy body is saying one thing, but you've taken on the overlay of someone else's pattern that may not be natural or truthful for you. If you pay attention when you experience mixed signals from other people's fields, you may notice it causes you to feel discordant or have an uncomfortable impression of untrustworthiness or incompetence—basically, you want to avoid that person.

When you match a field with a low vibration and feel worse for doing it, the action may be unconscious, but it's still your choice. The same goes for suffering people who you'd like to help or rescue. You don't have to feel bad because someone else is blocked. And you cannot force someone's personal field to change any more than they can force you to change yours. Free will is the name of the game. We can influence each other, though, and the sweet gets faster, more permanent results than the bitter. It's easier to influence others to raise their frequency and expand than it is to pressure them to change via threats.

Because we tend to match each other's frequencies, you might make a game of becoming a clear space in the world. You might "strike your tuning fork" to radiate high-frequency energy to everyone you encounter. Wise people serve others by being clearings in the unified field of humanity—so that whoever comes near, in thought, feeling, or physical form, also becomes clear to some degree via frequency matching. This clarity of your personal field is a function of a loving heart; it's as if the heart expands to become the entire personal field. A friend of mine calls this "the heart with no skin." *When the heart takes over, the soul embodies.* The soul's compassion vibration is truth, and somewhere inside every one of us is the knowledge that contracted states aren't what we want and aren't who we are. It means people are naturally inclined to open up and be more loving, and will always choose heart if given the chance. You can give them the chance.

• • • • • • • • • • •

Try This!
Let Your Heart Become Your Field

1. Close your eyes and be centered. Breathe easily and rhythmically. Imagine that the ball of energy radiating from your heart expands to encompass you in all directions, as far into space as feels comfortable. Feel its clarity and compassion filling your sphere.

(Continued on next page)

(Let Your Heart Become Your Field, continued)

2. Now imagine that that sphere of heart energy has been there all along, a condensation of energy from your soul that exists at a certain frequency—one that you have just remembered to match.

3. Let your soul's vibration, via the heart field, condense you into your mental, emotional, and physical form. Let its inner blueprint, with its innate wisdom, begin to subtly shift you into a new you. Suggest to yourself that, even if you forget, this repatterning will continue. Determine to feel your aura as your heart field as often as possible.

• • • • • • • • • • •

Also note that groups have inner blueprints, or morphic fields, created by the collective thoughts, emotions, and actions of the members. A group might be a species, a nation, a family lineage, or a football team. The members' individual personal fields merge to form a new mediating entity, and the group's inner blueprint evolves and shifts as the members evolve, come and go, and learn through group action. The same is true of a relationship between two people. When two people come together, they form a relationship field, or inner relationship blueprint, and it serves to guide the evolution of both people.

Influencing Inner Blueprints

You feel, know, and create things first in the energy world. In fact, it's much more effective, when you want to change something in the physical world, to work first on the inner blueprint of its pattern in the imaginal realm. When you use force and willpower to change physical results instead of changing the inner blueprint, the same form will continue to materialize, in spite of your best efforts. Your work life has an inner blueprint, as does your house, the projects you're involved in, and the things you're creating—and they can all be "tweaked." If you want to move or change your job, change its inner blueprint in your imagination and the external shift will happen faster and more smoothly. If you're making a sculpture or a painting, tune in to the artwork's pre-existing inner pattern, much as Michelangelo did when "freeing" sculptures from a block of stone.

You even use an inner blueprint when you communicate with others. Your words travel in the physical world, while your ideas, inner pictures, and emotions move through your personal field, then through the other person's field, and from there the meaning of the communication forms in their consciousness. They understand you to the extent their field is uncluttered, and to the extent your inner nonphysical images and feelings match your physical words. Words can cement communication or confuse it. Unless both personal fields resonate, the other person won't understand you.

The next time you communicate with someone, or pray for someone, you might try visualizing your fields connecting and mediating the process. Be in the experience of what you're communicating, take time to allow your words to accurately match your meaning, and send some love and appreciation along with your message: "The light in me greets, knows, and loves the light in you. I see the best in you." This greases the wheels.

If you begin seeding a crystal in a laboratory in New York, and two weeks later in Paris, someone starts doing the same thing, the crystal that is being seeded in Paris is going to develop more quickly because another laboratory has already executed the process in New York.

Pir Vilayat Inayat Khan

Michelle had trouble with her family of origin. Her parents were religious and conservative, and didn't understand why she left her hometown. They felt rejected and took every opportunity to make her feel guilty when she communicated with them. Her older sister, who stayed in the hometown and catered to their parents' wishes, seemed to hate her. She sarcastically criticized Michelle to her face, and told lies about her to family members and friends. She even tried influencing their parents to cut Michelle out of their will. The inner blueprint, or energy field, of Michelle's family was dominated by people who believed in deprivation, betrayal, attack, and self-sacrifice. Her parents and sister were rooted in fixed beliefs and avoided ownership of their negative emotions, preferring to project what felt uncomfortable onto a scapegoat—Michelle.

To begin to shift her family's pattern, Michelle first needed to understand that she was born into that family field because she overlapped with some of their qualities; they had a core resonance in common. She may have been similar to her family in previous lives, but now she was moving into a more independent, soul-based reality. Spiritually, Michelle chose a fast growth track; she birthed herself through the limitations of her family's group-mind field (which, in this case, was more like a minefield!). By doing that, she unwittingly challenged her family's worldview and they became defensive. Instead of following her lead, they tried to intimidate her back into agreement with them.

Since there wasn't much Michelle could do in the physical world to improve the situation, she needed to work on the inner blueprint of the family field. First, she stopped adding energy to her family's position of disowning her by discontinuing her resistance and hurt feelings. Then she visualized the family field filling with light and love. She saw each member connecting with their own home frequency and unique path to spiritual growth, and communicated telepathically through the fields that she believed in them. Meanwhile, in the physical world, she sent cards and called them as a validation of what she was doing in the non-physical world.

> The soul seems incapable of grasping anything
> that does not awaken the will to love.
>
> **Teresa of Àvila**

After a few years of doing this, Michelle's father died, and her mother had an emotional breakdown, during which she reached out to Michelle. Michelle was present and nonjudgmental with her mother, and her mother suddenly confessed that she had wanted to see the world but had gotten married too early; she had taken on family and church responsibilities and had always felt envious of Michelle's free-spiritedness. This conversation was a huge breakthrough, and the two became close again. New energy flowed into the family field. With the help of her mother, an opening occurred between Michelle and her sister. It took time and patience, but the family's inner blueprint evolved and the physical situation changed.

Whatever materializes in your reality reflects the quality of consciousness-and-energy in your personal field; your reality appears out of your field. Michelle was ultimately able to shift the vibration in her family because she maintained her own field at a compassionate frequency, didn't backslide to past vibrations, and held the other people's fields inside her as part of her field of compassion. *Your personal field is your interface with the unified field of consciousness-and energy; it's a set of instructions to the unified field.* It makes the impersonal personal and shapes the Flow into the sequences of experience you need for your evolution. The higher your vibration, the more completely the unified field sources you.

Finding the Unified Field Within Yourself

When you experience unity and cohesiveness inside yourself, you begin to experience the unified field. Here are a few ways to do this:

- **Unify oppositions by linking them together into one flow**. Notice when you define yourself as being one way, for example: "I'm so spacey!" Or "I'm too shy." Or "I'm just insensitive." These statements are one side of a polarity—one half of an either/or idea. You can't be one side without also being the other. So change your description: "I'm spacey *and* I'm also capable of concentration." "I'm shy *and* I'm also gregarious." "I'm insensitive *and* I'm also intuitive." Look for other either/or ideas and change them to "both/and" statements: "I use both my left brain *and* my right brain. I am both mental *and* emotional. I can focus tightly *and* broadly. I feel love *and* fear, confusion *and* clarity." There are many pairs of traits and qualities; linking them helps you feel the connectedness of the Flow, and feel more whole.

- **Sense the parallels among your various fields of consciousness-and-energy.** If you experience anger in your emotional field, notice how your physical field contracts in the same frustrated way and how your mental field holds a matching belief in frustration. If you experience luck, notice how your soul's field affects your mental, emotional, and physical fields, spreading spiritual truth everywhere through one harmonious resonance, making you feel good all over.

- **Use body, feelings, mind, and soul equally. Balance your activity between alone, relationship, and group time.** Look for coherence in your actions—that you are including each aspect of your makeup. If you've been at the computer for days, go for a walk in nature and feel inspired. If you've been working diligently building the deck on your house, read a stimulating book. If you've been with people nonstop, take some time for a solitary retreat. Let yourself notice when you're becoming lopsided, and round out your experience.

- **Let all your personality's aspects and talents live harmoniously together like a big family.** You are not just one way. You may have talent as a musician, a mathematician, a writer, and a dog whisperer. You may be a great public speaker, shy at parties, and a fabulous dancer. You may discover you have new talents: "I can cook! I'm athletic! I can speak another language!" Think of yourself as a big diamond with many facets, and let yourself frolic with all your selves. Show your many faces, and enjoy each and all as they play together. More facets are always surfacing, adding to the richness of who you are.

- **Feel into your body, and sense the energy and presence in every part.** In meditation, drop into your body, inside your skin, and into your skin itself, and feel your home frequency everywhere. Sense the living presence occupying every particle and space; there is no place in you that is empty. The unified field exists in you, as well as all around you.

Finding the Unified Field in Your Relationships

Practicing unity in relationships can be challenging, but relationships are the fastest way for you to experience the parts of yourself you've suppressed. The secret is seeing through oppositions, finding oneness in any twoness, and feeling the continuity of the Flow moving through the field created by both people. Here are a few tips:

- **Pay attention to inflows and outflows.** With relationships, you can more easily see how energy flows in and out of you because you have feedback from another person. Are you giving as much as you're receiving? What are other people giving to you? If you acknowledge it, you can receive it. What are you giving? Think in terms of consciousness-and-energy, not just physical things. See if you can feel giving and receiving happening simultaneously, balancing both people.
- **Notice the relationship field in addition to the other person.** What you think of doing in a relationship and what the other person does is coordinated by the relationship's field, or inner blueprint. When you consider the idea that there is a wise "guide," composed of both souls, helping both of you learn and grow, you may not polarize or collapse into an unhealthy, codependent merger so easily. The relationship field at its higher vibration is the heart field of both people.
- **Commit to return to the openhearted state whenever fear is triggered.** You're going to oscillate in and out of the experience of oneness, and in and out of fear—that's just part of clearing the clutter in relationships. Make a point of communicating in the physical and nonphysical worlds so both of you can return to the "soft heart" as soon as possible after a separation or fear experience.
- **Practice seeing the same issues in both of you in any given moment.** Instead of entering conflict, look for how you take opposite positions concerning one underlying issue. Speak to that unifying issue instead of holding separate positions. This mirroring—seeing yourself and your issue in the other person—leads to understanding based on

similarity, and the more you find the resonance of commonality, the more you see the soul in the other person. When souls see souls, there is deep communion and love, and a sense that "we come from the same place."

• **Make connections with others at a distance.** Practice communion with others who are far away or who you may not even know. Place attention on them and include them as part of your personal field. See yourself as inside their field. Bless them by seeing who they really are. If you want to speak to a friend, see your self talking to them with your fields merged. Just like your dog knows when you look at her and she turns to look back at you, see if you can feel the telepathic impression of consciousness-and-energy coming toward you from people at a distance. Who is thinking about you? Do you suddenly feel a desire to connect with someone?

> The last thing I want to do—ever—is to buy into the insidious delusion that spiritual lives and spiritual relationships are always quiet or always blissful.
>
> Marianne Williamson

Weaving Your Nonphysical and Physical Worlds Together

Though we may look separate on the surface—in physical reality—under the surface in nonphysical reality we all overlap fields and contain each other. In fact, you share a field with the entire world. When fields overlap and merge, everything inside the combined field knows about everything else. The idea of anything being impersonal, in the sense of being so distant you don't have to care about it, disappears. Instead, there is the realization that if someone or something appears in your field, you share a vibration and are somehow the same.

When you become part of a group, for example, the other people are actually materializing out of your field, and you from theirs—because your vibrations match in some way. If you think of your deceased father, he appears from your field to the extent you believe you can imagine him, and you appear to him to the extent he believes he can imagine you. Nothing and no one—no matter that they seem separate in physical reality—is outside of you.

Practicing unified field attention is a powerful way to accelerate your transformation, and seeing how nonphysical fields connect intimately with physical reality is extremely helpful. Here are a few ways you can practice unifying your two realities:

- **Treat the world as if it's conscious.** As often as possible, remember that the world is—right now, at this very minute—precipitating out of a field of consciousness-and-energy. And that living consciousness-and-energy exists through every part of it—through you and even through inanimate objects. This means you can know everything, and everything can know you. When you treat everything in the world compassionately, as a sentient being, the world will respect and honor you the same way.
- **Perceive with your whole self.** It's not just your eyes and brain that are attending to life. As often as possible, even when you're doing a routine chore, shift to your body and cells to see what they're noticing, then shift to your heart—or liver, or kneecap—to see what it knows. Let your energy body read the larger energy field. Occasionally, stretch out and expand your sphere to take in more of the unified field, without thinking about the specific things it contains. Let yourself feel how truly immense you are.

> You do not see the sky, you are the sky.
> You do not touch the earth, you are the earth.
> You do not hear the rain, you are the rain.
> You and the universe are what the mystics call "One Taste."
>
> Ken Wilber

- **Practice the art of correlation.** When you experience frustration in the outer, physical world, for example, you always simultaneously experience a matching contraction in your inner world of emotion and thought. Perhaps your plane is delayed for an absurd number of hours. If you look inside yourself, you might discover you're experiencing the same irritation and worry about your teenage son, who's not cooperating or communicating with you. When you experience an emotion in your inner reality, like feeling lucky, the same thing acts out in the physical world as an event—a great opportunity might fall in your lap. The inner and outer always correlate because there is no separation between the nonphysical and physical worlds.

There is one key insight in any moment. You may notice it first in your inner world as an energy state, thought, or emotion, or in your outer world as an event. Wherever you notice something—in your inner or outer reality—immediately look for its correlation in the other world and find the common theme. This way, you learn to see your life as one flow through one field.

- **Read your reality for deeper meaning.** Practicing the art of correlation leads you to guidance. For example, in the outer reality, your car has a flat tire. In the inner world, you see the flat tire relates to your hesitation to move forward on a new project. Noticing your hesitation, ask yourself why. You may discover you're going too fast and are missing key information, or that at heart, you really don't want to do the project.

If you're obsessed with getting married yet you keep finding partners who can't commit, you may not be committing to yourself in some way, or you may be looking to others to provide something you need to provide yourself. Maybe you're not loving yourself or your body. *The way the world treats you is the way you treat yourself.*

• • • • • • • • • • •

Try This!
Read Your Reality

1. Just as you would interpret a dream, watch your reality this week for scenarios and events that stand out from the norm, and interpret them symbolically.

You might keep a daily list of odd things people say to you, interesting images you see, or surprise exchanges you have with others.

2. Pay attention to your internal preoccupations, obsessive thoughts, "shoulds" and worries, "aha!" moments, and sudden shifts of emotion.

3. If you notice something in your external, physical world, find its correlate in your internal, nonphysical world—and vice versa. Ask, "How are these connected?" and find the underlying meaning.

4. Each time you find a correlation, take time to realize there is just one message or insight in any given moment.

• • • • • • • • • • •

Meeting the Love in Matter

Paying attention to fields of consciousness-and-energy reveals the universal presence of love. You can begin to experience the unified field by focusing on the present moment and uncluttering it. To find simplicity in the now, move out of language into your senses, intuition, and stillness. Experience "being with" what is. Be slow; there's nowhere to go and nothing that needs doing or changing. Listen for the velvety silence under the environmental hum of life's noises. Remember who is paying attention—it's you, the soul. Focus on feeling the presence of something universal and eternal in yourself, in the silence, in the air, and in what you notice. Focus on trusting who you are and what you perceive.

> Things flourish, then each returns to its root.
> Returning to the root is called stillness:
> Stillness is called return to Life,
> Return to Life is called the constant;
> Knowing the constant is called enlightenment.
>
> Lao Tzu

Place your attention softly on an object close at hand. Maybe it's a coffee mug. Take in its details as sense impressions—its color, shape,

213

pattern, texture, the material it's made from. Appreciate it for what it is. Keep your attention on it a few moments longer; be patient. Look deeper and feel farther into it. Be with it as though it's conscious. Grant it life. Look for how it's authentic, how it's beautiful, how it's loving.

By penetrating even more deeply into the mug with sustained attention, you can feel the presence inside it; you can feel its particles floating in space, oscillating in and out of the physical world. Pay attention a few moments longer. Your soul is letting you experience the heart of the coffee mug. You're seeing it compassionately, seeing its core substance as more "soul stuff" coming straight out of the unified field.

Now you realize that as you see the coffee mug as conscious—as you appreciate it and bless it by seeing that it's made of the same consciousness-and-energy that you're made from—the coffee mug experiences you, and appreciates you. You have activated the live connection with the world, the experience of communion. You have created a kinship experience with that part of the unified field that is shaping itself into a coffee mug—for you! You see how the mug is coming into existence to serve you and be with you. You thank it for helping you drink coffee, and it thanks you for asking it to come into existence to experience what being a coffee mug is. As you wash it and put it in the cupboard, you talk to it; you tend to it with great kindness and care.

Keeping Company with Your Unseen Kin

Your life—whatever is materializing in your sphere—is coming out of the unified field to be with you because something in you is calling it forth. And it's good to remember that the unified field is a field of consciousness made of limitless numbers of conscious beings, both physical and nonphysical—the collective consciousness. *All the phenomena of the world materializing in physical form is a stupendous act of compassion.* Every single thing is so beautiful in its motive to serve all other things. And you too—you are so beautiful in your existence, in your deep purpose to serve the rest of life.

Chapter 11: Practice Unified Field Attention

I had a realization a few years ago while I was doing a reading for a woman in Boston. Her circumstances were quite fortunate and her physical energy was robust, swooping with joy and power. She was not overtly spiritual, but I suddenly became aware of hundreds—if not thousands—of nonphysical beings occupying her field with her. I could feel how they loved her, how supremely service- and joy-oriented they were, and how delighted they were to help her with the projects and actions she undertook. She didn't consciously know they were there, but there was a quality to her energy that was welcoming and generous. All she had to do was ask and these invisible forces gladly assisted. In fact, they were waiting for her to ask.

Seeing this dynamic made me aware of the beings around me as well—I hadn't noticed them much before. Since then, I talk to them and ask for help, and I share various earthly experiences with them. I let them drive my car with me, write with me, and tend my garden with me. Nonphysical beings exist throughout the unified field, and are part of the "bigger you." They are available to help the "smaller you," just as you're available to help them by sharing your experience, and appreciating and acknowledging them.

We are all made from the same "star stuff," the basic building blocks of the universe. And whether that material comes from aggregates of cosmic dust, reformed primordial hydrogen, or even astral matter, its basic nature is that of particularized, frozen energy.

Richard Gerber

So now, when I stop and drop my attention into my moment—and into my coffee mug or little barrel cactus or computer—I imagine that the beings from the unified field are aligning with me to assist that object in coming into physical form. Maybe they're right there, inside, holding the form together. I thank them and enjoy the object, and the beings thank me. I see that when I pay attention in any moment, provision is being given by a host of beings who help shape the unified field into unlimited forms.

Perhaps the motivation for letting go of our Information Age screen addiction and furious multitasking will turn out to be an experience of profound love and connection with the life materializing around us—an experience of love and connection that can only be found through inner stillness.

Pay attention softly and purely, without clutter or biases, then pay attention a few seconds longer, and a few seconds longer. It's all about full engagement. Your attention ushers you into communion with the unified field, and the unified field reveals everything that's needed. Watch for the perfect coordination of need and results. The best answers—the ones that serve the most people as well as the planet—are to be had by finding the love in matter and letting that unifying consciousness guide you. Practice stillness so you can penetrate to the heart. Practice compassion so you can honor the loving consciousness and presence that lives and vibrates everywhere through the unified field—and is creating you right now.

> Hidden and buried, lost to man's knowledge,
> Deep in the finite, the Infinite exists.
> Lost, but existing,
> Flowing through all things,
> Living in All is the Infinite Brain.
>
> Doreal (translating *The Emerald Tablets*)

Just to Recap . . .

As you learn to experience the consciousness-and-energy world, you also learn to perceive and work with the fields that are inside every physical form—the inner blueprints. You experience how these fields give rise to forms, and how you can easily, and almost instantly, change the form of something by adjusting its inner blueprint.

We tend to frequency-match each other's fields and read them for energy information; sometimes you think you're feeling a certain way when really, the feeling belongs to a person you've matched. We can serve each other by keeping our own field vibrating at the level of the heart (or home frequency or soul), and others will tend to match us.

Once you recognize the concept of fields, you can feel the unified field as it interpenetrates your body, relationships, the groups you belong to, and even the inanimate objects in your daily life. Everything in the world is made of consciousness-and-energy, so everything is alive with presence in some way. You can honor the love in matter by penetrating into any object to feel its heart; when you do, you can feel how it loves you when you love it. And, you can feel how it's materializing with the help of many nonphysical beings. When you notice the nonphysical beings in the unified field and appreciate them, they gladly help you.

12

Practice Collective-Self Attention

How can it be that I am myself only?

Papaji

I am me and I am us. You are you and I am you. This is the new identity of the Intuition Age. Because spherical-holographic perception reveals your interconnectedness with everyone, and helps you experience the oneness tying us all together in the unified field, your identity changes. Just being your lone, personality-based self seems like a real limitation—and so boring—like an odd fiction you've talked yourself into believing. Feeling cut off, lonely, or abandoned seems like the strangest lie, like "How did I ever believe this could be true?" Your perception of yourself and your life ("Who am I?" and "What is reality?") takes a quantum leap, and you begin to practice the next Intuition Age attention skill: *perceiving and acting as an integral part of the collective consciousness.* In this chapter, we'll explore our expanding identity, the idea of group mind and group heart, and the new intimacy and ethics that are coming from experiencing ourselves as a collective self.

The Spectrum of Self

Your spherical field is constantly changing scope, and how much of the unified field you encompass in any moment determines your identity. The smaller your sphere, the more dense and individualistic your experience of self. The larger your sphere, the less dense your consciousness-and-energy, and the more you know yourself as a collective self, experiencing a group mind and group heart. We all constantly move back and forth through this "spectrum of self."

Especially in Western cultures, we tend to identify ourselves as individuals, each with our own distinctive personal history or story, which we recite often. Sometimes we identify with the relationships or groups we belong to: "I'm partner in a law firm," "I'm a Protestant/Catholic/Buddhist," or "I'm a conservative/liberal/independent." In other societies, the personal self takes more of a backseat, and family, tribe, or town identifies us. Today's higher vibration, though, is causing us to experience the entire spectrum of self: the individual with a unique body and personality, the intimate partnership, the family/team, and the country we live in. If UFOs ever do land and extraterrestrials make themselves known to us, I suppose we'll identify ourselves as earthlings too! There is no longer the luxury of being only one way. Around the world, in every nation, we are starting to fill in our identity gaps.

As you enter the Intuition Age, your identity expands even more—beyond these known physical identities to a larger, higher vibrational experience of self. You are living more in the nonphysical, spiritual world, so you see the nonphysical counterparts to each of the physical kinds of identity. You are a *soul*, you are in a *soul-mate* relationship and have *soul friends*, you belong to a *soul group* or *soul family*. You're on the same wavelength with these other souls—you and they have evolved along parallel paths and have had many of the same learning experiences, so you share similar tendencies, interests, and types of wisdom. As your frequency increases, you see how you share experience—and identity—with more and more beings. Eventually you expand to know: *I am the collective consciousness of all souls, and I am the entire unified field.*

Chapter 12: Practice Collective-Self Attention

Love is our true destiny. We do not find the meaning
of life by ourselves alone—we find it with another.

Thomas Merton

In the Intuition Age, you can experience all the varieties of identity, and one is no better than another; you need them all. It's important to be able to slide through the whole spectrum of self and not fix identity at any one level. That way, eventually, you can know yourself as the entire physical and nonphysical spectrum of self.

• • • • • • • • • • •

Try This!
Become Your Collective Self

1. Close your eyes, breathe fully und slowly, and center yourself in the middle of your sphere. Feel your body and your energy field; feel yourself as an individual.
2. Let your field soften and be fluid. Place your attention on a relationship you are involved in. Feel yourself and the other person merging your personal fields until both fields become one. In this state, you contain the other person and they contain you. You know the other person intimately as though you *are* them, and they know you the same way. Feel the relationship field; can you feel the purpose of the relationship? Make a note of anything you know or feel *as the other person*.
3. Let your field expand further. Place your attention on a group you're involved with. It might be your family or friends, or a team, a book club, or your colleagues. Imagine your field containing each of the other people's fields, and theirs include yours and the other members' fields. Feel the group mind and the group heart created by the merger. Can you feel the collective purpose of the group? What do you know or feel about the direction of the group and how it wants to evolve?
4. Imagine expanding your field even more. Place your attention on the country you live in. Imagine merging with the personal fields of all the people who live there with you, and imagine they are doing the same. Feel the

(Continued on next page)

(Become Your Collective Self, continued)

field of your country, and the group mind and group heart. Can you feel the collective purpose of your country? What do you know or feel about the direction of your country and how it wants to evolve?

• • • • • • • • • • •

Belonging and Becoming

Part of practicing the attention of the collective self is the ability to differentiate between *belonging* in a relationship or to a group and *becoming* the relationship or group as though it's an entity in its own right. When you perceive shifting your identity from an individual consciousness to a relationship consciousness or group consciousness, if you're in linear perception, focused in the physical world, the other people will seem separate from you. You'll seek to join them, be accepted, and "belong," seeing yourself as "part of" that relationship or group—yet still technically separate. However, when you're in spherical-holographic perception, focused in the nonphysical world, you include the relationship or group inside yourself, merge with its field, and "become" the consciousness of the relationship or group itself—and there is no separation at all. You understand both yourself and the other(s) equally, without biases, and you feel the potential of the relationship or group for evolution. You don't just belong, you *are* the relationship or group—the whole thing.

When you become a relationship or group consciousness, your wisdom and compassion increase because you're drawing from a larger pool of knowledge. You know everything everyone knows; you gain a composite mind and heart. You understand the other people from inside them, and they understand you the same way. Conflict dissolves, and trust emerges as the unifying principle in the shared field. Many basic ideas change their meaning; freedom, for example, transforms from the idea of "doing anything you want" to serving others when a need arises in the group. The collective inner blueprint guides everyone's unfolding. In the Intuition Age, this attunement to collectives—this becoming the collective mind and heart, and experiencing yourself as an "us"—will be much more common.

> A person who succeeds in any area is only creating
> more of a possibility for others to do the same.
>
> Marianne Williamson

Reincarnation: Just How Vast Are You?

Embracing the concept of *reincarnation* is a key part of identity expansion. Reincarnation—the idea that the soul has multiple lifetimes spread across time and space—is something some people "just know" is true, while others want proof. Many spiritual traditions around the world maintain that both reincarnation and life after death exist. And mystics who are deeply connected to the dynamics of the inner and after-death worlds, as well as many people who've had near-death experiences, or who have been regressed therapeutically under hypnosis, describe direct experience of life after death and the continuity of the soul's experience lifetime to lifetime. Science has yet to prove this, so it remains in the realm of subjective, intuitive, direct knowing. I encourage you to consider its reality.

> Thus finding myself to exist in the world, I believe I shall, in some
> shape or other, always exist; and with all the inconveniences human life
> is liable to, I shall not object to a new edition of mine;
> hoping, however, that the errata of the last may be corrected.
>
> Benjamin Franklin

Reincarnation is understood differently depending on your vantage point. From the linear, individual-self point of view, you might see a string of *past lives* running in a line from the distant past to the present, building upon each other and evolving toward the future. From this point of view, the lives are yours; you own them. There are time gaps between them, but they may have occupied the same locations. You may see that you have *parallel lives* as well—other personalities living right now, overlapping with you in time, but having gaps between them in space.

On the other hand, if you see reincarnation with spherical-holographic perception, you notice all your lives are happening inside you simultaneously. There are no past or future lives, just lives at different frequencies. All your lives influence each other—the lifetimes are interrelated, interdependent, and mutually sourcing.

> Our lives extend beyond our skins, in radical
> interdependence with the rest of the world.
>
> Joanna Macy

If you expand your sphere even more, you see you're also merged with other souls and *their* many lives. Because all souls and their lives are in your sphere, and in your present moment, you have access to all the knowledge and experience they have and are having—throughout all time and space. This propels you into the revelation that you are the collective consciousness of *all* earth lives. You can expand even further to include all the beings who have been around the earth but have never been physical. Your knowledge base is vast! Now you don't need to "own" the lives—they belong to, and are shared by, everyone. And still, every life, every personality, affects every other life. If you shrink your sphere back to your individual-self focus after having accessed that huge field of wisdom, you bring that knowledge back with you in a symbolized, encoded form. It may surface in you in a surprising way, in one of your moments, as you need it.

Soul Groups

Sometimes, souls incarnate together in groups to fulfill special functions on the planet. The Aborigines and other tribal groups are good examples; they act as keepers of ancient wisdom. Other groups, for example, incarnated sequentially through the lineages of the ancient

Egyptian pharaohs, then the Essenes, then the Gnostics, then to the Freemasons and Theosophy, then to the Transcendentalists and New Thought churches that arose in New England, and on to today—to help ground, and reground, important spiritual teachings in the West, passing them from time period to time period, country to country.

There are a number of specific soul groups, formed of enlightened beings, that have been identified by mystics and intuitives. The Great White Brotherhood, Sons of the Law of One, the 144,000, the Nibiruans, and the Pleiadians are a few that have been named historically. Recently, two more soul groups have been identified: the "Indigos" and the "Crystals." Though this seems highly esoteric and "out there" from our current point of view, as we progress into the Intuition Age, I believe we will feel the subtle vibrations of groups like these—groups who share a frequency and a specific purpose—and we will respect their particular contributions.

The newest two soul groups seem to naturally function at a higher frequency than most people. In other words, the souls in these groups didn't lose their higher consciousness by being born. For them, direct knowing, telepathic communication, instantaneous materialization, and group mind are the norm. The Indigos, in particular, are drawn to fast, nonlinear, mental processing and group activity. They connect naturally to technological advancement, can be impatient, and are natural rebels with a penchant for busting old systems. They are also highly intuitive and telepathic, and learn rapidly through direct experience.

The Crystals tend to be peacemakers and healers. They are so sensitive and vulnerable that they often go inward and disconnect as best they can to survive in a world where they don't yet fit. They are quiet and self-effacing, gentle and wise, highly empathic, cannot fathom violence and war, and require a great deal of alone time and connection with nature. Some intuitives suggest that the rise of autism in the world may be related to this soul group incarnating recently. Energetically, autism may be a way these souls can ground their high-frequency vibration into the world and still maintain a degree of insulation from global chaos.

Just as the more ancient soul groups, like the Great White Brotherhood, have worked to help humanity maintain a clear connection to the higher realms, these newer soul groups play an important role in anchoring the higher vibration of consciousness-and-energy into physical reality. And, they have a natural awareness of functioning as a collective consciousness, so they are subliminally introducing us to the idea of soul groups, helping us understand that our real "family" is a spiritual one.

On earth, you move through a sequence of collectives—for example, you may participate in sports groups, meditation groups, or book clubs, and though these are not necessarily soul groups, they point the way to collective consciousness. Your soul group is more like a pool of knowledge composed of beings who vibrate at a similar level of consciousness-and-energy. You may meet people who are in your soul group, and recognize them via a deep sense of familiarity, yet many of the beings may be nonphysical.

You can tune in to your soul group's collective consciousness for nurturing and guidance whenever you want. Remember that at your most expansive, you contain all soul groups. By becoming the "us" of your soul group, you can easily step up to the next level of the collective consciousness, and the next, identifying yourself with more and more kinds of beings—and understanding how much we all have in common—as though you're climbing a staircase to heaven.

> You are the meaning deepest inside things,
> That never reveals the secret of its owner.
> And how you look depends on where we are:
> From a boat you are shore, from the shore a boat.
>
> Rainer Maria Rilke

The Convening: Group Mind Materializes

A phenomenon is occurring, which my inner voice has called *the Convening*, and it is a function of frequency-matching. We are beginning to experience the spontaneous materialization of congregations and gatherings. As you dedicate yourself to living as your soul and allowing your personal field to stabilize at that high vibration, other people doing the same thing suddenly appear from your field as if they're materializing from another dimension. Simultaneously, you appear to them in the same way. We look around and find people who are truly on our wavelength—what a pleasant surprise! Each soul might joke, "I suppose you're wondering why I asked you all here . . ."

The Flow, which turns out to be the collective consciousness in motion, is moving us all into place to be ready for a new level of coordinated creativity. Out of the blue, you may want or need to move to a new location where you can find your Convening. You may become interested in a turn in your career path that puts you in touch with a new group, or you may begin to host gatherings in your home. As the Convening progresses, you discover that each person has a piece of the puzzle, with similar interest in an activity or project that can better the quality of life and speed conscious evolution. The puzzle pieces fit together perfectly, and results begin to materialize effortlessly.

• • • • • • • • • • •

Try This!
Call Forth Your Soul Group

1. Be quiet, close your eyes, calm yourself, and breathe easily. Tune in to your home frequency—the way you love to feel when you're at your best, happiest, most enthusiastic and open-minded. Imagine that vibration is a tone, and strike the tuning fork of that tone so it resonates through your body and all through your personal field.

2. Let your personal field expand to include more time and space, then imagine the tuning fork tone fully saturating your big sphere.

3. Ask your field to materialize people who vibrate at the same tone so they can find you and show up in your reality.

4. Feel this process beginning to occur, have faith in it, and relax your mind. You don't have to force anything. You have asked, and the process is responding.

• • • • • • • • • • •

How Groups, Organizations, and Collectives Are Transforming

Old Perception
Will-Oriented Model

Statement: I do _____.
Purpose: To survive, perpetuate

Actions to Achieve Purpose:

Ambition, accumulation, fortification, ego gratification, compartmentalization, attachment, control, competition, adherence to formulas

(change is seen as a problem.)

Goals:
- To conquer the environment
- To dominate or manipulate others into agreement
- To create safety through a consistent and/or expanding physical world (money, property, relationships, position, image)
- To control the Flow
- To be better than others
- To get (to take, rather than giving or receiving)

New Perception
Being-Oriented Model

Statement: I am _____.
Purpose: To create, serve, share, enjoy

Actions to Achieve Purpose:

Exploration, growth, curiosity, learning, receptivity, permission, respect, trust, cocreativity, cooperation, continual revisioning and redefining

(change is seen as an opportunity.)

Goals:
- To sustain the environment
- To experience more truth and harmony
- To explore the possibilities of creativity
- To serve all others as we serve ourselves: win-win-win
- To expand the experience of fellowship
- To focus universal principles into action and form
- To respect the self and others to the highest degree and bring out the best in everyone

Fig. 12-1

How Groups, Organizations, and Collectives Are Transforming *(continued)*

Old Perception	New Perception
Will-Oriented Model	Being-Oriented Model

Old Perception

Goals *(continued)*
• Task orientation
• Profit for its own sake, for survival, for ego gratification, for power over others

Results:
• Lack of trust, isolation, depression
• Demoralization, low motivation
• Poor communication, secrets, withholds
• Constant struggle to be productive
• Empire building, resentment
• Waste, laziness
• Profits generated from "have to"; after each success, power must draw upon will from scratch, with no inner purpose

Eventual Exhaustion (SYSTEM DIES)

New Perception

Goals *(continued)*
• To become one with the Flow
• To support societal evolution
• Process orientation
• Profit to increase opportunities for self-development, service, contribution to society

Results:
• Mutual support, trust, respect
• Healthy communication, openness
• More enthusiasm, motivation
• More responsibility, accountability
• Higher productivity, efficiency
• More effortless alignment, less waste
• Profits generated from a tensionless state of being; flow of profit accurately reflects the group harmony and alignment with purpose

Increasing Energy, Creativity, Life (SYSTEM EXPANDS)

Fig. 12-1

Hierarchies Are Morphing

Old, linear-perception group structures—hierarchies—are now morphing into free-flowing collectives of various kinds. Witness the rapid global proliferation of social networking sites, where an odd kind of unexpected intimacy has begun to spread, connecting people who've never met but share particular vibrational levels, interests, and communication styles. Witness the rise of the *crowdsourcing* phenomenon, where an anonymous group of volunteers is invited to collaborate virtually (via the internet) to solve a problem. This nonhierarchical way of working draws on the "hive mind" of collective learning and diversity—not necessarily on expertise—to find innovative solutions. The teams of people who show up are cross-disciplinary, from many walks of life, age groups, and world locations.

One interesting phenomenon in crowdsourcing: participation drops when anyone tries to predict answers or force the Flow in any direction. It is definitely not a top-down system where authority can cut off unsanctioned forms of creativity. This multidirectional connection of peers finds solutions that help everyone find further solutions. And in these spontaneously forming and dissolving virtual teams, participants enjoy pitching in and contributing, and don't seem to be motivated by ego gratification or profit. Instead, they thrive on collaboration.

Author and scholar Cathy N. Davidson describes a meeting she had with Jimmy Wales, of Wikipedia (the vast, online, crowdsourced encyclopedia). She says, "The key is to have many eyeballs and different kinds, even opposite and contentious ways of seeing. Without that calculated difference, you'll have a wearying consensus."[1] Because Wikipedia has discovered that the crowd is smarter than any individual, she wonders if the next step might be "a gigantic social wiki, where everyone in the world could contribute insights and solve world problems, editing one another, contributing, always knowing who said what, insisting on transparency, on clarity, and on the facts ... focusing on real problems that can be solved, that are doable."[2] When you think about the possibilities for innovation that can emerge from the collective consciousness—from soul groups of aligned, like-vibrational people—it's incredibly exciting and hopeful.

Enlightened Fellowship and Conscious Communion

We know a bit about practicing collective-self attention because we know the concept of *fellowship*. Fellowship, a term often associated with organized religion, is about coming together in commonality with others—with the idea that everything we do helps further others' growth. If I want the best for myself, I learn that provision comes from those I tend. I also realize the decisions I make for myself affect your life. For example, if I think I'm not good at public speaking, and I actually have a valuable message, if I stay home and watch television instead of giving a talk, I might deprive you of an insight you need to change your life. So when I am more of myself, it helps you be more of yourself.

Fellowship is related to *conscious communion*, a state in which you're immersed in the experience of one energy connecting all things, moving continually to carry knowledge and provision everywhere. All animate and inanimate things are in communion all the time. When I believe the best about you and see us as equals, it's quite probable that you'll live up to my vision of you—and vice versa. Magnify that to include everyone, and you can sense what might happen globally as a result of everyone holding each other in high esteem.

When I enter this felt-sense state of communion, the homogeneity of energy moving through all things makes me feel the world is quite personal—the air must know me! The tree must be aware of me because we're made of the same thing. There is familiarity, a cozy kinship feeling with all forms of life, and a flow of joy—I have friends everywhere! It makes me feel safe. Think of how, when children feel safe and protected, they show off shamelessly and play with abandon. I feel that way—like I want to create adventurously and move beyond my comfort zone, past the little bubble I've defined as myself.

Conversely, with collective-self consciousness my own personal issues and agendas become *less* personal. What I thought was so important and special—what has defined my identity—doesn't need promotion and protection. Why give *my* stuff so much attention when I'm in *everything*? And why think I'm the only one who has problems or talents? We all share these things equally. It's boring to stay so small all the time. I'm a huge "Us-ball." I'm personal *and* impersonal, individual *and* collective.

• • • • • • • • • •

Try This!
Join the Collective Consciousness at Night

As you fall asleep, imagine you're at the center of a huge ball filled with lines of light connecting millions of beings, who you might picture as points of light. Imagine receiving the threads of light as they come into your body from all directions, even from below, and let yourself be nurtured and softened by the connections. As you go to sleep, imagine you're not dropping down—not falling into sleep— but are expanding out to merge with more and more of the collective's big body, traveling through the millions of threads and points of light making up your expanded circulatory system. Notice what happens to your dreams.

• • • • • • • • • •

The New Intimacy and the New Ethics

Lynne McTaggart, author of *The Field*, says: "Quantum physicists had discovered a strange property in the subatomic world called 'nonlocality.' This refers to the ability of a quantum entity such as an individual electron to influence another quantum particle instantaneously over any distance despite there being no exchange of force or energy. It suggested that quantum particles, once in contact, retain a connection even when separated, so that the actions of one will always influence the other, no matter how far they get separated. . . ."[3] She describes how the discovery of nonlocality affected physics: matter could no longer be thought of as separate from energy, and actions did not have to have a cause that was observable—because life was now an indivisible web of interdependent relationships.

This scientific discovery relates to fundamental tenets of human behavior in the Intuition Age as well as the behavior of quantum particles. It helps us understand a new, total intimacy that is becoming the basis for our lives. As you understand quantum mechanics, you understand collective consciousness. And as you understand the dynamics of collective consciousness, the way you act changes: you know for sure how affected you are by everyone and how you affect everyone, which then affects you again. You realize the truth of the power of our intimate interconnectedness.

Morality and ethics have always been based on wisdom accessed by mystics. The problem has been that ordinary people who never meditated or experienced the principles of collective consciousness had to be guided—seemingly "from above"—by religion and government to maintain a semblance of order that might approximate universal truth. These laws and moral commandments were seen as coming from the outside world, and it was normal to feel we had to obey (or resist) their imposed authority. But now, we experience how the universal principles are inherent in our own nature, and we know them directly from inside. There is a new intimacy, not only with other beings but with the dynamics of consciousness-and-energy. We feel how these principles that have historically been the inner blueprint for our ethics really *do* provide the most practical and optimal way for us to function. And there is nothing to obey or resist.

With the experience of intimacy that collective-self consciousness brings, you naturally adopt a new kind of ethics—one that isn't imposed from the outside. Here are some of the important ideas:

- **Everything affects everything else.** Your life can be accelerated and made easier by other people doing good works and opening their hearts, even if they're on the other side of the planet. Likewise, by clearing *your* clutter and pain, you demonstrate clarity to the world and provide an inner blueprint that others can frequency-match to make it easier to clear *their* own pain. Good works are incredibly powerful.

- **Self-sacrifice denies everyone the experience of soul and slows evolution.** When you withhold your energy and wisdom, sacrifice your full self-expression, hesitate to move forward, or indulge in states like apathy and helplessness, you deny both yourself and others the benefits you all might receive from your unique kind of expression. If you don't share, others can't be fueled with what they need so they can give what they want to give, so more people can be fueled, and so on. By refusing to transmit consciousness-and-energy, you slow the Flow. And when many people do this, our collective progress toward conscious evolution is hampered.

- **Even the tiniest acts of violence and fear are felt by others and can affect them.** There are many ways we act irresponsibly, with subtle meanness, in our treatment of others. Sarcasm, indignation, egotistical superiority, avoidance, shunning, abandonment—even dismissive one-liners like "Nothing," "Fine," or "Whatever"—these are all ways we perpetuate violence. We are telepathic beings and we pick up on the subtext in communications—things like unspoken critical thoughts and hurtful intentions. Though these things may seem small, they wound others and feed the unconscious tolerance of, and reality of, pain and suffering.

  If you make excuses, pretend not to care, allow yourself to fly into rages, fling nasty comments or curses, judge people negatively, or don't believe the best of someone, you add pain to the collective consciousness and inhibit everyone's optimal functioning. At some point, we all must make a choice to eradicate these damaging habits, and as Buddhism advocates, "Do no harm."

- **Freedom equals service equals creativity.** When you live in your home frequency, you realize you have total freedom to feel the way you like to feel and create what you want to create. You also realize how fully you're merged with the collective—and all you really want to do with your freedom is help others receive what they need so they can express themselves authentically. After all, what fun is it to be conscious and living at a high vibration if others are stuck at a low frequency, in a sort of blindness? When others are suffering, they're not available to "come out and play." By expressing yourself originally, with enthusiasm, gratitude, and deep attention, your creativity and service become the same thing, and you produce beautiful, useful, inspiring offerings for the collective.

> If a man look upon any other man and estimates that man as less than himself, then he is stealing from the other. . . . You can forgive others effectively only when you have a sincere desire to identify them with their ideal.
>
> Neville Goddard

- **What you need is what you want; what others need is what you want to give.** In the collective self, there is a perfect fit of desires, opportunities, resources, and need. There is a synchromesh functioning that is nearly impossible to comprehend in its elegant efficiency: *Do what you love and it is the very thing you need and what is most useful to others.* Where do your curiosities, ideas, and urges come from? The collective plants them in you because you're the one who can offer what's needed. The collective causes you to want to do certain things, for your own and others' evolution. Remember, you *are* the "us." No one is making you do anything; you're working in harmony with the whole. You don't receive ideas by accident.
- **We naturally want to assist, cooperate, and cocreate.** You are supported in your self-expression, too. When you want to act on *your* idea, the help and resources show up for it to come to fruition. A management consultant friend of mine once told me that people really want you to be happy, so tell them what you love. They'll gladly help you get it.

I recently dreamed of meeting a group of firemen who had died in various tragedies. They were strong, warmhearted men standing around, just waiting for something to do. We joined together to heal a man who was sick, and they were very good at it. They told me to ask them for help any time I needed it, as they felt underused.

We're so used to the idea of competing and winning—of needing to be "the best." But that's not the way the collective-self consciousness works. We can only become our "personal best" when we are also cooperating and cocreating with others. It is others who bring out our best, and if we could look at competition as cooperation to bring out everyone's personal best, instead of as an experience of putting others behind us, society would shoot forward into conscious evolution!

> I stand up, and this one of me
> turns into a hundred of me.
> They say I circle around you.
> Nonsense. I circle around me.
>
> Rumi

Just to Recap . . .

We have a spectrum of identity that ranges from physical individuality to relationships to groups, and into the nonphysical experiences of soul, soul mates, and soul groups. With linear perception, we "belong" in relationships and groups, but with spherical-holographic perception, we become them. We can begin to understand how vast and inclusive we are by understanding reincarnation, then seeing how we have access to all lifetimes simultaneously. We can also attune to various soul groups—which we can experience as pools of knowledge created by the resonance of like-vibrational souls.

A new phenomenon is occuring—the Convening—where people of like vibration are beginning to "show up" in each others' fields and lives to work together. Old group structures like hierarchies are morph-ing into new, nonlinear structures. We are learning to practice fellowship and communion as we learn about a new kind of ethics based on a new intimacy. With these new values we are careful not to be violent in even the most subtle of ways, and we see that any form of self-sacrifice hurts others.

13

Practice Shaping the Imaginal Realm

*Imagination, the real and eternal world of which
this Vegetable Universe is but a faint shadow.*

William Blake

Imagination—that amazing ability to form new ideas, create something from nothing, and access possibilities not available to the physical senses—is actually the basis of the world! Your soul is imagining the world into existence and shifting your reality effortlessly as it accesses ideas from the unlimited unified field. Billions of other souls are imagining their worlds into existence too, and together, all these worlds overlap. When all the imaginations combine, we end up living in something akin to a wildly rapid-fire, complex video game, where we're playing off each others' latest creations while adding something new of our own.

You see the unlimited, effortless, and fluid nature of imagination in action in your dreams, yet you rarely realize the same principles are responsible for materializing the "movie" of your daily life. You shift from scene to scene all day, the same way you move from scene to scene in your dreams. Unusual things show up and happen: the café is populated with odd characters, the street is having its trees trimmed, the bus driver is unusually witty. Things happen in sequences you didn't plan: you go to the post office and run into a friend on the sidewalk first; you head to the market next and have a dead car battery when you come out; then the man who restarts your car utters something profound that makes you think. It's an exciting idea to consider—that you're imagining your reality, helping materialize the conditions of life by what you think, feel, and notice.

When we are children, imagination was second nature. But as school trained us to use our left brain, and as life taught us to be "adults," we progressively lost our imaginal skills. Now, most of us—shockingly—feel unable to dream or imagine a better life, so programmed are we to accept what is fed to us by outside sources, like the media. We don't question the subliminal messages or over-validation of stereotypes—and without questioning, there is limited curiosity, an inability to stretch creativity, and a lack of pure imagination. In this chapter, we'll explore the most powerful of Intuition Age skills: *the practice of accessing and shaping the unified field—the imaginal realm—to create a reality that evolves.*

You and the World Are All Imagination

Every possible reality exists in the *imaginal realm*. The imaginal realm is your deep inner world—the realm of the collective consciousness and the origin place of the Flow. It's a term used by psychologists like James Hillman to differentiate it from the negative or misguided connotations we have with "imaginary." As serious "adults," we usually equate imagination with unreality or escapism, yet the imaginal realm is just the opposite: it is super-real and causal. It is also David Bohm's implicate order, the realm that sources the explicate order, or outer world. Everything in your life begins in the imaginal, consciousness-and-energy world and projects out, or down in frequency, becoming a physical movie.

When you place attention on an idea, you call it forth from the field of the imaginal realm and it forms itself into a reality by first becoming an inner consciousness-and-energy blueprint. The longer you maintain focus on the idea, the more attention penetrates into the inner blueprint and the more physical it becomes. To enter the imaginal realm, you need only shift from your left brain to your right brain and be in the present moment. Let your Inner Perceiver access ideas for you, then notice what you notice. The ensuing translation of the nonphysical pattern into physical reality is relatively gradual with linear perception, but immediate in the Intuition Age.

One morning recently, I was sitting at a local bakery staring out the window in a slight daze, readying myself to write. The scene was full of tiny, enthusiastic, jumping toddlers holding hands with their mothers, coming from story hour at the library. Inside and all around me were clusters of retired folks, gathering to chat over a sweet roll. I shifted my gaze to the fresh flower in the vase on my table. It was an unusually large gerbera daisy, audacious in its riotous, school-bus-yellow radiance. Looking closer into its face, I saw it had three geometrically beautiful rings of petals in descending size and density. And it didn't stop there— it erupted in the very center with some extra tall, squiggly, lilac-tinted petals like fireworks, like an extra layer of icing on an already fabulously decorated cake. Life just couldn't stop! The soul of that plant *really* wanted to express itself. I realized I was imagining that flower in all its vitality and magnificence, along with the giddy toddlers and social seniors. I had forgotten I could be so creative.

I thought, then, how often we skim the surface and are dulled by what we see—until we really *look*. It's easy to think you're limited to the pool of stimuli you see in the fact-based world when you create new things—as though the new must relate to what already exists. Without questioning and some degree of dissatisfaction, without looking deep, you might resign yourself to a narrow supply of creative inspirations. Yet when you take time to stop and drop your attention into the moment and connect with what's showing up, you immediately return to a new experience of awe and inspiration, to finding the spirit inside things and the magic of imagination.

Whenever you find inspiration, you return to a direct connection with the imaginal realm. And when you enter it and feel it—without need for definition—the realm presents you with totally new ideas, inventions, stories, images, songs, dances, and shapes. Why a daisy with only three layers of petals? Why not seven layers! The inspirations come from the heart of the moment and don't necessarily relate to a cause-and-effect process that began in your past. Imagination has nothing to do with willpower; it is sourced by joy.

The imaginal realm does not function when you bring constraints, contractions, and conditionality with you when you enter it. It is what Carlos Castaneda's mentor, Don Juan, meant when he repeatedly told Carlos to "stop the world" so he would be able to truly "see." It's important when entering the imaginal realm that you totally withdraw attention from the solidity of the fact-based world—what Don Juan said was a just a "description" based on collective norms and values, seldom questioned, and reinforced continually by people we meet. Perhaps this is also what is meant in the Bible quote from John 10:17-18: "I lay down my life that I might take it again. No man taketh it from me, but I lay it down myself."

> We must first let everything go in order
> to get everything back at a new level.
>
> Wolfgang Kopp

By moving into your right brain, you allow anything that wants to come to you from the imaginal realm to simply show up. It is not up to your left brain to "try" to imagine something new; your soul and the collective consciousness are already imagining new realities for you, seeding you with them freely. They only await the receptive mind to grow. They come forth to meet the playful mind.

Cycles of Imagining and Creating

Imagining moves in cycles. It's helpful to understand how the Flow brings ideas from the imaginal realm into the physical world, then how it releases the creations and re-enters the imaginal realm to be renewed and begin a new cycle. I've mentioned the rocking, blinking motion of life—how the implicate (enfolded/nonphysical) order unfolds to become the explicate (unfolded/physical) order, then enfolds itself again; how the wave becomes the particle and the particle becomes the wave; how your one world dissolves into the many possible worlds, then reappears again as one world when you place attention back on it.

This oscillation of the Flow is an imaginative, creative cycle with three main phases. When you're familiar with the feel of each phase (detailed on the next page), and you know there is no scary end to the Flow just because one phase is changing to another, you can easily move through the cycle without a hitch. You'll see that in the first phase, an idea emerges from the imaginal realm and translates into your mind. In the second, the idea becomes a clear inner blueprint, gathers feeling and motivation, action follows, and a result materializes. In the third phase, attention is withdrawn, the result dissolves, and your consciousness-and-energy merges with the imaginal realm again.

Phase 1: Inspiration to Choice

In phase 1 of the cycle of imagining, the Flow begins its descent in frequency from the imaginal realm into matter. It brings the consciousness-and-energy of your soul and the collective into personal expression through you. Coming via intuition, the inspirations first impact your right brain and visionary sense. You receive an impression of a vision, a glimpse of a new reality, a feeling of a concept. Then your brain fleshes out the impression with sensory information, and it coalesces into a thought with feeling—an inner blueprint. When you can feel it fully, you choose it.

Phase 2: Action to Materialization

In the next phase, the inner blueprint descends through your brain into your body, becoming desire, motivation, and action, ending with a physical outcome, slowing in frequency at each step. There is a tendency at the end of the second phase for the Flow to become fixated in physical reality, the left brain, and linear perception. Looking forward, all the left

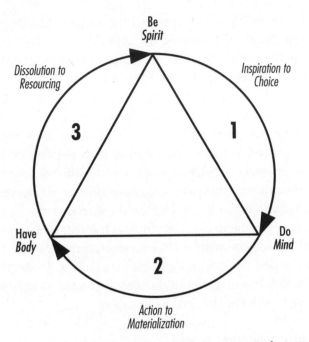

Fig. 13-1: The Flow of consciousness-and-energy moves from Being (spirit/nonphysical/imaginal realm) to Doing (mind/choice/action) to Having (body/form/results), and back to Being and the imaginal realm again.

brain sees is a big Void, and it's frightening. At this point, you may be tempted to repeat more of the same, or maintain your creation with willpower.

Phase 3: Dissolution to Resourcing

Finally, a simple task remains: relax, let go, and "be with" your creation the way it is, without attachment. Kick back and sigh contentedly. You have completed the cycle and are on last leg of the journey. Feel satisfied, take pleasure in your creation, learn from it, and be nurtured by it. Then let yourself be bored, disengage, soften your attention into meaninglessness. Get rid of clutter and "noodle around"—play, explore, and experiment. Before you know it, the glimmer of a new imagination appears from the mist, and the cycle begins again.

You're On the Cusp of a Big New Cycle of Imagining

You may feel stuck these days. The old is really old; the new hasn't quite shaped and revealed itself yet, but you feel it lurking behind the scenes. Why doesn't it come forth? Instead of complaining, compliment yourself. You're not just at the end of a normal cycle of imagining and creativity, you're at the end of an era! You're shifting from the Information Age to the Intuition Age. You've been imagining and materializing many cycles of growth to learn certain skills and lessons and reach this important turning point. You're legitimately bored now and ready to enter phase 3 of a major cycle of imagining. Your left brain may be causing you to think that what you've been doing is wrong, but it's not; it's just old. You're a success at materializing what you've had and do have. You *do* know how to imagine things into form!

Meanwhile, you may be dealing with a variety of dramas whose function is to catapult you into a high-frequency reality. You're going through a divorce, your car is stolen, you impulsively quit your job, your sibling must go into rehab. At the same time, you may be taking up odd new interests: the study of mediumship, energy healing, yoga, woodworking, painting, cultivating orchids, or wrapping yourself in colorful scarves. Your soul is showing you through symbolic acts that a cycle—a way of being—is over, and you need to let go. At the same time you're being drawn to immerse yourself in activities that shift you into your right brain. The new activities may or may not have anything to do with solving your main problem, but they are opening you to the feeling of a new reality.

It's not uncommon to feel frustrated and indulge in negativity as you face the unknown: "What am I supposed to do next? I can't see beyond the end of my nose." A client recently said to me, "Everything that was, isn't." Another said, "I am comfortably numb." It's important to remember that the left brain is speaking at this point, and it is blind to the truly new because it's so used to participating in and re-creating your familiar, fact-based world. So indulge in those frivolous activities that open your right brain and imagination. Your right brain *loves* the unknown!

Your needs are changing, and your soul and the collective consciousness are revealing glimpses of new ideas—though they may at first seem incongruous. One client who'd been a mathematician felt the urge to become a psychologist. Another, a realtor, wanted to create a museum to house collections of women's memorabilia. A secretary thought about going to Florence to study photography, and a martial arts teacher wanted to write screenplays. "Can I do it?" they all wanted to know. "Of course!" I responded. "How do you think you became a mathematician / realtor / secretary / martial arts teacher in the first place?" New dreams often sneak in and occupy space at the periphery of your consciousness, and you must soften your gaze to "see" them.

> Something inside of me has reached to
> the place where the world is breathing.
>
> Kabir

Blocking or Freeing Imagination

Your left brain can interfere and block the phases of imagining, or you can be in harmony with the Flow—in other words, there's a snagged path or a smooth path through the cycle. As you begin the process, on the snagged path, your left brain might throw up a smokescreen of self-doubts and "yes, buts": "Maybe this is a stupid idea;" "Maybe I'm not good enough;" "Maybe someone else has already done it;" "Maybe I'll lose everything I have." Or it might block the emergence of imagination with apathy, cynicism, fragmentation, addictions, or distraction.

On the other hand, on the smooth path—if you're in your right brain—you remain quiet and receptive, innocent and in "beginner's mind." You allow ideas to percolate up from your personal field and register in your consciousness with the glee of the excited child. You're curious and confident that the new idea comes to you because *it wants to happen*. As you begin to shape the imagination, you may receive "updates" from your right brain—ways the idea needs to adapt to have optimal success. You can revise its inner blueprint until the idea feels just right and totally enjoyable. Keep your attention on the living reality of the creation, softly, without being impatient or pushy. You have plenty of time to let the fruit ripen. This developmental phase is fun!

> Fixated on the need to have something to show
> for our labors, we often deny our curiosities
>
> Julia Cameron

As you move into the action part of the cycle, on the snagged path, your left brain may complain that you have to do everything alone, or that the people working with you are incompetent, or the process isn't going fast enough. Willpower and ego impose shoulds and make you frustrated at mistakes, stopping the Flow simply because it takes a new direction. Or you can be trapped in desire, the "I want it" stage, placing your imagined goal in the future and not letting go enough for it to emerge in present time.

When you're on the smooth path, you feel charmed, trusting that the Flow knows what it's doing. You step into the action stream and start your motion when it starts you, becoming one with it. You don't get ahead of yourself. The immediate process contains all the information you need about what the result is to be; the formula for the outcome is encoded in the Flow. You see how a slowdown in one spot often creates acceleration somewhere else. It all works out!

In the final phase, on the snagged path, your left brain may refuse to complete a project or let go and move on to something fresh and new. It might freeze in panic about entering the unknown—and losing everything "I've worked so hard to attain" or having to face uncomfortable things it's been successful in denying so far. On the smooth path, during the last phase you may simply realize you want to clear some old blockages and "lighten up" to move to a higher frequency. Or you may dive into the exquisite pleasure that rest provides. You soften your edges and surrender into the wonderful feeling of spaciousness, feel your heart, notice what's authentic for you, and amuse yourself.

Imagining something into reality becomes smooth and efficient when you maintain your home frequency throughout. The whole process is a just series of now moments, each of which you can occupy fully with your attention and presence—and enjoy. Keep your mood upbeat and childlike, and grease the wheels with cheerful emotions. Welcome each phase of the process for the specific kind of energy, consciousness, and fun it offers.

· · · · · · · · · · ·

Try This!
Take an Elevator to the Imaginal Realm

1. Close your eyes, center yourself in your body and the moment, and be neutral and receptive. Imagine that an elevator appears in front of you and the doors open. You step in and the doors close. The elevator goes up rapidly, through many levels, and comes gently to rest at *The Imaginal Realm.* The doors open and you step out.

2. Let yourself be surprised by what you see. Perhaps you're somewhere in nature, on another planet, or in a library or an artist's studio. Maybe you're in a crowd, at a seminar, or with a spiritual guide or animal. Maybe you've changed into another version of yourself or are wearing an unusual costume. The Imaginal Realm meets you with its own input, and you can interact with it. Each time you act, it responds. When you provide an idea, it provides an idea.

3. Here are some ideas for things to do in The Imaginal Realm: Enter your "workshop" and make something. Go for a walk in nature and see where it takes you, and who you meet. Meet a being from another planet. Meet a dead friend or relative. See yourself in a new kind of work or a volunteer activity, and try it out for a while. Design a hat. Design a chair. Design a car. See yourself at your ideal weight, in optimal health, and do various activities you might not have done before. Be an expert in an art form you've never tried. Do something you think you're afraid of—and succeed!

Go back in time and be a fly on the wall in the home of a famous person. Heal something that seems chronic in yourself or another. Communicate effectively with a difficult person. Look at something very close up, then at something very far away. Go into the center of the earth. Smell the most sublime smells that exist. Ask for expert help in solving a problem.

4. Come down in the elevator to your normal reality, and bring all the ideas and feelings from The Imaginal Realm back with you. Make notes in your journal.

· · · · · · · · · · ·

Your Dream World Is Practice for Your "Real" World

Sometimes, it helps to imagine you're playing "pretend" like you did as a child. Invent living, mini movies in your imagination, cast yourself in a starring role, and enter the movie. Involve all your senses. Run it for a while and see how you feel. Can you see yourself working with teens on an organic farm? If the imaginal movie doesn't feel quite right, change a variable. Maybe you want to work with teens and their parents to teach them to cook healthy food; maybe you want to work on an organic farm in Peru, or do a photojournalism piece for a national magazine on the best organic farms in Canada. In the Imaginal Realm, anything can combine, and variables can unfold in any sequence. Keep tweaking your dreams and inner movies until your body receives the tone of joy. That's when you really know what you want.

You can also program your nighttime dreams to bring you insights about what you might do next. Go to sleep with soft enthusiasm about adventuring into new territory or experiencing new states. Let yourself slide into the good mood of being at your next, more expanded level of life experience—as though it's already happening. Keep track of your dreams in a journal, and remember the fluid state you were in during the dreams so you can apply it later to daily reality. Once you experience a higher state in your dream world, you can drop it down in vibration to materialize as part of your life. Perhaps you dream you're acting in a play and receive a standing ovation. That state of smooth, flawless expression can translate directly to your upcoming talk at a professional conference.

Exercise your imagination muscle as often as possible. Rebuild its strength by playing with ideas. Fill your blank moments—instead of being spaced out, look at the people next to you in the checkout line and invent a personal history or future for each one. Look at the money in your wallet and imagine where it was before it came to you. Redecorate your living room in your imagination. If you could put a large sculpture in your front yard, what would it be like? If you could invent a new vegetable, what would it look and taste like? If you had a different name, what would it be? Play! Have you ever made a *vision board*—a collage of images that capture your imagination and things you'd enjoy having in your life? If so, you may have noticed that many of the things you wove together in imagery actually materialized a short time later.

• • • • • • • • • • •

Try This!
Imagine a New Invention

1. Close your eyes and center yourself. Imagine a huge building atop a hill. Walk up the wide path to the giant front doors, where the guard lets you in. Walk into the great, high-ceilinged rooms and notice the endless corridors of shelves stretching as far as you can see. On the shelves is an endless array of boxes of different sizes, shapes, and colors. Some are so big you have to get them down with a forklift, while some are so small you can only see them if you get up very close.

2. Let yourself wander around for a while, looking at the fantastic variety of boxes, wondering what might be inside each one—until one catches your attention. Take it off the shelf and carry it to the end of the aisle, where you find a private viewing room.

3. In the viewing room, remove the box's lid and see what's inside. It's a new invention! Take the invention out and examine it. Look for the instruction sheet that comes with it. What is the name of the invention? How is it to be

used? If you have difficulty understanding your invention, ring a buzzer and a guide will come in to explain it to you.

4. Return to normal awareness and draw a picture of the invention. Then write about it: How might this invention be a symbol for something you need in your life right now?

· · · · · · · · · · ·

Let's say you'd like to imagine a new computer into your life. Can you say "I really want it now" and mean it? By trying to answer with an absolute yes, you will immediately encounter any subliminal "yes, buts": "Yes, but I'm worried about the money." "Yes, but I have to sell my old computer first." "Yes, but what features do I want?" "Yes, but how will I transfer my files?" Take care of dissolving these blocks; there's a solution to each hesitation. Then bless your old computer for supporting you and being with you for so long. Treat it like a conscious being and love it. Wish it well so it can move to its next home, where someone else will love it. Release it to dissolve out of your reality.

> First thoughts have tremendous energy. The internal censor usually squelches them, so we live in the realm of second and third thoughts, thoughts on thoughts, twice and three times removed from the direct connection of the first fresh flash.
>
> Natalie Goldberg

Let the whole new imagination drop into the vibration of your present physical reality. Imagine how good you feel now that the new computer has become a normal part of your life. Feel it sitting on your desk: it's paid for, the files are transferred, you're using it, and all your doubts are in the past. Your body loves working and playing with it, and the new computer matches your home frequency. Can you relax happily, knowing the unified field is voluntarily shaping itself into a new computer on your desk? Remember that the field handles the logistics of how things materialize. It causes you to want to take the actions necessary for the computer to materialize. Before you know it, your imagination is real.

I Want a Do-Over! Revising Your Reality

There are times when you realize you've imagined a reality into existence that doesn't match your home frequency. It contains old-perception habits you're moving beyond, that you don't want now. Perhaps you landed a job in a bad job market, and now you discover your colleagues are petty, lazy, or unqualified—and you don't fit in. You bought a house but need to move to be near your aging parents, and now it won't sell. You put on weight during a period of depression, went through therapy, cleared the negativity, and now you want your body to match your new mood. You failed the bar exam twice, and you want the third time to be the charm. You developed an illness, and you want to "undevelop" it.

Here are a few important principles for revising your reality:

- **Just because you created a reality once doesn't mean you have to keep re-creating it again and again.** Because a reality exists doesn't make it sturdier, stickier, more stubborn, or more authoritative than any other reality. Physical realities are as ephemeral and fluid as the realities in your dreams. It's your left brain that causes the illusion of an unchangeable reality. Every reality emerges from and dissolves back into the imaginal realm *easily*. Put attention into a reality and it appears; withdraw attention from a reality and it dissolves. Don't let a reality have authority over you. You're the creator! Also, remember that boredom can be your friend. It can help you disengage and move onto something fresh and new more quickly.
- **Change your vibration and your reality shifts immediately.** When your personal vibration increases, your reality expands and improves; when your vibration drops, your reality contracts and degenerates to a similar degree. When you vibrate at your home frequency, you evolve naturally with the collective consciousness and your imaginations

become comparably sophisticated. The less clutter you have in your personal field, the faster you vibrate, and the faster the translation from imagination to form. You can't reject or get rid of a reality you don't like—there's nowhere to put it because there's no outside world. Just withdraw invested attention instead, and the reality dissolves back into the unified field.

- **You don't have to have all the answers or know exactly what to ask for.** Your soul and the collective consciousness are guiding the unfolding of your life. If you're relatively clear, you may see the new reality in a dream, recognize a new direction after friends mention intriguing ideas, or simply have someone invite you to do a new thing that turns out to be surprisingly absorbing. Even if you feel blocked and your growth has been stalled, when it's time to make a change, higher consciousness-and-energy can break through. Like a slingshot pulled all the way back, you can only hold that suspended animation so long before the release propels forward motion. Not to worry!

- **Start with the first thing: what's right in front of you.** The first thought and action is tied to the next thought and action, and the next. Don't wait to start; begin with the most mundane act just under your nose. As soon as you enter the Flow, its direction adapts to take you to your destination. You're like a spindle: the separate strands of ideas enter you from the imaginal realm, some magical sort of weaving happens in the middle, and finished yarn flows out from you into the physical world. The emergence of that woven yarn—your stream of creations—is continuous. Just start pulling it! It may change in color, size, or texture, but it keeps coming if you keep pulling. You keep pulling because you enjoy the surprise of what emerges.

- **Your inner and outer speech permit new realities to materialize—or not.** If you're caught in a reality you don't like and you complain, protest, or speak about how helpless you feel, the reality clings to you and follows you around. You're inadvertently giving the negative reality attention, keeping it alive and making it more powerful than you are. Instead, tell yourself that this reality materialized out of old perception and fear thoughts, and that you're making different choices now, based on maintaining your home frequency. Tell yourself it's easy to change to a new reality you love. Describe it to yourself; the positive speech carries energy to create the positive result.

• • • • • • • • • • • •

Try This!
Ask Good Questions to Find a New Vision of Reality

If you want something new to materialize in your reality but can't see what it is yet, here are some good questions to help you zero in. Write about the answers in your journal.

1. If I had an extra day to myself every week, what would I do that doesn't involve the concept of "should"?
2. How do I want to feel when I collaborate with others?
3. What things do I want to learn more about?
4. What places do I want to visit?
5. What groups would I like to join?
6. What creative art forms would I like to learn and practice?
7. What volunteer activities would I enjoy?
8. If I moved to a different house, what would it be like?
9. If I put three of my favorite activities together to make a job, what would it look like?
10. If I added more people to my life, what would that look like?
11. If I added more silent, alone time to my life, what would that be like?
12. What are my deal breakers concerning relationships, family, work situations, home life, travel, body, and health?
13. If my income doubled, what would I be doing?
14. What's an ideal next phase of life—one that includes things I want to do and need to learn?
15. What would a lateral shift in my work look like? What would a 50 percent expansion of my work into new areas look like?
16. What's even better than what I was thinking?

• • • • • • • • • • • •

Imagining Better Realities for Others

Shaping the imaginal realm does more than improve your own life—it can serve the people you're involved with so they can flourish too. One of the easiest ways to do this is to revise the way you see others. We all make snap judgments that place people above or below us—someone seems gorgeous, perfect, brilliant, and hilarious; or wimpy, unkempt, stingy, shallow, or snobby. The lists go on and on. Try this instead: notice your first impression about another person, then imagine they are also the opposite of that. If you think they're stupid, imagine they actually have a high IQ. If you think they're clumsy, see them as an expert athlete or dancer, too. If you think they're perfect, see them making mistakes like the rest of us. The point is to see others as human and multifaceted, capable of magnificent things, silly things, and even dark things. When you do this for others, you give yourself the same gift. And it's a great way to entertain yourself while you're waiting at the airport or doctor's office!

Vote for people's best selves, and leave the negative images on the cutting room floor. When the speaker stands up in front of the audience, picture her doing her very best and enjoying her own presentation. When the bank teller looks bored and tired, picture him smiling and connecting with each customer in an interested way. When the stooped senior walks hesitantly down the sidewalk with her cane, picture her body without pain, with fresh energy feeding all her organs and cells.

Prayer and Blessing

Because you are so telepathic, when someone prays for you, you can receive more than their positive intent. If their imagination for you is slanted according to what they think is "good for you"; if their prayer has a specific, limiting form; if they don't acknowledge the purposefulness in your immediate experience—the prayer can be like a wet blanket thrown on top of you. You must then telepathically sort through the new clutter and dissolve the parts that aren't useful, so you can receive the truly helpful bits.

Prayer works best when you first accept the other person's situation. This can be difficult. Does the other person's reality trigger repugnance or your deepest fears? A couple I know is caught in a situation where his illness triggers her fear of abandonment, so some of her desire to help heal him comes laden with fear. This doesn't help him as much as her totally calm and trusting efforts might, because he now has to overcome her fears, in addition to his own, to heal. So first, release fear and recoiling. A suffering person is learning something from their situation. They've drawn a fear up from their subconscious, are "looking at it" intensely by experiencing it, and are totally able to release the condition once they learn what they need, to free themselves and evolve.

There is a high-frequency form of prayer I like to call "the art of blessing." Because the ultimate healing power—the highest frequency of consciousness-and-energy—is spread evenly through the entire unified field, we don't require a higher power outside us to do the healing work for us. *This power is already inside all of us.* We can *imagine* healing occurring, though—by focusing attention on the ideal, harmonious self and the experience of unity inside everything, and activating it. This is a big part of facilitating healing for others by blessing them. Blessing is a lost art of imagination that comes from experiencing our own highest truth and oneness.

My intuition tells me that in ancient times, because there was no refrigeration and food was often tainted, people learned to meditate and bless their food to treat it before they ate it. They looked beyond the food's outer form and imagined its inner light or energy body. Then they communed with that ideal inner blueprint—the pure essence of the food—and communicated with it.

The one who prepared the food might say, "I see who you are, oh peach, oh potato, oh squash, oh dove. You embody the quality of sweetness, of power, of earth, of gentleness. You are beautiful and radiant. I see you as the Creator intended you to be, and I love you for your true self. I ask that we become one—that you give yourself to me to nurture me. And I will give you all my love and appreciate you. As I eat you, I will take your essence into myself and let it flow through me. I will let you live through me. We will know each other's true selves." In this way, people could derive benefit from less-than-fresh food.

I imagine, then, that blessing became a form of healing animals and people as well. To hear "Bless you!" may have originally meant that you had been seen by a wise and loving person, all the way to your core—that your beauty and truth had been witnessed and thus made real. If it could be real to a wise person, it could be real to you too.

Forgiveness

As a child, it always seemed that when someone had "done me wrong," to forgive them meant I had to tolerate their selfish, oafish behavior. Nothing seemed to be evened out by saying, "It's OK. No problem." Lecturer and author Joan Borysenko describes this well when she says, "Forgiveness is not the misguided act of condoning irresponsible, hurtful behavior. Nor is it a superficial turning of the other check that leaves us feeling victimized and martyred. Rather, it is the finishing of old business that allows us to experience the present, free of contamination from the past."[1]

The more I've felt into what forgiveness is, the more I see it as an imaginal realm practice, not unlike the art of blessing. First, it is the ability to expand beyond judgment to allow a higher perspective—to let something be without reacting in indignation or with even the slightest feeling of self-sacrifice or vengeance. Holding a grudge denies the other person—and you—freedom. When you forgive, you reimagine the situation in a win-win-win way. In your revised reality, the other person acts respectfully and supportively, and you reciprocate. Energy flows and consciousness is not blocked. The other person feels your validation of their true self—not their fear-based, injurious self— and is better for it.

If you haven't forgiven yourself, this is just as powerful. Imagine the person you think you've injured, and see them not holding a grudge. "It's all water under the bridge," they say, and they mean it. Then imagine yourself not holding the regret, remorse, or guilt. What you did or didn't do before, imagine yourself doing it now the way you really want to, from your heart.

What if the person you hurt was *you*? Maybe your past self made a mistake that's had repercussions in your life for years. In your imagination, see yourself making the mistake then rectifying it right away. Or picture yourself in a reality where you didn't make the mistake, and allow the wisdom to ripple through your life until it reaches your present moment. Receive the benefits you want. The secret to shaping the imaginal realm into a reality that helps you evolve is to always occupy the imagined reality and *be the fulfilled wish*. Imagination can bring a magical, uplifting reality for you, and it can help heal you and others as well.

Free will actually means *freedom to select any idea you desire.*
By assuming the idea already to be a fact, it is converted into reality.
Beyond that, free will ends, and everything happens
in harmony with the concept assumed.

Neville Goddard

Just to Recap . . .

Imagination is a powerful, creative force. We bring our imaginations into form by paying attention to them, and we cocreate our reality with all other beings. Just as we dream fluidly, we create reality fluidly. Outside influences like our educational process and the mass media tend to separate us from our imagination, even making it seem frivolous. But you can rebuild your imagination muscle by playing with ideas, creating little movies in your mind, tweaking the variables, and entertaining yourself with made-up scenarios. You can go to the Imaginal Realm as if it's a real place where you can have magical, effortless, creative experiences. Imagination is sourced by joy.

You can easily reimagine and revise a reality you've already created. When you start a flow of imagination, it takes you to things that are on purpose for you and moves through three phases: from *being* (spirit) to *doing* (mind) to *having* (body) to *being* again. You can imagine better realities for others, as well as yourself, by seeing them as multifaceted, and by blessing and forgiving them—seeing their essential, true self.

14

Practice "New Human" Abilities

Our normal waking consciousness, "rational consciousness"
as we call it, is but one special type of consciousness,
whilst all about it, parted from it by the filmiest of screens,
there lie potential forms of consciousness entirely different.

William James

In the Intuition Age, what used to be supernatural becomes natural and normal. What we've known as human becomes "new human." Today's high-frequency reality is refining our sensory perception and allowing us to run more energy through our circuits and brain tracks. Just as there are things we couldn't have known about before now, there are abilities we haven't been able to develop in the old climate of slowness and limitation. There's a reason our movies and books are filled with stories of superheroes with superpowers today—the collective consciousness is priming us to be able do many amazing new things, without the aid of technology.

In this chapter, we'll look at another Intuition Age attention skill: *focusing consciousness-and-energy to expand your perceptual and physical abilities.* We'll explore some possible "new human" abilities, and yes, it may sound like science fiction or fantasy, but I encourage you to allow the possibilities—even if they're slightly beyond your comfort zone. These new abilities don't need to be dramatic or violent, as Hollywood likes to portray them. Some may occur innocently, naturally, and even seem matter-of-fact. You may one day hear yourself say, "Weren't we always able to read minds? Doesn't everyone know how to materialize objects out of thin air?" Of course, we must remember that it's always a little difficult to imagine what a transformed reality will be like when perceiving it from the previous reality!

Dream of the "New Human"

On my first trip to Peru and Machu Picchu in 1987, I had many instructional dreams and visions, some of which occurred while I was awake. I felt close to levitating or teleporting at one point, and was almost constantly in a state of communion with beings that seemed "intergalactic." As odd as that sounds, I was in the force field of Nazca, Cuzco, Machu Picchu, and Lake Titicaca—one of the highest frequency places on earth that I've experienced so far—and there seemed to be little difference between my normal physical reality and a nonphysical one populated by shamans and seven-foot-tall people. It was almost the equivalent of a near-death experience.

When I returned to Peru in 2009, after *Frequency* was published, I awaited the spiritual messages and experiences I might have with great anticipation. And guess what? Nothing happened! It wasn't until I was home that I began to have a recurring dream that progressed gradually, night after night, for a week. In the dream, I saw a close-up of a man's head, neck, and shoulders from behind. He was naked, muscular, and bald; and tiny, blue-black, curling tendrils were gradually emerging from within his body to become visible just under his translucent skin. It was like an intricate tattoo growing ever more detailed, complex, and beautiful as the sequence of dreams progressed. The design was three-dimensional, spanning across his skin and penetrating down into his body; I could see into his tissues. Finally, a voice said, "This is the 'new man.'"

I didn't know what to make of the dream until I shared it with a friend who was studying shamanism with anthropologist and author Alberto Villoldo. She said, "I know the Inca have a prophecy about the emergence of the new human that is occurring now. Maybe that's what it's about." I got that truth-signal shiver; I hadn't mentioned Peru. It turns out Villoldo had been talking about a period of change the Incas call the "pachacuti," that is in full swing and promises the emergence of a new human—what he calls "homo luminous"—after a period of turmoil. Pachacuti (also known as Pachacutek) was also a great Inca leader, who represents a spiritual prototype—a luminous one who stepped outside of time. He is viewed as a symbol and a promise of who we all might become.

Thinking back to my dream, I realized the spiral designs I saw emerging from the man's body were a new kind of internal circuitry—something interdimensional—like tiny wormholes in physics. The image seemed to be saying that our energy would soon be moving in entirely new ways, and this fit with everything I'd been seeing about the end of the linear geometric worldview. I knew the new spiraling circuits would take us into greater abilities, greater knowledge, and greater connection with our unified-field origins. Villoldo says the prophecies "speak of evolution taking quantum leaps, of the body never dying, of reshaping ourselves into a new species within our lifetimes."[1]

Superpowers and Superheroes

From Superman, Batman, Spider-Man, and Ironman to Wonder Woman, Catwoman, Lara Croft, and Electra—superheroes and heroines have never been more popular. Television programming is full of protagonists who see visions, talk to ghosts, jump through time, have total memory recall, and dream mediumistic dreams that solve crimes. An autistic boy assists the unfolding of people's destinies through immersion in mathematics. Investigative crime teams are composed of people with expanded abilities, like superhuman strength, mind control, reading electronic signals from the air, clairvoyance, clairaudience, and clairsentience. We even have heroic sorcerers, vampires, and werewolves. And in all this, technology isn't responsible for the superpowers in the slightest—they are natural and innate talents. We can't get enough of this stuff! *Why?*

I think we're saturating ourselves with the idea that the supernatural is becoming natural and that we, too, might do magical, marvelous things—all on our own without the latest electronic gadgets. Of course, in the early stages of getting used to the idea that we are far more than we ever imagined, there's a tendency to see expanded human abilities as "special"—that if we could develop even one or two, we'd be more special than other people. And, of course, this is quite satisfying to the ego.

I remember that, when working in teams with other intuitives and trance mediums in my early years, it was the young men who wanted to have psychic phenomena happen around them—maybe it's akin to the adrenaline rush of driving a sports car really fast. Without fail, they spoke longingly about wanting to levitate, teleport from one location to another, or move things with their mind. The women, on the other hand, wanted to be precognitive counselors and heal others with energy. I couldn't help but wonder about the various core motivations and how they might influence the development of expanded abilities.

· · · · · · · · · · ·

Try This!
A Day Without Technology

1. For one month, take one day a week where you're totally away from the computer, cell phone, calculator, and television. Let voicemail pick up your messages, use telepathy and intuition, practice connecting with the environment and the life inside things. Be creative and see what comes *out of you* instead of taking things in from other sources. Be in nature, be alone, be quiet for extended periods, and work with the imaginal realm.

2. During these no-technology days, notice what functions technology has been fulfilling for you, and see how you might do the same thing with your own inner consciousness-and-energy skills. Build your consciousness-and-energy muscle.

· · · · · · · · · · ·

If you've thought about having "superpowers," you might ask yourself, "What is my motivation for developing an expanded, 'new human' ability? And what is the proper context for allowing the new ability to surface in me?" To be able to do things others can't, can easily slide you back into ego and stuckness, separating you from the collective consciousness and blocking the Flow through you. The more attached you are to the specialness of having an expanded ability, the more likely the ability can become skewed, or malfunction, or stop.

To add another complication, linear perception causes most people to be skeptical, suspicious, and downright fearful of expanded abilities, since they "aren't normal" and are often associated with evil or charlatanism. If you demonstrate heightened powers, you may provoke condemnation from others. And if abilities open suddenly, as they can with a blast of kundalini energy (what's often called *spiritual emergency* or *kundalini psychosis*), your emotions and common sense can go haywire.

It's important to pay attention to these caveats. Without the discipline of a spiritual practice, expanded abilities can overwhelm the left brain and cause chaos in your personality or environment. For example, people with expanded abilities often have erratic, intense energy that can cause machines around them to break down. Ted Owens, known as "PK Man," claimed to be able to psychokinetically control the world's weather, influence the outcome of football games, and produce UFOs on demand—by using his mind. His emotions weren't that stable; he was often motivated by spite and ego, punishing people he didn't like by supposedly sending a hurricane their way. Others gifted in these ways have been persecuted or have become unhealthy physically—hypernervous, dangerously overweight, plagued by environmental allergies, partial paralysis, or chronic pain. It's best to allow expanded abilities to develop gradually, in conjunction with the increasing frequency of the planet. If expanded abilities serve your evolution process, they'll occur for you naturally, in a balanced way.

• • • • • • • • • • •

Try This!
Read the History of an Object

1. Ask a friend to choose a common object from her home—something with a known history—and bring it to you. It's best if your friend knows a lot about the object. It might be her grandfather's silver watch; a book that belonged to her aunt; a key to her storage shed; or a ring, small statue, or special mug from her childhood. It's important that your friend be able to verify the history.
2. Hold the object and sit quietly. Describe to your friend all the impressions you receive from the object in as much detail as possible. Then ask her how accurate you are.

• • • • • • • • • • •

In fact, when there is a broad, inclusive spiritual context for expanded abilities, they *can* occur naturally and calmly, as extensions of your consciousness-and-energy, often for a specific purpose—then they may subside until they're needed again. As your frequency increases, your understanding of how normal these abilities are also increases. If you're a huge sphere of consciousness-and-energy, and everyone and everything is inside you, intimately interconnected with no gaps, it makes sense that you could telepathically know another's thoughts, for example—they're communicating inside your own big mind.

It also makes sense that you could move energy with your attention to materialize or dematerialize an object, or move an object through space. It would be no problem to change your identity to such a degree that your physical look, or even your reality, might change in an instant. You could know your own and others' future or past lives, or talk to dead people and nonphysical beings. And if you can dematerialize and materialize an object, then it's not much of a stretch to apply the same principles to lightening your body and levitating, or dematerializing yourself from one location and rematerializing in another.

> Everything that happens in all material, living, mental, or even spiritual processes, involves the transformation of energy. . . . Every thought, every sensation, every emotion is produced by energy exchanges.
>
> J. G. Bennett

When I was first developing my intuitive ability, I was exposed to people who demonstrated a variety of these phenomena, and because of this, I came to know how possible these things are. I worked with Hans Holzer, the parapsychologist and ghost hunter, in New York City, and saw the effects that nonphysical entities could have on photographic film. Later, an amazing healer dissolved a tumor and knitted a broken bone in my foot, in the twinkling of an eye. I worked with several full-trance mediums and some shamans, around whom odd phenomena regularly occurred. Some of them were eerily precognitive. Around one medium with whom I spent a lot of time, it was common for objects to dematerialize, materialize, and teleport, and she even had voices, supposedly of spiritual guides, imprint on blank audio cassette tapes. A shaman once appeared to me as real as day in his energy body, from a thousand miles away.

Expanding Your Idea of What's Normal

Expanded abilities can develop in people who've had a near-death experience, a traumatic accident, or major surgery. It's as though the dramatic shock to the energy body and the mind cracks them open so more of the soul can flood in, bringing heightened consciousness-and-energy. Often, after recovering, people feel different, or even think they've somehow traded places with another, more evolved soul. As far as I can tell, it's really an increased capacity to embody more of one's own unlimited soul and the collective consciousness. The traumatic event acts as an excuse to be new—a sort of shortcut to expanded consciousness. Many people have shared stories with me about this. Marie told me that, "At nineteen, I was in a fatal car accident. I died for a few seconds. When I woke after being in a coma for three days, my intuitive abilities had sharpened, and I had a scar on my left hand in the shape of a crescent moon and a star."

These days, with the world's acceleration, expanded abilities are likely to develop without trauma, just by keeping your vibration at the level of your home frequency, working to become more transparent, and settling into the realization that you are much more than you've ever thought. You'll find, too, that as one ability opens, it's tied closely to other abilities, and several may occur in rapid sequence. For instance, becoming more clairaudient and clairsentient (hearing and feeling with the inner senses) can greatly enhance your telepathic ability, because telepathy is about sensing subtle impressions and sounds. The ultrasensitivity of your physical body may help you sense nonphysical beings because you more closely match their frequency now. Just practicing materializing the kind of job, relationships, and reality you want can assist you in learning to work with psychokinesis or apportation (moving and materializing objects with your mind). And if you learn to dream lucidly—to control your movements from within your dream state—perhaps eventually you'll be able to time travel!

Opening "New Human" Abilities

In general, to begin to develop expanded abilities, try the following things:

- **Ask yourself if there is a need and a strong, sincere interest in being able to know and do more.** Being a curiosity-seeker won't take you deep enough. Impatience won't get the job done. You need honesty, patience, and persistence.

- **Pay close attention to your growing ultrasensitivity.** What is your Inner Perceiver causing you to notice? If you pay attention a little longer and penetrate a bit further into the moment, what do you notice? Ask yourself, "What else am I aware of? What's happening just below the surface of this scene? What is that man or woman thinking or feeling?" Focus on your physical senses becoming more acute—to the point where you can sense with your inner hearing, inner sight, inner touch. Can you hear colors or see through your skin? The goal is to increase alertness and the amount of detail you can hold in your field of attention.

> To discover the truth in anything that is alien,
> first dispense with the indispensable in your own vision.
>
> Leonard Cohen

- **Pay attention to people and situations, and look for energy irregularities and blockages.** When you sense something of this nature, bless the area by imagining it whole, free of fear, and flowing. Notice when you're too cold, too hot, hungry, or tired, and focus on changing your bodily experience with your imagination until you feel comfortable. The point is to find something you want to change, then do it in your inner world until you're satisfied. See how the outer world shifts as a result, and validate what you did by enjoying it.
- **Scan the list of abilities in Figure 14-1, and notice how you already do some of these things, or are bordering on being able to do them.** Did you have a dream that came true? Did you know a friend was about to get sick? Did you think about a friend and she called an hour later? Did you clear a blockage from your past, and the next day, a colleague said, "Wow! You look different today!"? Did you walk in the front door and have a quick impression that your dead aunt was standing in the living room? Validate your budding abilities, and they increase.

Some Expanded "New Human" Abilities

Enhanced Physical Skills and Senses	Decoding energy information with ultrasensitivity; hyperacuity; increased energy flow and coordination; control of bodily functions (as with yogis); synesthesia / sensory crossovers and combinations; clearing energy blocks and healing energetically; sensing earthquakes, EMFs, pollutants
Development of the Inner Senses	Clairvoyance, clairaudience, clairsentience, clairgustance, clairscentience; seeing auras, sensing events at a distance, reading bodies and life patterns, seeing/hearing/sensing discarnate beings, empathic resonance, tasting or smelling nonphysical things, dowsing, kinesiology
Telepathy, Mind Reading, Psychometry	Communicating without spoken words, across distances and dimensions, often between languages; interspecies communication; reading the history of an object by touching it
Precognition and Past-Life Recall	Knowing things from other times and locations, remote viewing, divination, accessing the Akashic Records, interpreting symbols
Interdimensional Communication	Communicating with discarnate beings via full or partial trance mediumship, working with nonphysical beings through ceremony and ritual/shamanism, psychography/ automatic writing, xenoglossy/ speaking in tongues

Fig. 14-1

Some Expanded "New Human" Abilities
(continued)

Lucid Dreaming	Controlling the dream state from within it, interdimensional movement
Out-of-Body Experience (OBE), Near-Death Experience, Astral Travel, Bilocation, Time Travel	Conscious movement to points outside the body in time or space, perceiving visitations from others who are out of the body, being in two places at once
Shape-shifting, Alchemy	Changing your appearance and form, sometimes even from human to animal; transforming one physical substance into another
Psychokinesis, Apportation, Teleportation, Dematerialization, Levitation, Ascension/Descension	Moving objects with focused attention, materializing and dematerializing objects, moving objects from one place in time and space to another, raising an object off the ground, moving your physical self out of form into spirit and back

Fig. 14-1

• • • • • • • • • • •

Try This!
Play With Telepathy

A friend's three-year-old son told her he could read her mind. "Try it," he said. "Think of something and think it to me LOUD!" You might try this with someone you know.

1. Think of a friend or colleague. Focus your attention into the middle of their head, the center of their heart, and into every cell of their body. Give them the feeling that you are there; strike the tuning fork of your home frequency

(Continued on next page)

in their field. Tell them you'd like to connect in the physical world. Then let go and relax. See if they call or write. If not, repeat.

2. Think of someone you know, and let an image of them appear in your mind. See them doing something, feel how they're feeling, get a sense of what they're thinking about, and what color they're wearing. Imagine you're standing with them, and they notice you. Then call them and make contact; tell them what you just did, and see how accurate your impressions were. Ask them if they'd be willing to do an experiment with you—to notice when you're focusing on them, and when they do, to contact you.

3. Focus on a dead relative. Picture them and ask them to enter your consciousness spontaneously—perhaps in a dream or in a moment when you're slightly absentminded—and place an impression of a communication in your field that you'll be able to translate. It might be a feeling state, a word or phrase, or a symbol. You might try this repeatedly, for a month, and keep track of what you get in your journal, looking for inner meanings.

• • • • • • • • • • •

- **Let your abilities develop first in your inner world, in your imaginal realm.** With all your senses actively involved, imagine moving the salt shaker an inch across the table with your attention. Imagine touching an object and knowing where it came from or who it belonged to. Imagine disappearing from the spot you are occupying, so you're invisible, then imagine reappearing five feet to the side. Play with creating these realities in your imaginal realm again and again until it feels normal to be able to know and do these things. Expanded abilities begin in the nonphysical world, where they're normal. When they can slide effortlessly into the physical world, they'll be normal here too.

- **Practice keeping your consciousness-and-energy at the level of your home frequency.** Think of yourself as being able to run more energy through the circuits of your body when your frequency matches your soul. Picture yourself as transparent so there is less clutter interfering with the translation of your imaginations into matter.

Let this become a normal state of mind, and let your body relax into the reality of this.

> Gradually, we realize that the Divine Form or Presence
> is our own archetype, an image of our own essential nature.

> Ken Wilber

- **Practice remembering that your inner consciousness-and-energy world is merged totally with your physical world.** Both worlds are in the present moment, affecting each other constantly. If you can create the inner blueprint of an expanded ability and feel it as though it's real, it's not far from being physical. It's right there, about to animate your reality. All you need to do is remove resistance or incredulity about it being possible. Give permission.
- **Remember that all the motive force for doing or knowing in an expanded way does not have to come from your body.** The field around you contains particles and energy, the objects in the field contain particles and energy, and your consciousness easily flows through the whole of it. You can animate the particles in the salt shaker, the air, and the table by asking the collective consciousness to assist in moving the salt shaker to a different spot in your field. *All expanded powers are a collaboration* between you and the field.
- **Imagine the thing you want to know or do, make it very real, then remove your attention and focus on it peripherally.** Do this casually, softly, as though your body or your heart is paying attention, not your eyes and brain. Relax. Being forceful doesn't work. The release allows the energy to flow.

• • • • • • • • • • •

Try This!
Shape-shift into an Animal

1. Imagine you're out in nature and walk into a clearing. Be still and look around. An animal or a bird will emerge from the landscape and make

(Continued on next page)

itself known to you. The animal is choosing you, and has a message or lesson for you, so trust what comes.

2. Imagine you can step out of your own body in your energy body and slide into the animal's body to become harmoniously one with it. Feel yourself adjust to the new body shape. Be comfortable looking through the animal's eyes, fitting into the animal's head and limbs, feeling its heart, and so on.

3. Then let the animal take you somewhere to show you how it understands the world and navigates its environment. How does it sense and know things? Your animal can talk to you telepathically and transmit patterns of knowledge directly into your body. When you've received the message or lesson the animal wants to give you, thank the animal, slide out of its body gently, and come back to your own body.

4. What did you learn by being this animal? Why did this animal pick you today? Write about it in your journal.

• • • • • • • • • • •

Listen to the Stories! They're the Tip of the Iceberg

We all have stories about expanded abilities, but so often we gloss over them, seeing them as aberrations or a form of entertainment for our friends. By taking these stories seriously, however, you can open to greater things.

Something unusual happened once when I was driving the hour and a quarter from my house to work in Menlo Park, California. It was a drive I made every week. I knew the route by heart and the landmarks at each fifteen-minute interval. I looked at the car's clock that day and saw I was at the wrong landmark; I was fifteen minutes farther along than usual. "I'm making great time," I said to myself, while also thinking it odd. When I exited the freeway, I was back on schedule, having lost fifteen minutes in the space of a few miles. I knew I hadn't made a mistake. Then it dawned on me that I may have experienced something like teleportation, but my left brain couldn't handle the anomaly and returned me to my regularly scheduled reality.

Beyond my body, my veins are invisible.

Antonio Porchia

Some more stories: Kaz, in Japan, after fasting for ten days, smelled what he calls "a very rare, tiny, small smell." It was a minty odor. He looked everywhere around his room—opened the windows, checked the hall—but couldn't find the origin of the smell. And it didn't fade. Finally, he realized it was the scent of toothpaste, and it was coming from his mother's bathroom, in a distant part of their house. He said, "It showed me how much I could be one with nature or my surroundings, and that we all have such an instinctive ability."

Carrie says she's terrible about calling people, but before her grandfather died (and later, her grandmother), she swung into gear and reached out. She says, "I actually called my grandfather at the moment he died. I find this heartening because it is a confirmation that we are all connected and always communicating beyond physical limitations."

Hugo tells of a time when he was in the army and met a fellow soldier who confided that he could read using his fingertips. The man agreed to a test, so Hugo bandaged the man's eyes and put a bag over his head so there was no way he could see. Then Hugo opened a book to a random page. The soldier placed his fingertips on the first word and began reading as if he were looking at the words with his eyes. Hugo then gave him a photo, and he touched the image and began describing it in full detail. Hugo says, "Ever since that day, my mind has been open to all possibilities!"

During a business trip to Baltimore in 1996, I had a sudden mood change and became unreasonably upset simply because a client was late. Then, as I sat with the woman, doing her reading, I heard people talking in the hall of the house where I was working; I thought someone had come home from work. My client pointed out that we were alone, but I didn't believe her. I came back to normal

273

consciousness and went to look—sure enough, no one. After the session, I felt like a stone and couldn't keep my eyes open. I fell onto the sofa and went into a heavy, jerking sleep that one of my friends calls a "coma nap."

I awoke when my host came home. I was still unable to focus and had to teach in a few hours. She plied me with coffee, but I remained a zombie. "Do you mind if I sleep on the way to the seminar?" I asked. At the seminar, I described what had been happening. Amazingly, six of the participants had had similar distraction and agitation. About 8:30 PM, we all felt much better, and were rolling along in good humor and mental clarity. It wasn't until the next morning that I heard that TWA Flight 800 had exploded near New York close to 8:30 PM, only a few hundred miles away.

> We cannot live only for ourselves. A thousand fibers connect us
> with our fellow men; and among those fibers, as sympathetic threads,
> our actions run as cause, and they come back to us as effects.
>
> Herman Melville

What had happened? Did my body feel the approaching "event waves" of the explosion and respond, like animals do to upcoming earthquakes? Was the bulk of my consciousness drawn into higher realms to help the people who were about to die? Were the voices I heard related to the accident victims? Did the event begin in the higher dimensions long before the physical explosion occurred in real time? And when the actual physical event occurred, was the psychic tension released?

This experience was so dramatic that it broke through from the nonphysical dimension and totally disrupted my physical life. The same thing happened before September 11, 2001, and I now believe it was a kind of astral projection or bilocation experience, where I was trying to be in two places—physical and nonphysical—at once. So much of my energy went to the accident victims in the higher realms that I literally couldn't stay conscious in my normal reality.

· · · · · · · · · · · ·

Try This!
Travel through Space and Time

1. **Visit someone energetically.** Picture someone you know in a place they might routinely be: your mother at her desk, your brother cooking at the stove, a friend in her garden. Imagine yourself in the same time and space with them, as though you're actually there. First, feel yourself to be in your energy body, then imagine you are "filling in" and becoming solid—as if you can reach out and touch the other person, and can speak and real sound will occur. Greet the person by name or get their attention in a way that feels real to you. Tell them something important, and touch them gently. Let yourself feel it as tangibly real. Practice this repeatedly and see if the person responds. Perhaps they'll see you flash on and off in their kitchen, or dream about you, and call. Notice any insights you receive while visiting them.

2. **Practice bilocating.** While you project to another location to visit someone energetically, as in the previous exercise, simultaneously imagine yourself in your current location. Hold both images and feeling experiences as real. You may need to shift to a slightly higher viewpoint, or expand your sphere, to hold both comfortably.

3. **Try time travel.** Just as you placed yourself in another location in the previous exercises, imagine another time, preferably in your past, so you can recognize it. Go there in your energy body and slide into the body you had then; look out through those eyes. You are a visitor, so just go along with yourself as you perceived and made choices at that time. Notice your environment in great detail, and feel your motivations, interactions with others, and the way you felt about yourself. Infuse love into that body from your present energy body—gently, unobtrusively. You might even insert a positive message to help your past self.

· · · · · · · · · · · ·

There are things we don't know yet about the mechanics of high-frequency, "new human" abilities and how the subtle dynamics of consciousness-and-energy can actually affect our physical reality. I was once told by a spiritual being, speaking through my friend and colleague, trance medium Kevin Ryerson, that the phenomenon of *spontaneous combustion*, where a person's body burns up in seconds or an extremity of the body burns to ash (without pain), is caused by the consciousness projecting into another point in time and space, and not returning to the point where the physical body exists. There isn't enough presence to keep the body in form, so it basically disintegrates. It was an eye-opening insight for me, helping me see there was so much more to know about the "invisible reasons" for things we don't yet understand. "New human" abilities may not yet be normal, simply because we haven't yet understood their inner blueprint.

When we develop the habit of doing things first in the nonphysical world to source the action and form in the physical world, we'll relax about the "weirdness" of all these supposedly supernatural abilities and phenomena. It will instead be a case of how much imagination we have and how much we know for sure that our applied attention is a force that facilitates the materialization of realities. We'll see that these skills—these abilities that previously seemed so unusual in the physical world—are nothing special in the nonphysical worlds. In fact, it's our "supernatural" abilities that stay with us and carry over to our nonphysical life after death.

> Real science can be far stranger than
> science fiction and much more satisfying.
>
> Stephen Hawking

Just to Recap . . .

In the Intuition Age, what used to be supernatural becomes natural and normal. Psychic abilities and expanded powers are a result of bringing flows from the nonphysical world into the physical without reducing their frequency. Our books, movies, and television shows are filled with examples of superpowers these days, showing us that we can—and long to—do things that are beyond the scope of technology. When seeking to open our abilities, it's good to be clear about motivation and have a spiritual context and practice, because the energy required can be disorienting.

Many expanded abilities may develop softly and gradually as our frequency increases and the need for them arises. One new ability may connect to a variety of others, then deepen. There are principles of consciousness-and-energy that affect phenomena on earth that we don't understand yet, but they will be revealed in the transformed reality. Anything is possible in the nonphysical realm, and part of what keeps the "new human" abilities from becoming physical is a lack of imagination and the belief that they can't really be real.

15

Practice "Pretend Dying"

Everyone is committing suicide. The eternal, blissful,
natural State has been smothered by this ignorant life.

Sri Ramana Maharshi

This isn't a spooky chapter, I promise! It's about the fact that, as we
enter the Intuition Age, we're having the kind of transformational
experiences, due to the acceleration, that used to be available mainly
through the dying process, and in the period of adjustment right after
death. Death used to be our only form of transformation—but because
we rarely died consciously, we were oblivious to how it worked. The difference is that today we can be fully conscious of experiencing the
stages involved in shifting dimensions—in effect, "dying" without leaving this world. We can do these things intentionally and benefit from
them. So what I mean by "pretend dying" is to fully imagine dying
without actually doing it physically.

If we can do this, we can demystify death for ourselves, and when the
time comes for us to "transition" from our predominantly physical focus
to a predominantly nonphysical one, we'll have done so much of the work

279

already that the shift will be effortless and painless. It will feel fluid and comfortable rather than wrenching and foreign. We have a chance to eliminate one of our greatest fears, and that is incredibly exciting!

If we can understand the nuances of the death process and what happens right after, we can practice one of the most important Intuition Age attention skills: *seeing and feeling through the physical world's veil of solidity to enter the freedom, love, peace, and joy of the spiritual world, without having to die to do it.* We can practice learning about the stages in the great "transition" and work through them in our imagination. We can enter nonphysical life and live in it according to its rules, while we simultaneously live a physical life according to *its* rules. Coming and going with the Flow can become second nature to us. Eventually, we won't experience death as separating us from anything or anyone—in fact, it will connect us to each other more than we thought possible. And, as has been prophesied, we may not even die—we may experience something akin to transmutation or ascension. As they say on *Star Trek*, "Beam me up, Scotty!"

Let's Loosen Up Our View

Many people have technically "died" for brief periods and returned, others can communicate with people who have died and are living in the nonphysical reality, and some have mapped the territory of consciousness through focused meditation and out-of-body journeys. They all have stories to tell about what the process of dying is like. Many of them report—ironically—that life on earth feels more like death, while being nonphysical feels joyful and free. It is birth that many souls dread, they say; it's the immersion phase of our growth process that can make us feel heavy, dull, and out of touch with the astonishing qualities of the spiritual realm.

I once saw Krishnamurti speak, right before he died, sitting in an apple orchard in Ojai, California, wrapped in a blanket. He said, "The only death is ego." I could easily see, all at once, that *everything is life, except for the fixations and contractions we hold where we don't experience consciousness-and-energy.* So here's an interesting proposition: What if we could make our physical experience match the experience we have in the higher dimensions of consciousness-and-energy? What if there were nothing to resist in either being born or in dying? What if we realized we were always alive? Wouldn't this radically change us and the world?

Death seems mysterious and frightening because it exists in a huge gap in our perception of the Flow. We blank out when we try to remember what happens during this dimensional transition because we dread the idea of the Void. *Nothingness! Ugh! Shudder!* Because of this fear gap, we don't experience the continuity of consciousness-and-energy between the physical and nonphysical realms, or experience the true unity of the dimensions. We forget to connect the last phase of a creation/imaginal cycle to the new first phase of the next cycle, and we forget to notice that cycles repeat and have no end point. We often totally forget to experience the nonphysical reality, because we can't see it. This limited view locks us into polarities—here and not here, form and no form, real and unreal.

Physical death may be part of our earthly reality simply because we haven't experienced how we exist before, during, and after form appears and disappears, or because we haven't yet reached the frequency where our polarized idea of life and death can be eclipsed by a more comprehensive understanding. Perhaps the physical process has materialized out of a global inner blueprint of negative thought and emotion, and if we can update our inner blueprint, the phenomenon of death might adapt in some surprising manner. Here are some ideas that can help shift our notions of death:

- **We need to examine our descriptions.** We say "life and death," implying that physical experience is life, while death equates with no life—as though there is nothing beyond form. Actually, life equates with consciousness-and-energy, and is the true substance of the entire unified field. Life is everywhere, in everything (both physical and nonphysical), and cannot end. The more accurate description of the worlds, or states of being, might be "physical and nonphysical life."

- **We believe the life and death states are separate, yet they're not.** Physical life is a specific frequency of consciousness-and-energy, as are the nonphysical states like emotion, thought, and spirit. The states are continuous—they interpenetrate and cocreate each other. There is no "other side." We don't "cross over."
- **The Void is *full*, not empty.** "No-thing-ness" is actually an experience. It's about being unlimited and free from having to live in just one node of the grid of time and space. The Void is really a Great Spaciousness, and in it we have easy access to everything in the imaginal realm, or unified field, all at once.

> Without the rigidity of concepts, the world becomes
> transparent and illuminated, as though lit from within.
>
> Sharon Salzberg

- **Death seems shocking because we don't feel into it.** When we become skilled at experiencing energy and the subtle states of consciousness, we feel what happens in the supposed gap between being physical and nonphysical. We see there is no shocking end, just a continuing series of frequencies and noticings. Since these states interpenetrate, moving between them is just a shift of attention.
- **We're always nonphysical *and* physical.** When we dream, we're in our nonphysical self, and even as we work at our desk, our nonphysical energy body is in us, and around us, sourcing us. After we "die" and are living in the nonphysical realms, our soul still simultaneously lives in both states, projecting multiple physical lifetimes throughout time and space.

• • • • • • • • • • •

Try This!
Loosen Up Your Viewpoint

1. Imagine you're looking out from your eight-year-old self's eyes and feel that consciousness; then imagine you're in the present moment at your current

age, looking on the world from this point in time and space. Go back to your child perspective, then return to your adult perspective again.

2. Next, shift to your dream-world vantage point and feel how easily you can create and change the scenes of your dream reality. Then shift back to the slower, denser physical world and feel how things work here. Return to your nonphysical dream reality, then come back to this one again.

3. Imagine yourself before you were born into this lifetime, then imagine yourself in the midst of this lifetime. Now, imagine yourself after this lifetime.

4. Write about your insights in your journal.

· · · · · · · · · · · ·

Near-Death Experiences Show We're Always Conscious

Dr. Sam Parnia is one of the world's leading experts on the scientific study of death. He was involved in an international project, known as AWARE (AWAreness during REsuscitation), that began in 2008 and explored the biology behind near-death experiences. He describes how when the heart stops and no blood reaches the brain, brain activity ceases within about ten seconds. Yet when people "die" and are resuscitated after a few minutes (and up to an hour later), 10 to 20 percent report having had consciousness throughout the entire period, and a number of them have *near-death experiences* in which they experience a realm of life after death. Parnia says we simply cannot continue to assume that the mind and the brain are the same thing.

Of course, not everyone who clinically dies and comes back has a near-death experience. But those who do are remarkably consistent about what they see and feel, and these results hold true cross-culturally. Actor Peter Sellers had a near-death experience after a heart attack and described what happened: "I felt myself leave my body. I just floated out of my physical form, and I saw them cart my body away to the hospital. I went with it. . . . I wasn't frightened or anything like that because I was fine; it was my body that was in trouble."[1]

Most people describe similar things: moving through a bright tunnel at high speed with no discomfort; meeting a powerful spiritual being who appears as a brilliant light radiating love and gives them a profound sense of peace, sometimes releasing intense emotions; and meeting people they know who've died, and recognizing them from their "essence."

Many report time and space occurring all at once, often experiencing a "life review" where they simultaneously feel every experience they've had and recognize how their choices affected others—and their own life. They report being able to see, hear, smell, feel, and taste more vividly, and frequently describe colors or music unlike anything they've experienced on earth. In one way or another, they realize they're not finished with what they want to do in their physical life, and they shift back into their body—even though most feel great joy and bliss in the nonphysical state.

Ernest Hemingway, in *A Farewell to Arms*, gives us a visceral feeling of the experience: "There was a flash, as a blast-furnace door is swung open, and a roar that started white and went red and on and on in a rushing wind. I tried to breathe but my breath would not come and I felt myself rush bodily out of myself and out and out and out and all the time bodily in the wind. I went out swiftly, all of myself and I knew I was dead and that it had all been a mistake to think I just died. Then I floated, and instead of going on I felt myself slide back. I breathed and I was back."[2]

I've had a number of near-death experiences—in my dreams. In one, as I was dying, I was curious to see if it hurt to die. So I slowed the process way down, and instead of leaving my body and floating up, I descended through my tissues and cells, looking for a final point of connection to life in my body. Then suddenly, I was "out"! No pain, no snags, no discomfort of contraction or pressure, no consciousness of the actual transition experience. It literally was a "blink." I was expanding through space, free as a bird, and it felt great! Oddly, I had no concern for my body and personality. This new state, which felt so familiar, was so much more "real" than ordinary reality, and such a relief.

When I think back on the experience, I sense much of the exhilaration was because I was free of the tyranny of my left brain. In fact, *death may be nothing more than a forced shift from your left brain to your right brain and beyond.* If you practice shifting to your right brain and its free, formless, magical reality while you're walking around in your body, perhaps dying won't seem so final and frightening; it's one way you can practice "pretend dying." Once you identify yourself as consciousness-and-energy, there's no end to you.

. . . .

Try This!
Have a Near-Death Experience in Your Imaginal Realm

1. Close your eyes and center yourself. Enter your imaginal realm. Let yourself be alert, with full sensory, energetic, and emotional consciousness, and know you're perfectly safe physically. Begin an imagination journey where you see yourself leaving your body by either going down into the particles and out, or out through your skin.

2. Now imagine that a powerful force draws you into a tunnel of light through which you travel at great speed, coming to rest in a bright area where you encounter an extraordinary being made of light. This being surrounds you in a love so strong that it might make you weep, swoon, or experience ecstasy. Be at peace here and receive anything you need. You may hear celestial music.

3. As you become used to the light and love, people you've known in life, who have died, appear. They may or may not be in a recognizable physical body, but you know them and they communicate with you. Make note of what they say.

4. Next, notice that time, space, and knowledge are all available simultaneously. Your attention focuses on your current lifetime, and you receive an impression of your entire life. Certain times may stand out, like times you were not as kind, loving, courageous, or balanced as you really wanted to be. Just notice these times, and in your heart, determine to change your behavior. Bless any people you have harmed, at any level. Forgive any who have harmed you, even if it was unconsciously done.

(Continued on next page)

(Have a Near-Death Experience in Your Imaginal Realm, continued)

5. Imagine that you now feel the remaining tasks, life lessons, and purpose you still have in your current life. Feel the rightness of going back and the peacefulness of your choice. Allow yourself to be drawn smoothly back into your physical body, perhaps with heightened consciousness, and slowly return to the scene of your present moment.
6. Make notes in your journal about what you learned and experienced.

. . . .

Practice "Pretend Dying" by Becoming More Transparent

The transformation process is taking you through stages meant to help you clear clutter—the fears, ignorance, and inauthentic ideas you live by that don't resonate with who you are. By dissolving these low-vibrational thoughts and emotions, your soul can translate your destiny accurately into your life, and the Flow can help you evolve. Transparency, which I touched on in chapter 10, is a state of clarity, nonattachment, and fluidity that allows you to shift effortlessly back and forth between form and essence—in effect, integrating the nonphysical and physical worlds.

It is the clutter you unconsciously hold that makes you feel opaque, solid, separate, and alone; it acts as a "veil" between worlds, cutting you off from your nonphysical roots. As this chapter's opening quote from Papaji intimated, holding the clutter is a kind of suicide. The clutter is largely to blame for the erroneous concept that "death equals nothingness." When you clear the clutter, transparency remains, and it reveals the "fear-less," consciousness-and-energy world with all its benefits.

Remember that you can practice the following things to become transparent: Stop contracting, holding, and needing to control the Flow. Release fear, attachments, ego, and fixed beliefs and emotions. Develop a trust born of soul-group kinship and home-frequency resonance. Embrace what comes, engage willingly, be authentic, do your creative part with joy, and contribute with generosity. Be with whatever phase of the creation/imaginal cycle you're in, knowing it leads to another phase that's just as interesting.

The more transparent you become, the more you see the physical and nonphysical worlds as one gigantic reality with no dividing line. You know the full spectrum of self—who you are at every frequency—and what you're capable of doing. Perhaps when we become fully transparent, birth and death will transform into descension and ascension, materialization and dematerialization. In our transformed reality, I imagine we'll be conscious of the involution-evolution journey at every step along the way and we'll never get stuck in an immersion phase.

> It appears to me impossible that I should cease to exist,
> or that this active, restless spirit, equally alive to joy
> and sorrow, should be only organized dust.
>
> Mary Wollstonecraft

When you're transparent, you don't hold tightly to defined identities and worldviews. You can easily change your point of view, and your reality follows suit. It may be that dying physically is just a shift of viewpoint: *Now I'm here as physical me; now I'm here as nonphysical me.* When you dream, you unconsciously practice this easy, rapid shifting of attention between dimensions. You might think of dreaming as another way to practice "pretend dying."

"After-Death" Frequencies of Consciousness

The Monroe Institute, founded by Robert Monroe, is a worldwide organization that helps people learn to journey beyond the frequency of their body to higher states of consciousness. Over many years, participants have mapped a variety of levels or frequencies of consciousness—and many that occur after death. Their work provides a strong indication that there *is* a continuing progression of growth in the nonphysical world. Death is not an end.

The first after-death level the Monroe Institute journeyers report is a frequency we occupy when we die in a state of dementia, delirium, coma, or being anesthetized. It is also at this level that people who don't believe in an afterlife may "sleep" for an indefinite time. Eventually, they become conscious of their new reality, often with the help of spiritual guides and counselors who work with them telepathically and energetically.

The next experience is associated with people who feared death, who don't know they've died, or who cannot overcome a limiting idea or emotion. This is typical of suicides, addicts, or people who die with resistance, bitterness, or grief. Again, they may remain in this relatively stuck state until they are helped and educated by spiritual guides and counselors.

The next levels of after-death consciousness increase in frequency, yet there is still some fixation. Here, people hold fixed beliefs and expectations concerning what the afterlife will be like. If someone believes they'll hear trumpets when they reach heaven, they do. If they believe in a religious figure, they find him or her. If their family is important, they remain involved with their familial patterns. At some point, again with the aid of helpers, these people discover other possibilities and move on to a higher, more fluid frequency of consciousness.

It's important to remember that the movement through these higher states of consciousness is not linear—it's a continuation of the evolution process, of the expansion of our spherical reality. Once free of limiting kinds of consciousness, people experience something commonly called "The Park"—a sort of reception center that appears as a huge, green, tranquil park with gorgeous trees and lawns. Here, people reconnect with loved ones, work with guides to understand what they were learning in their life, go to a rejuvenation center to recover their energy, look at possible future lives, learn in the vast Akashic Records library, or relax and play until they're ready to expand to higher frequencies of consciousness. Some people also train as "rescue workers," guides, and counselors, so they can to drop back to lower frequencies to free souls stuck in various limited realities and bring them up to a frequency where they can evolve further.

Beyond this, there is a higher frequency experience where we connect with enlightened teachers, saviors, and prophets, and it is here where souls rest while they integrate the experiences from all their lives. There are higher levels yet; one interesting one is called the area of "the Gathering." Here, we meet extremely high-frequency, impersonal, intergalactic intelligences who have gathered around the earth to witness an important event that will occur here. They want to help us.

There are many lessons to be learned about the true nature of higher dimensions and the true nature of the soul. I've given you a quick overview of some of the possible after-death experiences so you get an idea of how we continue evolving in nonphysical life.

What Often Happens After Death Can Be Learned Now

As you can see, many of the after-death experiences reported by the Monroe Institute relate to dealing with unconsciousness, or fixed emotions and beliefs. In physical life, habitual emotions and beliefs become rooted in your energy body through repeated validation. When you leave your physical body, you live and travel in your energy body, and these ingrained patterns are still there. You may leave behind illness and physical pain but not deeply embedded emotional pain and negative thought.

In addition, if you're afraid of dying, if you're in resistance, or if you're unconscious when you transition to nonphysical life, you may not know what has happened to you—much the same way denial in physical life causes you to miss important information. If you're strongly attached to people or places when you transition, you may still be attached to them afterward. This is what creates the phenomenon of ghosts and earthbound souls, by the way. Much of this kind of carryover clutter can be reduced by clearing yourself while you're still physical. If you do, you can skip over the first few levels in the after-death world, going straight to a higher level of consciousness-and-energy.

If you're open-minded and transparent, there can be many love-promoting insights immediately after death. I learned this firsthand

How to Practice "Pretend Dying"

Become Transparent	Clear fear, other people's overlay ideas, soul-blocking behaviors, negative thinking
Release Attachments	Let go of your holding patterns: where you hold on to fixed ideas, feelings, possessions, and habits; where you hold back from full self-expression, hold forth to dominate others, hold back or out with stinginess and conditionality
Practice Ego Death	Release the need for limited, defined identity; the need to be better than others so you can feel good about yourself; the need to be right, to control reality
Develop Trust	Cooperate with your Inner Perceiver and the Flow; validate how things are working perfectly for your evolution
Maintain Your Home Frequency	Repeatedly choose to return to your preferred state—to feel how you like to feel—when knocked off center by the world's ignorance and suffering; practice positive inner and outer speech
Practice Perceiving from Your Right Brain, Heart, Cells, and Personal Field	Shift from your left brain as soon as you notice fixations, too much language, or the need for definition and proof; expand your sphere for higher perspective; work with intuition and direct knowing

Fig. 15-1

How to Practice "Pretend Dying" (continued)	
Practice Integrating the Physical and Nonphysical Worlds	Feel how consciousness-and-energy underlie and penetrate everything, how form arises from the unified field and dissolves back into it; practice feeling your energy body
Practice the New Attention Skills of the Intuition Age	Shift from the linear to a spherical reality, affirm unity, work consciously with the collective consciousness and the Flow, regulate and hone your use of focused attention
Develop Telepathy and Imaginal Realm Abilities	Practice communicating now with nonphysical beings via meditation, focused attention, and other frequency-increasing activities (all skills that you'll need to function easily in the nonphysical reality)

Fig. 15-1

when my father died in 2000. He was alone, three thousand miles away, and wasn't found for four days. I was worried about what he experienced when he died, and after I finally settled down, I decided to enter a deep, meditational state to attune empathically to his death experience and go through it with him. He was sitting in his chair, and I could feel him go blank just before his heart gave out. I could feel the effect of the years of frustration, anger, and resentment that had plagued him, as well as some thoughts of failure where he hadn't acknowledged everything he had accomplished physically and emotionally.

He'd been a bit afraid of dying, but it wasn't painful. And as he found himself out of his body, seeing his body in his chair, he commented, "That wasn't so bad." He was only worried about his little dog, left alone in the house without him, but knew people would find and care for it.

He was amazed that much of the emotional torture he'd been living with was suddenly gone; it had fallen away with his physical body. He saw how it had largely been maintained by his pessimistic attitude; his chronic upset was reduced now that he was free of the repeating cycles of negative emotion generated chemically by neurotransmitters in his body. There was forgiveness work still to do, but it wasn't overwhelming at all.

In the last years of his life, he'd been a loner, and he was now surprised to find himself surrounded by many friends and family who'd come to welcome, praise, and love him. In rapid succession, he shifted to a realm where spiritual guides and counselors helped him process what he'd achieved in his life; he had completed some karmic debts, built strength of character, been loyal, used his abilities, and been a good father. He also saw how he'd hurt others because he had been hurt.

Then came an interesting revelation. He felt how the overlaps with family members—especially those facilitated through DNA and physical, cellular resonance—had added richness to his life, teaching him important nonverbal lessons via osmosis and intuition. I felt how I had contributed to him this way. These revelations came all at once, and precipitated an overwhelming sense of love in him, and in me.

He also experienced the support and lessons he gave to others in the same way. I could instantly feel how the wide way I carry my chest and shoulders was him in me, showing me through an inner posture how to be steady, wise, safe, and calm. I could feel his way of walking in me, showing me how to persist and keep on going. A voice said to me, "This is the recognition of the gifts that are given." After this point, I let him go, as he seemed to move on quite rapidly, and I only felt him laughing and making jokes.

This experience really opened my eyes. I saw and felt compassion in action, and the great harmony of the unified field returning us all to our natural state of love and joy. The sad, awful experience of "death" transformed into an astounding process of healing and restoration. It also made me realize that if my father could have done the clearing, processing, and learning before he died—in other words, if he could have practiced "pretend dying" as a way to eliminate the needless snags in the transition to nonphysical life—his death itself would have been so much more full of love and joy. Dying consciously seems a vital part of the transformation process in the Intuition Age.

In order to awaken in the transcendental dimension, you have to shift your thinking so that space is not relevant anymore, nor time. The consequence is that you discover having always existed, and you are not located in space.

Pir Vilayat Inayat Khan

Releasing Attachments and Ego

When you transition to nonphysical life, one of the biggest adjustments is detaching from all the definitions of self—your earthly identity—as well as from your habits, possessions, and relationships. It doesn't mean you stop loving the people you've loved, just that you allow the way you experience each other to change. The following meditation is a mini death-and-rebirth exercise, where you first dissolve attachments, then let yourself experience spaciousness, then bring back those things you really want in your life—the way you want them to be.

• • • • • • • • • • •

Try This!
Release Your Earthly Attachments then Bring Them Back

1. Close your eyes and center yourself. Imagine you're surrounded by a field of fresh, glossy, soothing diamond light that extends as far into space as you can track. This is the light of your true self, and it can transform anything that isn't in harmony with your highest destiny. You can send things you no longer need into it, to be dissolved. Whatever you need for your evolution can also magically appear from it.

2. Soften your edges, relax your cells, and let all the patterns that make you who you are rise from their storage places in your physical, emotional, and mental bodies to float in the space around you.

(Continued on next page)

(Release Your Earthly Attachments then Bring Them Back, continued)

3. Next, we're going to proceed through three lists of physical, emotional, and mental things you may be attached to. Focus on the feeling of each one and your connection to it, then release it into the field of diamond light, letting it burn away in the purifying, spiritual radiance.

4. Feel the freedom as you release each item. Let yourself become more and more pure consciousness and energy, with no limits. Feel your soul essence. Rest in the spaciousness.

Release What You Have

- *vehicles—cars, boats, planes, campers, motorcycles, bikes*
- *equipment, gadgets, tools, computers, phones, appliances, furniture*
- *clothing, shoes, jewelry*
- *home, other properties*
- *money, investments, valuables*
- *friends, family, pets, partners, enemies*
- *talents, strengths*

Release What You Do and Think

- *job, professional role, achievements*
- *roles in the family, in religion (church), with friends (social)*
- *hobbies, leisure activities, sports, fitness level*
- *eating, drinking, sleeping, sexuality*
- *habits, addictions, weaknesses*
- *opinions about your likes and dislikes*
- *beliefs about why you're good and not good*
- *ideas about what you have to do or "should" do*
- *ideas about what you owe others and what they owe you*
- *worldview and cosmology*

Release Your Emotions and Identity

- *emotional pain from the past, regrets*
- *feelings of sacrifice, unfairness*
- *feelings of lack of freedom, restriction*
- *fears*

- *your gender*
- *your name, history, ancestry*
- *your physical body, any pain and illness*

5. Rest for a while in the openness. When you're ready, go through the lists in reverse order, adding back in only what you intuitively, enthusiastically, and authentically want in your life. Let your reality take shape in a high-frequency way. It's OK to not have as much clutter or need for identity. Come back and feel a new, more elegant way of living.

• • • • • • • • • • •

This exercise can be quite helpful if you're having massive endings, purges, and ego death as part of your transformation process. Letting go in your physical reality is easier when you're willing to release attachments in your imaginal realm first. Once you consciously experience the freedom and openness that comes after letting go of anything, it's much easier to simply "be with" what you have or don't have, allowing the Flow to bring what you need, and clear away what you don't need.

If the soul is immortal . . . it takes nothing with it to the next world except its education and training; and these, we are told, are of supreme importance in helping or harming the newly dead at the very beginning of their journey there.

Socrates

Important Skills for Nonphysical Life

Thanks to our dream life, we are fairly well-prepared for how things function in the nonphysical world. When we first transition into the nonphysical to live for a while, I imagine it's like riding a bicycle—you don't really forget how to get around. There are several attention skills you'll probably use more than anything else, however, so it's a good idea to develop expertise with them now so you can carry them over with you without forgetting. *The first ability is a combination of intuition and direct knowing, empathy and direct feeling, and telepathy and direct communication.*

Being in the nonphysical realm is a lot like living in your right brain—language as you know it doesn't exist, logic doesn't exist, separation doesn't exist, and your brain doesn't exist. Communication via direct knowing does exist, and compassionate empathy greases the wheels to bring understanding. Your whole energy body becomes your organ of consciousness, a vibrational transmitter and receiver capable of integrating complex concepts and bodies of knowledge all at once.

With intuition and direct knowing, if you think of someone in the nonphysical realm, they think of you. It's instantaneous and mutual—there's nothing in the way. If you want to create something, others know and want to help you. Heart becomes the field of consciousness-and-energy you live in. If you communicate telepathically to another being, you also communicate to the whole soul group that vibrates at a similar frequency. The group may respond as though it *is* the individual, and this all happens at the same time. Because everyone is merged via consciousness-and-energy, there is one voice in the many. Communications "occur" from within and throughout your entire energy body, as subtle impressions or bloomings of understanding.

To practice this now, try assuming that other people communicate like this naturally all the time, beneath their habits of logic, mental biases, personality types, and absentmindedness. At heart, they are "all heart." Assume that if you think of someone, they can feel you and know what your intent is. Assume that underneath, everyone is an expert intuitive and telepath. Then validate yourself when you receive an impression concerning another person—or an intuition about anything. Act on it. Follow up in whatever way seems most appropriate. Make this an active part of your life.

> All goes onward and outward . . . and nothing collapses,
> And to die is different from what anyone supposed, and luckier.
>
> Walt Whitman

The other attention skill that's so important in the nonphysical realm is the ability to focus attention and work with imagination to create realities.

I've already touched on this in chapter 13, but in the nonphysical realm, it's more obvious that you're working with consciousness-and-energy as the creative medium, since there are no physical results. There's no left brain, so focusing functions differently—much more softly, naturally, rapidly, and fluidly. Creating realities occurs instantly, and each reality lasts as long as you maintain it in your field of attention. If you want to change a scene, you just visualize where you're going and feel yourself there, much as you do in dreams.

If you want to do something you didn't get a chance to do while you were physical, you can do it in your imagination. Maybe you want to design and build a house. As soon as you start imagining it, it takes shape. Change the color of the door, the placement of the windows, the location from an open field to a beach, and it changes instantly to incorporate the new imagination. The entire creation is in your imaginal realm, because that's where *you* are now.

If you don't believe in imagination, or if you're not used to using your imagination to create and dream your physical life into existence, you'll feel frustrated and handicapped in the nonphysical world until you get the hang of it. If you're in the habit of jumping from thing to thing, with the attention span of a flea, you may carry that inability to concentrate into nonphysical life, hampering your ability to create and move calmly from one imagined reality to the next. In the higher dimensions, your vibration is your reality, just as it is in the physical world, but it's much more evident. You are more conscious of actually occupying frequencies and being able to change frequencies by changing your attention. By making a practice of accessing new imaginations consciously and materializing them with attention now, in the physical realm, you can carry that skill with you into nonphysical life, too.

The Active Side of Infinity

The goal in practicing "pretend dying" is to merge your physical and non-physical realities, find the same principles at work in both, and develop the attention skills that work well in both. A big part of this practice is to maintain memory and continuity of purpose between the physical and nonphysical worlds, then to bring your spiritual inner blueprint back into your next incarnation without distortion, as just another new focus of attention. You are weaving of the worlds together into a fine, conscious tapestry with no loss of wisdom.

Carlos Castaneda speaks of this practice of carrying consciousness between realms in his book *The Active Side of Infinity*: "Don Juan described the total goal of the shamanistic knowledge that he handled as the preparation for facing *the definitive journey*: the journey that every human being has to take at the end of his life. He said that . . . shamans were capable of retaining their individual awareness and purpose after death. For them, the vague, idealistic state that modern man calls 'life after death' was a concrete region filled to capacity with practical affairs of a different order than the practical affairs of daily life, yet bearing a similar functional practicality."[3] Castaneda said that shamans called the experience we enter immediately post-death "the active side of infinity."

As you progress naturally through the process of transformation and enter the Intuition Age, you're discovering the same wisdom and abilities that shamans and other enlightened beings have discovered. You're transforming as we speak, rapidly adjusting your idea of "normal" to include much more than has ever been thought possible—from fanciful human superpowers to instantaneous healing to interdimensional travel and communication.

Should it be so surprising, then, that the Intuition Age might also transform your very notion of life and death? Does consciousness-and-energy stop in its rocking journey between particle and wave? No! It's a continuum. You and I are simply larger particles and waves in the continuum. We blink into physical life and relax back into nonphysical life; we are "born" into one world as we "die" from the other—and we are both movements and both worlds.

Now, with consciousness-and-energy filling in the artificial gaps where we haven't paid attention before, we're beginning to experience this simultaneity and ever-presence of life. If you pay attention, you can experience the truth—that there is no death except for the whirlpools that capture and trap consciousness-and-energy, caused by fear and the left brain. As you learn to keep your attention free-flowing, you regain access to the trapped parts of life. Then it dawns on you that *all you are is life, that all you are is consciousness and energy.* You are totally free to come and go, in and out of physical reality, whenever you please. You can focus your imagination and attention to precipitate various frequencies of reality, and you can move in concert with all other beings. You have arrived—everywhere and nowhere!

In the Intuition Age, sliding into physical life may not require physical birth, and sliding back into nonphysical life may not require physical death. Like so many of the great masters the earth has known, you, too, may be able to ascend and descend, to appear and disappear, in a twinkling—in harmony with the desire of the Flow.

What reason have they for saying that we cannot rise from the dead?
What is more difficult, to be born or to rise again; that what has
never been should be, or that what has been should be again?
Is it more difficult to come into existence than to return to it?

Blaise Pascal

Just to Recap . . .

We say death is the "final frontier," but in the Intuition Age, our ideas and experience of dying will transform, just like everything else. We can help demystify this experience now by seeing how the nonphysical and physical worlds are merged, how the process of involution and evolution is continuous, and how we exist inside every part and aspect of life. There is really no such thing as death—unless we see our stuckness in ego or the immersion phase of our consciousness journey as a kind of death.

Many people have had near-death experiences or have explored after-death states in deep meditation. They report that there is a progression of experience in the nonphysical realms, and many of the early stages have to do with removing fixations, blockages, and clutter. The next stages pertain to sorting through and understanding what has been learned in the lifetime through a filter of compassion. After that, we remember how living in the nonphysical dimensions functions and continue to learn and create in the imaginal realm.

Learning to do these things consciously while still physical can make the actual experience of "transitioning" effortless and joyful. I call this practicing "pretend dying"—doing the work you might normally do during and immediately after death, *now*, in your imagination. It's also useful to build skill with direct knowing, telepathy, compassion, and imagination now in preparation for nonphysical life. As the Intuition Age progresses, we may not need to die and be born to experience both the nonphysical and physical aspects of ourselves we may descend and ascend.

Final Thoughts

*We must walk consciously only part way toward our goal,
and then leap in the dark to our success.*

Henry David Thoreau

A s I said in the beginning, I am going through this acceleration
of consciousness-and-energy, with its concurrent acceleration of
time, right along with you. As I tune in to the moment, feel into life,
and merge with the Flow, I receive glimpses of what we may become as
we shift into our transformed state as "new humans"—and what reality
may be like in the Intuition Age. I am passing along what I know so far,
though I'm sure the view will continue to expand. You can see for yourself too, right now—you should have all the orienting concepts and
navigational skills you need at this point to do just that. I am convinced
that, though there are troublesome phases, difficult things to face, and
deeply ingrained habits to break, we're going to rise into the high-
frequency life like a happy helium balloon.

Still, it helps to have a rough map, to have a sense of where the road
goes. And where the map has blank spots, you have your intuition and

trusty Inner Perceiver. Know that there is a sanity to the way this evolution is unfolding, even if your left brain doesn't understand it. Know that there is a transformation process underway that is helping you, not destroying you. It's helping you understand, gradually and compassionately, what's coming and what you need to do to move through the narrows and come safely out the other side. *Just listen.* Allow yourself to be impressed with new patterns. Trust that your body knows how to adapt itself to higher levels of energy and begin functioning in a new way. Choose and act on what you love. Be generous and never sacrifice yourself. You actually *do* know what to do when you stop listening to your dominating left brain.

It's reassuring to remember that the future isn't "out there" anymore. It's inside your sphere of consciousness-and-energy, at a slightly higher frequency than that of the moment you're creating now. You can raise your vibration and be there, and all the futuristic ideas I've been describing will suddenly seem so normal! Mine is definitely a message of hope: I see a positive, exciting vision and always have. And in the end, isn't it more productive to feed a positive vision with your attention than to add energy to the reality of fear, pain, suffering, and Armageddon?

Raise Up Your Arms!

You never know what's going to capture your full attention. For me, recently, it was when I saw a little girl enthralled with a friendly dog outside our local coffee shop. She squealed and raised her arms up over her head in a gesture of outright glee. I remembered how often I have seen little kids do the same thing at the beach, facing the ocean, as the waves first tickle their feet. Perhaps it is the sheer stimulation of something so great, so overwhelming, that makes the innocent child want to connect with it—to embrace it with their entire little body. When do we lose the urge to make this gesture?

I can't remember the last time I saw an adult raise his or her arms in glee—save for the occasional football player making a touchdown. Do we become so weighed down by gravity or encumbered by carrying heavy bags that we can't move our arms up anymore? Can we only raise our eyebrows? Children's arms rise of their own accord, no effort required. Try it! When you raise up your arms and spread your fingers in this unselfconscious way, something happens to your heart: it widens and opens, and the lungs take in air in a big, enthusiastic gulp. It feels really good.

> I would like to step out of my heart
> and go walking beneath the enormous sky.
>
> Rainer Maria Rilke

Why do I think of this now, at the end of this book? Perhaps it's because the book's title has the word "leap" in it, and I want us to remember that, though transformation has its difficult passages, overall we are in a process of joyful return. *Leap!* The word definitely needs an exclamation point after it. And *you* need an exclamation point after your soul! The nonphysical world, the realm of your soul and spirit, is arriving, appearing, revealing itself openly—inside, throughout, and all around your physical reality. You are regaining memory of astoundingly good stuff, and there is so much more to recall that is going to light you up!

The purity of the way consciousness-and-energy functions is right under your nose; it's in the air like the scent of fresh-baked bread, drawing you forward. You can't miss it. The Intuition Age is transforming you at your core, and simultaneously, it's transforming science, psychology, medicine, business, government, and even history. Areas of study can't be separated much longer, as they are all merging into one another, affecting each other. Secrets are being revealed, the hidden is coming to light, and the emergence of wisdom and truth is happening everywhere, through every particle of light on the planet.

You may have waited for science to prove new things to you, but in the Intuition Age, the source of truth is within you and every other person—we *all* have direct access to universal principles and wisdom, and know in our own way. You can now know at the same time that science knows. And contributing your perspective to the world is vital for all of us.

The "Writers in the Sky" Check In

When I ask the "writers in the sky," the nonphysical beings I imagine writing with me, "What would you like to say now, at the end?" this is what they say:

"This is not an end but the beginning of an experience of self that is endless. And being endless is far from being frightening; once you leave your left brain, you adore space and freedom and limitlessness, and fear dissolves completely. We have spent time explaining the stages of transforming from old perception to the new consciousness of the Intuition Age, and though it may seem like it will take years, it can truly occur in an instant.

There is every reason to abandon negativity and embrace the positive view. When you can see through the illusion of your solid world, you experience the astonishing amount of help you have in transforming your reality. There are billions of nonphysical beings and nonphysical aspects of every physical being, and we abide full time in the truth of the way the spiritual realm functions. The collective impact of our deep wisdom can dispel any lie, any misunderstanding, any superstition that might plague you. We are your true family, ever at hand.

The steps to attaining transparency and living in the diamond light are not at all difficult, especially if you don't think they're difficult. Your transformation is not in the future, since there is no future anymore; you're already transformed. All that remains is for you to practice experiencing your transformed self in your imaginal realm until it becomes second nature and drops into your physical reality. Then, as we like to say, 'And so it is.'"

Final Thoughts

Oh they but mock us with a hollow lie,
Who make this goodly land a vale of tears;
    For if the soul hath immortality,
This is the infancy of deathless years.

And if we live as God has given us power,
    Heaven is begun: no blind fatality
Can shut the living soul from its high dower
    Of shaping but a glorious destiny!

Alice Cary

Acknowledgments

Even though an author likes to think, "I wrote this book," it really turns out to be a cocreation—and the end product is the better for it. I want to thank Martha Beck for her generous, humorous, irreverently reverent attitude and for taking time out of her busy schedule to write a great foreword for me. The highly professional—and kindhearted—crew at Beyond Words and Simon & Schuster came through again, on this, my third book with them. Thanks especially to Cynthia Black, Ruth Hook, Anna Noak, Lindsay Brown, Sheila Ashdown, Jennifer Weaver-Neist, and Devon Smith. There are many more behind the scenes working enthusiastically on promotion and sales. Susie Surtees, in Australia, with her good ear and bright mind, was a saint for patiently reading every bit of the first draft. I am grateful to Rod McDaniel for the contribution of his prodigious quote library, and to Brad Bunnin for his kindness and diplomacy. I must also thank

Acknowledgments

my mother, Skip, for her unfailingly positive support. My sister Paula, brother-in-law Allan, and nieces Valerie and Julia have also been on my side from the get-go. And thanks to Anne and John Lewis and Karen Harvey for their help locally when I've needed it, and to Pam Sabatiuk and Steve Steinberg for their moral support.

Notes

Chapter 1

1. Barbara Hand Clow, *Awakening the Planetary Mind: Beyond the Trauma of the Past to a New Era of Creativity* (Rochester, VT: Bear & Company, 2011), 38.

Chapter 3

1. C. G. Jung, *The Structure and Dynamics of the Psyche,* trans. Gerard Adler and R. F. C. Hull, 2nd ed., vol. 8, The Collected Works of C. G. Jung (Princeton: Princeton University Press, 1969), 158.
2. James H. Austin, *Zen and the Brain: Toward an Understanding of Meditation and Consciousness,* 2nd ed. (Cambridge, MA: MIT Press, 1999), 40.
3. Rick Hanson, *Buddha's Brain: The Practical Neuroscience of Happiness, Love, and Wisdom* (Oakland, CA: New Harbinger Publications, 2009), 5.

Chapter 5

1. Jill Bolte Taylor, *My Stroke of Insight: A Brain Scientist's Personal Journey* (New York: Plume, 2009), 140.
2. Ibid., 141.

Chapter 7

1. Satprem, *The Mind of the Cells or Willed Mutation of Our Species*, trans. Francine Mahak and Luc Venet (Paris: Institut de Recherches Évolutives [Institute for Evolutionary Research], 1982), 13.

Chapter 8

1. Neville Goddard, "No One to Change but Self," 1948 Lessons (Lectures) Series, Including the Questions and Answers, no. 4: http://freeneville.com/free-neville-goddard -lectures-1948-4-no-one-to-change-but-self/ (accessed November 4, 2012).
2. Michael Talbot, *The Holographic Universe: The Revolutionary Theory of Reality* (New York: Harper Perennial, 1992), 50.

Chapter 9

1. Jon Kabat-Zinn, *Wherever You Go, There You Are* (New York: Hyperion, 1994), 4–5.
2. Cathy N. Davidson, *Now You See It: How Technology and Brain Science Will Transform Schools and Business for the 21st Century* (New York: Penguin, 2012), 6.
3. Ibid., 56.
4. Charles A. Lindbergh, *The Spirit of St. Louis* (New York: Simon & Schuster, 2003), 387.
5. Ibid., 386.
6. Ralph Waldo Emerson, *Ralph Waldo Emerson: Selected Essays*, ed. Larzer Ziff (New York: Penguin, 1982), 39.
7. Gaston Bachelard, *The Poetics of Space* (Boston: Beacon Press, 1994), 195.
8. James H. Austin, *Zen and the Brain: Toward an Understanding of Meditation and Consciousness* (Cambridge, MA: The MIT Press, 1999), 549.

Chapter 10

1. David Bohm, *Wholeness and the Implicate Order* (New York: Psychology Press, 2002), 188.
2. Cathy N. Davidson, *Now You See It: How Technology and Brain Science Will Transform Schools and Business for the 21st Century* (New York: Penguin, 2012), 55–56.

Chapter 11

1. Norman Friedman, *Bridging Science and Spirit: Common Elements in David Bohm's Physics, the Perennial Philosophy and Seth* (St. Louis, MO: Living Lake Books, 1990), 235.

Chapter 12

1. Cathy N. Davidson, *Now You See It: How Technology and Brain Science Will Transform Schools and Business for the 21st Century* (New York: Penguin, 2012), 229.
2. Ibid., 230.
3. Lynne McTaggart, *The Field: The Quest for the Secret Force of the Universe*, rev. ed. (New York: Harper Perennial, 2008), 11.

Notes

Chapter 13
1. Joan Borysenko, PhD, *Fire in the Soul: A New Psychology of Spiritual Optimism* (New York: Grand Central Publishing, 1994), 128.

Chapter 14
1. Alberto Villoldo, "The Inca Prophecies of Hope and Revelation," *Insight Healthy Living Directory* website (2009): http://www.insightdirectory.com/articles-/80-the-inca-prophecies-of-hope-and-revelation-by-alberto-villolodo.html (accessed November 4, 2012).

Chapter 15
1. This account of Peter Sellers's near-death experience was published in Shirley MacLaine's book *Out on a Limb* (New York: Bantam, 1986; page 172).
2. Ernest Hemingway, *A Farewell to Arms*, The Hemingway Library ed. (New York: Scribner, 2012), 47.

Glossary

Absolute, the: See *Awareness*.

Akashic Records: The library or memory bank of the planet composed of everything every individual or species has experienced. (See also *causal realm*.)

apportation: An expanded human ability; moving and materializing objects with the mind.

ascending flow of perception: The process of becoming conscious of something—of learning—as consciousness-and-energy rises up the spine and moves sequentially through the reptile brain, midbrain, and neocortex. (See also *descending flow of perception*.)

ascension: The ability to raise the frequency of one's body, emotions, and mind beyond the vibration of the physical world, so the body disappears into a higher dimension without physical death. (See also *descension*.)

astral realm (dimension/plane): A segment of the emotional realm; a frequency or level of consciousness containing fear-based perceptions; a frequency of consciousness connected with etheric energy. (See also *emotional realm* and *etheric energy*.)

attention span: The length of time one can concentrate or hold a focus of consciousness.

Glossary

attention: The act of noticing specific kinds of consciousness and things; the adjustable lens of perception that reveals varying amounts of reality.

attunement: Adjusting the vibration of your body, emotions, and mind to match a particular frequency, usually of a higher vibration.

aura: See *personal field*.

Awareness: The original, unmoving, nondual state of being, beyond consciousness, beyond the unified field; consciousness unaware of itself.

be with: To bring presence and focus fully into the moment; to include and appreciate life the way it is. (See also *mindfulness*.)

bilateral integration of the brain: The equal use of both the right and left hemispheres of the neocortex, creating a sense of balanced perception. (See also *vertical integration of the brain*.)

bilocation: The ability to focus one's consciousness in two places at once, sometimes with the simultaneous appearance of the energy body or physical body in two places.

brain-mind: The kind of consciousness, or mind, focused through the physical brain to produce the experience of the personal self or personality. (See also *universal mind*.)

causal realm (dimension/plane): A frequency of consciousness and a realm of experience containing the evolutionary plan and inner purpose for each individual and group; the home of the Akashic Records. (See also *Akashic Records*.)

cellular consciousness: The vibratory frequency of the collective of all the cells in one's body that produces a specific kind of consciousness; the nonlocalized "brain" of the whole body itself.

centeredness: The experience of residing in the centerpoint of any field of consciousness, whether it be a physical body, organ, or cell, or a nonphysical focus, like the experience of one's family, destiny, or past lifetime. (See also *multiple centeredness*.)

chakra: A vortex-like concentration of spinning, subtle energy located primarily along the spine; one of seven main centers of spiritual force in the etheric body.

clairaudience: The inner sense of hearing; the ability to hear voices, music, and sounds without the aid of the physical ears.

clairsentience: The inner sense of touch; the ability to feel or sense nonphysical energy fields, discarnate entities, or patterns of knowledge without using the physical body. (See also *psychokinesis*.)

clairvoyance: The inner sense of sight; the ability to see visions, past or future events, or information that can't be discerned naturally through the physical eyes.

Glossary

collective consciousness: A field of consciousness formed by many souls vibrating at the same frequency, experiencing shared knowledge and mutually inclusive creativity. (See also *soul group*.)

collective unconscious: The vast consciousness contained in the unified field that has yet to be made conscious to an individual personally.

compassion: A pervasive understanding that knows love as the core of every being and situation. The virtue that gives rise to one's desire to alleviate another's suffering.

conscious communion: The act of merging with someone or something else, sharing a common experience, and experiencing intimate fellowship or rapport. (See also *empathy*.)

consciousness-and-energy: The basic substance of the unified field, two aspects of the same thing that affect each other in equal measure.

consciousness: The fundamental sense of presence; a feeling of being, existing; the experience of "I am." (See also *presence*.)

contracted consciousness: Perception that is affected by fear, that reduces or blocks the flow of energy and the experience of the soul. (See also *expanded consciousness*.)

Convening, the: A phenomenon that occurs when people achieve and maintain matching frequency levels, and spontaneously appear in each others' personal fields or lives.

corpus callosum: A broad band of nerve fibers joining the two hemispheres of the brain.

Creation: The bringing into existence of the universe or unified field; the process of materializing an imagined reality by an individual. (See also *Word, the*.)

dematerialization: The process of dissolving a physical form back into the unified field. (See also *materialization*.)

descending flow of perception: The process of materializing or creating something as consciousness-and-energy drops sequentially through the neocortex, midbrain, reptile brain, and into physical form. (See also *ascending flow of perception*.)

descension: The process of dropping one's consciousness in frequency from the nonphysical, spiritual realms until the body appears in form without physical birth. (See also *ascension*.)

destiny: Life after the soul has integrated fully and consciously into the body, emotions, and mind; one's highest frequency life.

diamond light: A way to imagine the substance of the soul; the qualities of diamond light convey the experience of purity, clarity, incorruptibility, and enlightenment.

dimensions: Levels, domains, worlds, realms, planes, or frequencies of consciousness-and-energy progressing from physical to etheric to emotional to mental to causal, and on into levels of the Divine. As consciousness-and-energy expands through the dimensions, increasing in frequency, greater unity is experienced.

Glossary

direct experience: A live connection with the world, where one experiences situations immediately without pausing to analyze and compare; full engagement with each action in each moment. (See also *conscious communion*.)

direct knowing: The ability to understand something in the present moment without logic and proof; instant comprehension by conscious communion or "feeling into." (See also *intuition*.)

dissonance: When vibrations of different wavelengths meet, create instability and chaos, and demand resolution. (See also *resonance*.)

Divine, the: A nonreligious way to refer to the Godhead or Creator; an experience of perfect, transcendent force, truth, love, and oneness with the universe.

ego death: The experience of shifting from fixed and limited left-brain definitions of self and life into an open, fluid, expansive sense of self and life generated by the right brain.

ego: The sense of individuality based on fear, self-preservation, and separation from the whole.

emotional realm (dimension/plane): A frequency, level, or domain of consciousness generated by emotion and containing feeling states related to both fear and love/joy. (See also *astral realm*.)

empathy: The ability to use one's sensitivity to feel "into," "with," or "as" another person, group, or object, resulting in compassionate understanding.

energy body: See *etheric body*.

energy information: Data carried directly by vibration registering on the body and in the personal field, without language.

enlightenment: The achievement of total clarity about the true nature of things, and a permanent state of higher wisdom, illumination, or self-realization; the awakening of the personality to its divine identity; the final attainment on the spiritual path when the limited sense of "I" merges into the Absolute.

etheric body: The higher frequency energy body, or subtle body, that catalyzes the physical body, often seen clairvoyantly as light, and in shape, is parallel with its corresponding physical form. (See also *inner blueprint*.)

etheric energy: The vibratory frequency that is one level higher than matter; a malleable form of "subtle energy" that acts as a kind of modeling clay or energetic blueprint for the physical world. (See also *inner blueprint* and *personal field*.)

evolution: A phase of growth in which consciousness ascends in frequency from the finite to the infinite, from the physical to the nonphysical, leading to more advanced forms of life. (See also *immersion* and *involution*.)

Glossary

expanded consciousness: Perception generated by love, that increases the flow of energy and reveals the soul. (See also *contracted consciousness*.)

explicate (unfolded) order: A term coined by physicist David Bohm for any physical reality precipitated from a nonphysical one. (See also *implicate [enfolded] order*.)

feel into: The ability to penetrate into a person, object, or energy field with one's attention to merge with it and become it briefly; to allow subtle information to register on one's body via conscious sensitivity, as if one is the object of observation. (See also *empathy*.)

felt sense: The impressions or direct experience of a person, object, or energy field, registered on the body and mind through conscious sensitivity.

fetal origins: The study of the effects of the conditions encountered in the womb and how the nine months of gestation wire the brain for survival.

field: A region in which a particular condition prevails, especially one in which a force or an influence is effective. (See also *morphological field*, *personal field*, and *unified field*.)

Flow, the: The natural, continuous, fluid, wavelike, oscillating movement of life and any process; a state in which one is fully immersed in what they are doing, characterized by a feeling of energized focus, full involvement, and enjoyment.

frequency-match: The process of attuning one's personal vibration, whether consciously or unconsciously, to the vibration of another person or place.

frequency: The number of waves that pass through a specific point in a certain period of time; the rate of occurrence of anything.

geometry of perception: An inner blueprint or underlying, geometric pattern of consciousness that governs the way perception functions.

harmony: A pleasing combination of the elements in a pattern that stresses the similarities and unity of all the parts.

hologram: A quantum mechanics explanation of reality that suggests the physical universe is a giant time-space hologram, where the entirety is within each facet, leading to the concept that every moment— past, present, and possible—exists simultaneously. Likewise, every place exists everywhere. Also, a three-dimensional image (originally generated by a laser).

holographic perception: An underlying geometry of perception that allows for perception from multiple points of view, each center containing the totality of every other center, where the end result is an experience of inseparability and oneness. (See also *linear perception* and *spherical perception*.)

home frequency: The vibration of one's soul as it expresses through the body, emotions, and mind; a frequency of consciousness-and-energy that conveys the most accurate experience of heaven on earth. (See also *soul*.)

Glossary

horizontal integration of the brain: See *bilateral integration of the brain.*

imaginal realm: A frequency of consciousness that contains all creations and worlds as potential realities; a term to differentiate from "imaginary" (that which is unreal or based on fantasy). (See also *implicate [enfolded] order* and *many-worlds theory.*)

immersion: A phase of personal growth between involution and evolution, in which consciousness becomes stuck in the three-dimensional, physical reality, often accompanied by suffering. (See also *evolution* and *involution.*)

implicate (enfolded) order: A term coined by physicist David Bohm for nonphysical reality, which contains all possible physical realities. (See also *explicate [unfolded] order.*)

initiation: A rite of passage; a transformation in which the initiate is "reborn" into a new role or level of knowledge.

inner blueprint: The underlying and evolving pattern of one's life purpose; it includes a mix of love and fear, wisdom and ignorance, and can be cleared to raise one's personal frequency; the nonphysical etheric or subtle energy pattern that gives rise to a physical form or process. (See also *etheric energy* and *personal field.*)

Inner Perceiver: The wisdom of the soul inside a person, sometimes known as the Revealer or inner voice, that directs one's attention to notice things that aid in learning life lessons and expressing oneself authentically.

Intuition Age: The period following the Information Age, where perception accelerates, and intuition and ultrasensitivity take precedence over logic and willpower; the time on earth when soul awareness saturates the mind, transforming the nature of reality.

intuition: Immediate knowing of what is real and appropriate in any situation, without need for proof; perception that occurs when body, emotions, mind, and spirit are simultaneously active and integrated while focused in the present moment; a state of perceptual aliveness in which one feels intimately connected to all things and experiences the cooperative nature of life.

involution: A phase of growth in which consciousness descends in frequency from the infinite to the finite, from the nonphysical to the physical world. (See also *evolution* and *immersion.*)

karma: A theory that the negative or positive energies one sends out come back to the sender in like kind, either in this life or another lifetime; the idea that the soul corrects ignorant experience by reenacting similar situations for the purpose of learning.

kundalini: A yogic term describing the body's vital force as "coiled" at the base of the spine and able to rise up the spine (like a snake) when activated, bringing breakthroughs in consciousness.

Glossary

kundalini psychosis: A syndrome that occurs when the kundalini is "awakened," especially suddenly or dramatically, causing destabilization or profound psychological transformation in what is termed "spiritual emergency." (See also *spiritual emergency*.)

left brain / left hemisphere: The left side of the neocortex, governing rational, logical, analytical thought; compartmentalization; language; and the definition of meaning. (See also *right brain / right hemisphere*.)

light body: See *etheric body*.

linear perception: A geometry of perception characterized by cause-and-effect logic, the analysis of steps required to achieve a goal, and thinking along lines in time and space; perception that causes the illusion of separation and gives rise to fear. (See also *holographic perception* and *spherical perception*.)

many-worlds theory: The idea in physics that the world is split at the quantum level into an unlimited number of real worlds, unknown to each other, where a wave evolves instead of collapsing or condensing into a specific form, embracing all possibilities within it; the idea that all realities and outcomes exist simultaneously and do not interfere with each other.

materialization: The process of bringing an idea into physical manifestation. (See also *dematerialization*.)

mental realm (dimension/plane): A frequency, level, or domain of consciousness generated by thought, containing both fixed beliefs and inspiration.

midbrain: The middle of the three primary divisions of the human brain (between the neocortex and the reptile brain), that helps process the senses, perceptions of similarity and connectedness, and affection. (See also *neocortex* and *reptile brain*.)

mindfulness: The act of paying close and loving attention to what is in the present moment. (See also *conscious communion*.)

monkey mind: A term, primarily from Buddhism, describing a mental state of restlessness, distraction, and hyperactivity.

morphic field: A term created by biologist Rupert Sheldrake to describe a field of consciousness-and-energy around a morphic unit (physical form) that organizes the unit's character, structure, and pattern of activity. (See also *morphic resonance*.)

morphic resonance: A term invented by biologist Rupert Sheldrake to describe the feedback mechanism between a morphic field and its corresponding forms of morphic units. The greater the degree of similarity, the greater the resonance, leading to habituation or persistence of particular forms.

multiple centeredness: The ability, with spherical-holographic perception, to occupy many centerpoints simultaneously and know the whole from any point in the unified field. (See also *centeredness* and *centerpoint*.)

319

Glossary

myelin: A whitish insulating sheath around many nerve fibers, increasing the speed at which impulses are conducted.

narcissism: Excessive focus on oneself, often marked by a sense of grandiosity, a craving for admiration, and the need to have others validate one's worldview.

neocortex: The topmost, most evolved level of the triune human brain, divided into left and right hemispheres, and involved in higher functions such as spatial reasoning, conscious thought, pattern recognition, and language.

neurogenesis: The process of generating new neurons, something that wasn't thought possible until Fernando Nottebohm's research with songbirds in the 1960s.

neuroplasticity: A new view of brain science that holds that there can be changes in neural pathways and synapses due to changes in behavior, environment, and neural processes.

new attention skills: Ways of using perception to reveal and maintain the experience of the transformed reality, or Intuition Age.

nonphysical realm (dimension/world): The reality or experience of consciousness-and-energy vibrating at a higher frequency than the physical world, containing thought and feeling. (See also *implicate [enfolded] order*.)

One, the: See *Divine, the*.

oneness: The state of being unified or whole, though comprised of two or more parts as the oneness of the Divine.

overlays: Unconscious, limiting beliefs one inherits in infancy and early childhood, from parents and other influential people, that emphasize particular behaviors.

parallel and past lives: The idea that souls are composed of thousands of aspects that incarnate into the physical world to experience individual lives. The myriad lifetimes of one soul can be separated from each other through time (past lives), giving the impression of sequential occurrence, or several lives may exist at one time (parallel lives) but be separated by location.

passive aggression: A type of behavior characterized by indirect resistance to the wishes of others and an avoidance of direct confrontation; acting in a subtly hostile way while maintaining the guise of friendly cooperation or support as a way to exert control over one's life.

perception: The act of becoming conscious of something.

personal field: The subtle energy around and through the physical body comprised of an individual's pattern of etheric, emotional, mental, and spiritual consciousness-and-energy; sometimes seen clairvoyantly as color and able to be photographed by special cameras; also known as an aura.

Glossary

personal vibration: The vibration that radiates from a person in any given moment; a fluctuating frequency that is a combination of the various contracted or expanded states of one's body, emotions, thoughts, and soul.

personality: The individual expression, or personal reality, of a soul in any given lifetime; the combination of characteristics forming a person's distinctive nature.

physical realm (dimension/world): The reality or experience of consciousness-and-energy vibrating at a lower frequency than the spiritual, nonphysical world; the three-dimensional experience of reality based on time, space, and matter. (See also *explicit [unfolded] order.*)

pineal gland: A small, conically shaped endocrine gland located near the center of the brain, between the two hemispheres, and believed by some to be a point of connection between the intellect and body, and a center of soul force in the body. (See also *third eye.*)

presence: The experience of the soul in the body in the present moment; the experience of soul in any physical form. (See also *soul* and *consciousness.*)

projection: Casting one's mind into thoughts of the past, future, fictitious realities, other locations, or other people's realities; blaming others for what one doesn't want to acknowledge about oneself, or seeing traits in others that one cannot see in oneself.

psychokinesis: Obtaining information by touching objects. (See also *clairsentience.*)

quantum mechanics: A branch of theoretical physics explaining the behavior of matter and energy at atomic and subatomic levels.

reincarnation: See *parallel and past lives.*

reptile brain: The first and oldest part of the human triune brain, located at the top of the spine in the brainstem; concerned with instinct, emotion, motivation, and fight-or-flight survival behavior.

resonance: The vibration produced in an object due to the vibration of a nearby object; the regular vibration of an object as it responds to an external force of the same frequency. Waves that vibrate at the same length create resonance. (See also *dissonance.*)

right brain / right hemisphere: The right side of the neocortex, governing pattern recognition, direct experience, intuition, creativity, and spiritual experience. (See also *left brain / left hemisphere.*)

Schumann Resonance: A low-frequency, global electromagnetic resonance (first measured by Nicola Tesla) that can be used to monitor global temperature; some call it a "tuning fork for life," acting as a background frequency that influences biological oscillators in the brain.

shape-shifting: The ability to make physical changes in oneself such as alterations of age, gender, race, or general appearance; or changes between human form and that of an animal, plant, or inanimate object.

Glossary

Shift, the: Transformation of human consicousmess; a change of consciousness from linear perception to spherical-holographic perception. (See also *Intuition Age* and *transformation*.)

skillful perception: A Buddhist term describing a way of perceiving oneself and one's reality where one heals suffering and does not add more of it to the world.

soul family/friends/group: A collective of people or beings with parallel experience and matching frequencies who are intimately simpatico and mutually sourcing, with many overlapping interests and dreams. (See also *collective consciousness*.)

soul mate: A person from one's soul group who becomes a life partner or lifelong friend, acting in a way that helps materialize one's destiny.

soul: The experience of the Divine expressing as individuality; the self-aware, spiritual life force or essence that is unique to a particular living being, carrying consciousness of all actions. The inner consciousness in a person that exists before birth and lives on after the physical body dies. (See also *home frequency*.)

spherical perception: A geometry of perception in which one experiences the self as the center of a spherical field of energy—one's personal field; the sphere expands or contracts to include as much consciousness-and-energy as is required in any given moment. With this view, there is nothing outside the self or sphere, producing an experience of unity. (See also *holographic perception* and *linear perception*.)

spherical-holographic perception: A new geometry of perception eclipsing linear perception in the Intuition Age; in it, one is always in the center of a spherical field of consciousness-and-energy and also capable of resonating into any other centerpoint in the unified field, knowing the totality from any point.

spirit: The nonphysical part of self and reality; a high frequency of consciousness that reveals the unified field and universal mind.

spiritual emergency: See *kundalini psychosis*.

strike your tuning fork: The act of imagining that one's body and energy field are composed of the soul's frequency, then activating that resonance and imagining that it, like a tuning fork, will radiate the vibration into everything it touches.

subconscious mind: Mental activity that functions just below the threshold of awareness; the place where all experience is stored as sensory data; the part of one's awareness where memories based on fear are stored or repressed.

subtle energy: See *etheric energy*.

telepathy: The transfer of thoughts, feelings, or images directly from one body and mind to another without using the physical senses.

teleportation: The movement of objects from one place to another without their traveling through time and space.

Glossary

third eye: An inner, nonphysical "eye" that provides perception beyond ordinary sight; thought to be connected to the opening of the pineal gland and expressing through the brow; a gateway leading to inner realms and higher consciousness. (See also *pineal gland.*)

transformation: A complete change of physical form or substance into something entirely different; a total shift in consciousness that alters the way reality functions.

transparency: A state of clarity and openness characterized by trust, spontaneity, and full engagement with the Flow in any given moment; enlightened awareness. (See also *personal field.*)

truth and anxiety signals: Generated by the reptile brain, the subtle, instinctive expansion or contraction responses of the emotions and body that indicate either safety and truth or danger and inappropriate action.

ultrasensitivity: A condition of increasing alertness and receptivity to nonphysical "energy information," conveyed directly by vibration to one's body and personal field; caused by the acceleration of energy in the earth's field.

unified field: A universal sea of consciousness-and-energy that underlies and pre-exists physical matter; a state, force, or "ground of being" that is the constant of the universe and connects everything in a single, unified experience. Gravitational and electromagnetic fields, the strong and weak atomic forces, and all other forces of nature—including time and space—are conditions of this state.

universal mind: Consciousness focused at the level or frequency of the unified field, resulting in the experience of self as a collective consciousness; the unified experience and wisdom of all sentient beings through all time and space. (See also *unified field.*)

vertical integration of the brain: The equal use of the three levels of the brain (reptile brain, midbrain, and neocortex), in both the ascending and descending flows of perception, so there are no gaps in consciousness to disrupt the perception of unity. (See also *bilateral integration of the brain.*)

Void, the: The unknown or collective unconscious.

willpower: Control deliberately exerted to do something; a deliberate or fixed desire or intention focused with a degree of force.

win-win-win: A solution or situation in which all parties, both physical and nonphysical, human and nonhuman, benefit.

Word, the: A way of referring to the original power that created the universe; the force that set the oscillation of life—the original vibration—in motion.